Sociology of Family Life

David Cheal

First published 2002 by
PALGRAVE MACMILLAN
Houndmills, Basingstoke, Hampshire RG21 6XS and
175 Fifth Avenue, New York, N. Y. 10010
Companies and representatives throughout the world

PALGRAVE MACMILLAN is the new global academic imprint of
St. Martin's Press LLC Scholarly and Reference Division and
Palgrave Publishers Ltd (formerly Macmillan Press Ltd).

ISBN 978–0–333–66578–7 paperback

This book is printed on paper suitable for recycling and
made from fully managed and sustained forest sources.
Logging, pulping and manufacturing processes are expected to
conform to the environmental regulations of the country of origin.

A catalogue record for this book is available
from the British Library.

Library of Congress Cataloging-in-Publication Data

Cheal, David J.
  Sociology of family life / David Cheal.
    p. cm
  Includes bibliographical references and index.
    ISBN 0–333–66575–9—ISBN 0–333–66578–3 (pbk.)
    1. Family. I. Title.

HQ728 .C445 2002
306.85—dc21   2002017002

10 9 8
12 11 10 09

Printed and bound in Great Britain by
CPI Antony Rowe, Chippenham, Wiltshire

I dedicate this book to my children, Joanne, Karen and Tanya. They have always been supportive of my writing, and they have been a constant source of encouragement to me.

Contents

List of Boxes

Preface

The main purpose of this book is to serve as an introduction to the sociology of families and family life. In an earlier time, the book might have been entitled *The Sociology of the Family*. However, that terminology would be controversial today for many sociologists. Calling our subject matter 'the sociology of the family' might seem to suggest that there is a single social unit called 'the family', which is both a cultural universal and a normative model that people are expected to follow. Most sociologists do not hold either of those beliefs today. Consequently, neither belief is endorsed in the present book. On the contrary, the emphasis here is upon diversity and upon the complexity of family studies when diversity is taken seriously. If some types of families are discussed more than other families in the pages of this book, it is simply because most readers can be expected to have a greater familiarity with certain family forms rather than others. Further details on the precise reasons for calling this book the *Sociology of Family Life* are discussed in the Conclusion.

This book was written mainly for students who are starting out on the sociological investigation of family issues. It is intended to provide them with an overview of some of the things that sociologists have been saying about family life in recent years. Therefore, the book does not claim to introduce any major new ideas into the discipline of sociology, nor is it intended to provide any new directions for family studies. Rather, the emphasis is upon reviewing a variety of contributions to family studies made by many sociologists, in order to demonstrate the value and relevance of a sociological perspective in this field.

It is hoped that this book will be helpful to students who are encountering sociology for the first time, as well as students who have already taken one or two social studies courses but who are just beginning to study family issues. For the latter students, more advanced material is presented in the boxes. An important way in which this book tries to help all students is through an extensive glossary. The glossary includes short definitions of many of the terms discussed in the text in order to clarify students' understandings of major concepts. Each term defined in the glossary is identified at an appropriate point in the text in *italics*.

Concepts are an important focus of the present book. Ultimately, it is through the concepts which we use in sociology that we phrase a common set of questions and debate the different answers to them. There are, indeed, many different answers to be found in sociology. That is because of the contrasting theoretical approaches that different groups of sociologists have adopted, and because of the many different experiences of family life that different people can have. Nevertheless, sociologists are able to communicate with one another because of the common stock of knowledge upon which we all draw. That common stock of knowledge consists mainly of concepts. Those concepts have many different origins, but they circulate within sociology because people in many different places have found them to be useful for purposes of sociological description and explanation.

Sociology is an international discipline, and the concepts that we use have been created by sociologists in a number of countries. A deliberate effort has therefore been made to acknowledge that fact in this book. In addition, the book attempts to introduce students to some of the different patterns of family life that can be found in different countries, and especially on different continents. Selected results are presented from a sampling of interesting studies in a variety of places. The findings have been selected because they have the capacity to make us think about family issues in a different way than we might otherwise do. It is therefore in the spirit of a stimulus to thought that the present book is offered to the reader.

DAVID CHEAL

1

Introduction: Asking Questions

The main reason for asking sociological questions about family life is because families take many different forms. None of us can possibly have personal experience with all types of families. Sociological research is therefore needed to describe family variations, and to show us how the varieties of family living compare. Three basic questions about families are discussed in this chapter. These questions are:

■ Who are family members?

■ What do families do?

■ And how are families connected to other groups?

CONCEPTS

family boundaries   kinship terminology
family   nuclear family   household   polygyny
polyandry   polygamy   extended family
secularization   cohabitation   structures
functions   roles   functionalism   nurturant
socialization   functional prerequisite   structural
prerequisite   patriarchy   ethnomethodology
division of labour   positivism   breadwinner/
homemaker family   longitudinal data   economic
determinism   family strategies   fertility
population aging

All of us can identify within ourselves feelings, interests and beliefs that were shaped by family members who were close to us when we were children. We can also observe, by comparing our own experiences with those of other people, how some families provide better opportunities than others to help individuals obtain the things they want. In these ways, family living has influenced how we grew from childhood into adulthood. It has therefore helped us to become the kind of adult that we are today.

The sociological approach to families begins in our individual understandings of how we are affected by the time we spend with other family members. It emphasizes how individuals' activities and personal characteristics are affected by the circumstances of living in interaction with other people. As sociologists, we are not interested only in our own lives but we are also interested in the family lives of other people, including people whom we have never met. We want to know how families of different kinds, in different places, produce different outcomes.

Family life is often subject to change, either in our own experiences or in the lives of the people around us. Immigration and alternative lifestyles on the one hand, and the disruption and reconstitution of families on the other hand, are giving us more encounters with unfamiliar ways of living. Over our lifetimes we can expect to be exposed to many different ideas on family life. Mental flexibility about fundamental personal relationships is, therefore, a practical requirement for successful living now. Here, the sociological viewpoint can help us adapt to the changes in our own lives, and it can help us adjust to the differences among the people we meet. Family sociology for the twenty-first century must be open to many possibilities. That means asking some very basic questions about how family life works.

At the heart of the sociology of family life there is a small set of questions, which all sociologists ask. Sociologists may answer those questions in different ways, and they often disagree with one another about which answer is correct. However, the fact that they ask the same questions does give the discipline a core subject matter.

Sociological enquiries deal with contexts of interaction, such as family groups. There are three basic questions about families as social groups. One or more of these questions is involved in all sociological investigations into family life. They are:

- Who are family members?
- What do families do?
- How are families connected to other groups?

Who Are Family Members?

If asked, we are all capable of identifying who are the members of our families. On certain special occasions, such as annual celebrations or family reunions, we may make mental lists of the family members who should receive gifts or invitations from us. Sometimes, on occasions such as weddings, or in wills for the inheritance of property, lists of family members are formalized and written down. Such lists become public evidence of the people who are most important to us. A family list separates people who are emotionally significant to us from the rest of the population, so that we can have special kinds of interactions with them. People who are not on the list are excluded. If those people find out that they have been excluded, they may feel 'left out' of our family life.

The inclusion of some people in family events, and the exclusion of other people, is referred to by social scientists as drawing *family boundaries*. Family boundaries are barriers that separate people who are inside the family from people who are outside the family. Sometimes those barriers are very visible, such as the walls around a dwelling or a fence around a family compound. Other barriers are less visible, such as the interaction processes by which some people are selected for inclusion in family activities while others are not.

Naming people as family members is one important way of drawing family boundaries. Children are therefore usually taught from an early age who their family members are, and how to name them correctly. Learning how to name family members involves more than just giving the correct personal name to an individual. It also involves the correct use of *kinship terminology*. Words such as 'sister' or 'uncle' are used to classify different family members according to their kinship relationships.

Drawing family boundaries in appropriate ways, including the proper use of kinship terminology, are rarely seen as important issues in most of adult life. We are likely to become aware of the significance we attach to these social processes only when rules of boundary maintenance which we take for granted are broken (Boss, 1987). An unexpected breaching of family rules may cause humour or sadness, depending on how it is done and who is most affected. For example, in many western societies today, problems of ambiguity about family boundaries can be observed among elderly people suffering from Alzheimer's disease.

More people are living longer in technologically developed countries like the United States, but we have not yet found reliable ways to prevent mental deterioration and loss of memory. Confusion about social relationships some-times results. There is a confusing sense of loss, that someone who is still physically present has somehow slipped outside the family circle (Boss, 1999). The question asked at the beginning of this section – 'who are family members?' – is not a trivial question here. Because this question of being inside or outside a family boundary is so important to most people, it is also an important topic for sociology (Wilson and Pahl, 1988).

In the discipline of sociology, questions about family membership very quickly turn into questions about defining the concept of the family. That is because how we define what a family is determines how wide we set the family boundaries, and that in turn determines how many people are counted as being inside the boundary. The typical family that sociologists describe may appear to be a small group or a large group, according to the way in which it is defined. If we use a narrow definition of 'the family', families almost always appear as small groups. But if we use a broad definition of *family*, it will be seen that families are sometimes small groups and sometimes very large groups. In this book we will use a broad definition of family. For our purposes, a family is considered to be any group which consists of people in intimate relationships which are believed to endure over time and across generations (Cheal, 1988).

There is no single concept of the family which is true for all historical periods and in all places. Definitions of family are relative to the social and cultural environments of people who think about families and who talk about families, as they go about their daily lives (Flandrin, 1979; Trost, 1990). As social scientists, sociologists spend a lot of time thinking about families and talking about families. We draw our images of families from our cultural environments, and then we clarify those images into specific concepts used in sociological theories (Gubrium and Holstein, 1990).

In the middle decades of the twentieth century many sociologists thought about the family as a small group, or *nuclear family*, composed of a legally married couple and their children, for as long as the latter lived at home. This group of people was described as living together in a permanent arrangement (at least until the children moved out), separated from the rest of the world by the walls of the family dwelling and by societal guarantees of family privacy. The family and the *household*, or economic group, were often considered to be identical for practical purposes. The nuclear family was considered to be the basic unit of household production, such as food preparation.

The 'isolated nuclear family', as this type of family was sometimes called, was especially popular in most of Europe and North America during the period of reconstruction after the Second World War. It provided the basis for early definitions of family in the growing discipline of sociology. As well, it provided the basis for procedures that governments used to collect information about families. The isolated nuclear family became the standard social scientific model of families in the Anglo-American countries, and it continues to be an influential ideal for many people today (Smith, 1993).

Sociological images of the isolated nuclear family have reflected a particular set of cultural traditions, based in part in the Christian religion and derived mainly from regions in northern Europe. Definitions of the family as a small group created by a permanent, legal bond between one man and one woman continue to be useful, in places where those cultural traditions remain in force. However, outside those places narrow definitions of family life are not always useful starting points for sociology, because different cultural traditions may produce very different family forms.

In the Middle East, Palestinian family life was traditionally organized in ways which were quite different from the isolated nuclear family (Abdo-Zubi,

1987). To begin with, a form of marriage called *polygyny* – that is, the marriage of a man to more than one woman – has existed among the Palestinians. The opposite of polygyny is *polyandry*, that is the marriage of a woman to more than one man. Polygyny and polyandry are both forms of *polygamy*, but polygyny is by far the more common of the two.

According to Muslim tradition, a man can marry up to four wives. In practice, this form of marriage in Palestine, as elsewhere, was found mainly among the wealthier classes since few men could afford to maintain several households (see also Al Khateeb, 1996). Another important feature of traditional Palestinian family life was a form of *extended family*, called the 'hamula'. The hamula consisted of a number of households whose male heads were linked to one another by descent from a common male ancestor. The members of the hamula lived in the same village, where the head of the hamula was the chief decision-maker. The head of the hamula was usually the oldest man in the village. He made decisions for his wives and children, as well as his younger brothers and their wives and children, and his unmarried sisters. The head of the hamula arranged the distribution of land for the production of food, and he represented the hamula in its external political relationships (historically, mainly with Turkish overlords, then the British, and then the Israelis). In addition to making major economic and political decisions, the head of the hamula also had the major say in decisions about family relationships, including the choice of marriage partners for children of the hamula, and divorce.

Family life for a member of a traditional hamula must have been very different from that of an individual in an isolated nuclear family. Family boundaries were wider and they included more people, and relationships with kin affected vital aspects of daily living. Today, most Palestinians no longer live in traditional hamulas, and more of them live in nuclear families not unlike those found in Anglo-American and European countries. Even so, modified hamula ties continue to be important for many Palestinians, especially in agricultural regions and in urban political organization of Arab communities in Israel (Al-Haj, 1995).

Clearly, thinking about 'the family' only as a nuclear family of husband, wife and children would be a restrictive viewpoint in crosscultural studies of family life. It is also a limited point of view from which to study the Anglo-American and European societies today. All of those societies have changed since the 1950s, and they continue to change in ways that are producing increased family diversity. Shifting patterns of migration have brought more different people from many other places into the countries of the northern hemisphere. Also, there have been major economic, social and cultural changes, including extensive secularization.

Secularization is the process by which religious institutions and religious beliefs exert less and less influence on social life over time. In places like Sweden, Finland, the Netherlands, and the Province of Quebec in Canada, the decline in the influence of traditional religious beliefs has been accompanied by a greater tolerance for unmarried lifestyles (Buunk, 1987; Kontula and Haavio-Mannila, 1995). This does not mean that family life has become entirely absent here. Rather, it means that in many cases family life has evolved into a new form, which is based on *cohabitation* instead of legal marriage (Hoem and Hoem, 1988; Palomba and Moors, 1995; Wu, 2000). Emerging forms of family life such as unmarried cohabitation have received greater attention from sociologists in recent years, because they are gaining greater social acceptance in a number of countries (Wu and Balakrishnan, 1992).

In countries like Canada and Australia, government legislation and court decisions have been extending legal definitions of family beyond the nuclear family model of heterosexual marriage and fixed, biological links between parents and children (Bala, 1994). Unmarried heterosexual cohabitation, also known as 'common law marriage' in Canada and 'de facto relationship' in Australia, has gained substantial legal recognition similar to formal marriage (Nicholson, 1993). This has happened partly in response to demands for less discrimination against alternative lifestyles. It has also been done in part so that governments can gain greater control over the new families, including more taxation powers.

A similar process of change seems to be occurring in a number of places with respect to homosexual cohabitation. There has often been a great deal of controversy over whether or not two people of the same sex who live together are 'really' a family or not. Jeffrey Weeks (1991) has described how in England it is sometimes argued that homosexual live-in relationships should not be recognized by public agencies, since it is claimed that they are merely 'pretended family relationships'. However, the dominant trend seems to be one of growing, if hesitant, social recognition for same-sex couples in England as in the United States (Rosen, 1999). That is because changing values, and new lifestyles such as long term cohabitation, are leading towards broader legal definitions. Those definitions stress the extent of practical support which exists between two or more individuals rather than their biological or sexual characteristics, or their official marital status (McRae, 1993).

Changing legal definitions of social relationships today are part of a continuous process of the collective redrawing of family boundaries. That process occurs partly in reaction to, and partly it encourages, more complex family relationships. In Chapter 2 we will examine selected aspects of contemporary family complexity. We will describe some of the forms it takes, and we will see what sociologists have had to say about it.

What Do Families Do?

Greater family complexity and broader definitions of what a family is have helped to focus more attention on what families do. As Elizabeth Silva and Carol Smart note, 'In this context of fluid and changing definitions of families, a basic core remains which refers to the sharing of resources, caring, responsibilities and obligations. What a family is appears intrinsically related to what it does' (Silva and Smart, 1999: 7). As a result, contemporary definitions of families used by some sociologists and social policy analysts, as well as by workers in a number of service professions, have tended to place less emphasis on family *structures* and more emphasis on family *functions*, than in the past (Bala, 1994).

The structure of a family consists of a set of positions, or *roles*, within the family, and the patterned interactions between them. For example, the definition of the nuclear family which was given earlier, as a legally married couple and their children who all live together, is a description of a certain type of family structure. The description of the family structure tells us who the family members are (for example, husband and wife), and it tells us what the relationships are between them (for example, marriage). However, it does not tell us what the family members do together, nor does it tell us what consequences their activities have.

The things that family members do are easy to identify. They give and lend money, they get children ready to go to school, they prepare and share food, they have sex and express love in other ways, and so on. But what is the significance of all these activities, from a sociological point of view?

One view holds that the activities carried out by family members are family functions, that is activities which fulfill certain of the members' needs. Those activities often fulfill needs of people outside the family as well. For instance, we can see that in traditional rural families, like the Palestinian hamula, people cooperate in the production of food and in defence against enemies. These particular family functions may not be important in most urban contexts today, but even in modern nuclear families people do carry out some activities to meet their needs. Preparing meals, and caring for sick children and adults, are obvious examples. Mutual protection is also still a function performed by urban families. Parents 'streetproof' their kids about what to do in the presence of sexual predators, or in some cases what to do when they hear gunfire on their street.

Functional definitions of families focus on what people do together, and especially on what they do to support each other. One such definition states that a family is a group of people who assume responsibility for some of the following functions (Zimmerman, 1988; Vanier Institute of the Family, 1994):

1. physical maintenance and care of group members;
2. addition of new members through procreation or adoption;
3. socialization of children;
4. social control over members;
5. production, distribution, and consumption of goods and services; and,
6. maintenance of motivation and morale through love.

Defining families in terms of these functions is socially inclusive, since any group of persons who agree to support one another in these ways is counted as a family.

Functional definitions of families, which stress financial and emotional support and physical care, are sometimes preferred in the professional discourses of people in social service occupations, such as social workers and lawyers (Minow, 1998). That is because a functional definition of the family helps to get around a potentially difficult problem, namely how to avoid excluding people who want to be considered as having equivalent rights to family members. Access to children, and the right to receive services intended for families, can depend heavily on whether or not a particular individual is counted as a 'real' member of a family.

Today, there are many people who have personal relationships which do not fit into the mould of the nuclear family. Nevertheless, they often want to have their relationships publicly recognized as family relationships, in practice and – increasingly – in law (Arnup, 1997). These claims arise from situations such as when a member of a same-sex couple wanted to arrange the funeral of his long-term partner, but his efforts were overwhelmed by the stronger legal rights of the deceased man's parents (Weeks, Heaphy and Donovan, 1999). Claims made by partners in cases like this involve bending and stretching institutionalized family structures, by emphasizing voluntary choices about relationships rather than fixed social positions within a nuclear family. Flexible definitions of family life that emphasize functional relationships between individuals are often advanced by those individuals who feel excluded from the privileges of family membership.

If functional definitions of families are increasingly attractive to some people, they are also rejected by others. Those who are opposed to functional definitions of the family include people who want to hold onto traditional, and especially religious, meanings of family life. They believe that homosexual couples are morally wrong, and that they should never be considered as families in the same way as heterosexual couples.

Opponents of the functional approach to families also include some sociologists. They point out that not all families function well. Some families are dysfunctional, even though from the outside it can be hard to tell them apart from functional families.

Issues are further complicated by the fact that functional relationships can easily slip into dysfunctional relationships. When love turns to hate in moments of intense emotion, it is hard to say what is the real state of the relationship. We have to face the paradox that families are contexts of love and nurturance, and they are also contexts of violence and murder (Collier, Rosaldo and Yanagisako, 1992; Duffy and Momirov, 1997).

Standard sociological theory has emphasized the pleasant side of families. In the past, sociologists tended to look at family activities only from a functionalist point of view. *Functionalism* is a theoretical approach which stresses the positive benefits of families. (See **Box 1.1**). Families are therefore often

Box 1.1   How can we define family? Answer one: It is a structure that fulfils a function

Many definitions of 'family' have been proposed in the social sciences, but there is not complete agreement about any of them. There are challenging arguments to be made against each approach and social scientists will continue to debate how to define family.

Functionalist definitions of family were very influential during the middle decades of the twentieth century, first articulated by the anthropologists Bronislaw Malinowski (1884–1942) and George Peter Murdock (1897–1985), and later by sociologists such as Ira Reiss. These influential men claimed that 'the family' is a universal institution. They believed that 'the family' is found in every human society because it performs certain basic functions for the maintenance of social life.

Ira Reiss (1965) argued that '*nurturant socialization*' of the newborn child is a *functional prerequisite* for every human society, and he further claimed that a 'small kinship group' is a *structural prerequisite* for the fulfilment of this function. He therefore defined family as 'a small kinship structured group with the key function of nurturant socialization of the newborn.' Among the many problems with this definition are the following. How do we classify couples who do not have children? Are they to be excluded from the concept of 'family'? What exactly is a 'kinship group'? Reiss suggests that a kinship group is based on biological ties of descent, real or fictive, that give people rights over children. How, then, should we classify surrogate mothers? And who exactly provides 'nurturant socialization'? If a couple leaves their children with foster parents during the working week, and the children live with them only at the weekend, which is the family here? If a mother gives her child to her own mother (the child's grandmother) to care for throughout most of the year, but visits the child from time to time, is she a member of the child's family or not?

In addition to the conceptual difficulties that arise from attempting to apply the above definition, there are certain practical problems that can follow from using it as a basis for social policy. If parents do not provide nurturant socialization for their children, should they be denied rights over the children because they are 'not really family' to them? Who has the right to make such decisions? How are these decisions connected to power relationships? And what are the implications for different social groups?

described as adaptive systems, which respond creatively to the stresses that are caused by unmet needs. Functionalist sociologists also argue that the reason why families exist is because of the functions which they fulfil. That is to say, family structures are thought to have evolved in the past because they helped human populations to survive. According to this point of view, families are thought to still be evolving today in order to help us cope with our changing economic and social environments. Functionalist sociologists emphasize how families continue to be essential for the maintenance of other social institutions, for example through the moral education of children who grow up to be decent, law-abiding members of society.

On the other hand, there are some sociologists who argue that the family is 'anti-social' (Barrett and McIntosh, 1991). What they mean by this is that family life, as most of us have known it, is thought to interfere with the full realization of human potential. Critical sociologists state that families are inward looking. They argue that a society which emphasizes family values tends to place a higher priority on private interests rather than public interests. When individuals are encouraged to put the interests of other family members first, they are obliged to be honest, fair and generous toward the people in their family. However, they may not feel that they have to treat people outside their own family in the same way. Public morality is likely to suffer as a result, and communities will have little capacity to cope with social problems. The isolated nuclear family may be functional for its members, but dysfunctional for society.

Feminist critics suggest that families are not always functional for all of their members, and they ask the question: functional for whom? They then proceed to point out the existence of inequalities within families. Family activities often place more restrictions on the personal liberties of wives than they do on husbands. That is mainly because women are more likely to have the primary responsibility for the care of young children, who need constant attention. It is also partly due to the predominant relations of power and influence between the sexes. (See **Box 1.2**).

Feminist sociologists have drawn attention to the power that older men have traditionally exercized over women and children. This kind of power is referred to as *patriarchy*. The traditional Palestinian hamula, for example, was organized along patriarchal lines. Decision-making power was exercized mainly by the oldest male, in his role as the head of the hamula. The patriarch of the hamula exercized power directly over his wives and children, and indirectly through his younger brothers. His brothers, in turn, exercized power over their wives and children, in their roles as heads of households.

Patriarchy was a stronger principle of social organization in Palestine in the past than it is in most western countries today. This does not mean that patriarchy is confined only to the Middle East; nor does it mean that it has existed only in the past. Patriarchy, and patriarchal images of families, still influence how many people experience family life today (Haj-Yahia, 1998). The influence of patriarchal ideas is sometimes reflected in the manner in which official reports present information about families.

During most of the post-Second World War period, governments collected statistical information about family income mainly from one family member

Box 1.2   How can we define family? Answer two: It is an arbitrary social construction

In opposition to those who claim that the family is a universal, and essential, social structure, there are social scientists who claim that 'the family' is ultimately an arbitrary social construction. The latter theorists take a quite different approach to the problem of definition in family studies.

It has been argued from a feminist perspective that 'the family' is not a natural social phenomenon at all (Collier, Rosaldo and Yanagisako, 1992). Rather, it is seen as one element in an ideology that idealizes 'nurturance' because it is thought to be lacking in an impersonal, bureaucratic, industrial society. This ideology, which we have inherited from the nineteenth-century reaction against excesses of industrialization, places a special emphasis upon nurturance by women (because of their role in reproduction). It therefore ties women to 'the family'. This ideological construction of the family is thought to be imposed upon modern societies by agencies of the state through law-making and law-enforcement. Attention is therefore drawn away from a supposedly universal definition of 'family', and toward the legal definitions of family and family relationships which are found in particular societies at particular points in time. Those definitions are believed to be open to change through political action.

Other social scientists, working mainly from the tradition of *ethno-methodology*, have arrived at similar conclusions about the way in which the public meaning of 'family' is a result of ongoing processes of the construction of meaning in social life (Gubrium, 1987; Holstein and Gubrium, 1999). These observers not only discuss social processes in legal institutions, but they also describe the subtle ways in which discourses about families create social effects in institutions such as hospitals and social service agencies. Here, they stress the ambiguity that frequently occurs in practical accounts of what 'really' counts as a family relationship, as well as the contested nature of the meanings of everyday family events.

Conflicts around the meaning of 'family', and uncertainty about what it 'really' is, have led some theorists to claim that we do not know what it is and furthermore we should not even attempt to define it (Bernardes, 1985, 1999). From this point of view, every definition of 'the family', is an ideological concept that must be understood within its political context.

In contrast to the approaches described here, some social scientists (that is, *positivists*) are likely to feel that it will be very difficult to produce a general body of theory about family life, based on testable propositions, if we do not develop a precise, and generalizable, definition of the family unit.

(usually an older male) identified as the 'head of the household'. This way of collecting information was based on the convenient assumption that in every family there was one person, usually the husband or the father, who managed most of the money for the family (Marsh and Arber, 1992). In contrast, information about children's health or children's education is usually collected from the mother, on the assumption that she is the person most knowledgeable about the child.

Social research into families often displays assumptions and practices concerning how tasks are divided within families. Traditional ideas on the *division of labour* between spouses, with husbands looking after the money and wives looking after the children, have had a considerable influence on the social organization of family activities, and on the conduct of social research.

How important the division of labour is in families today is open to debate. The roles of wives and husbands have clearly changed in certain respects in recent decades. But how much change has there been, and have the roles of men and women changed equally? What kinds of activities do women and men perform in families today?

We see here that questions about what families do very quickly turn into questions about what particular family members do, and with whom. Partly for this reason, and partly because of the criticisms of sociological functionalism mentioned earlier, the focus in family sociology has tended to shift away from the study of functions toward the study of interactions and transactions, or in other words, family practices (Morgan, 1996).

Family practices consist of all the ordinary, everyday actions that people do, insofar as they are intended to have some effect on another family member. One of the main things family members do is talk. They talk as they go about their daily routines in the household. They talk when they visit or phone distant family members who want to be informed about what is going on within the family. By communicating the meanings they give to experiences, family members construct a shared knowledge of each other's lives and their relationships with one another (Berger and Kellner, 1964). Shared knowledge of each other's needs and desires is the basis for practical exchanges of goods and services in transactions between family members.

In some instances, we can see that people who occupy different roles within the family contribute different things in their transactions with other family members. Family transactions then take the form of social exchange. One person gives one thing, and they receive a different thing in return. Exchange transactions like this are often important in marriage, especially when there is a sharp division of labour between husband and wife. An extreme example of this is a type of nuclear family known as the breadwinner/homemaker family.

The *breadwinner/homemaker family* was a very influential model for family life in the 1950s and 1960s. It is still found today, but it is no longer as prevalent as it once was. Economically, the breadwinner/homemaker type of family is based on a clear division of labour between the spouses, who therefore have quite different experiences of marriage. The husband earns all of the family income, and the wife does all of the housework. The effect of this arrangement is to produce an informal exchange within marriage, of money for services. Neither partner can provide for themselves alone, but by exchanging their resources of money and labour they can meet most of their needs.

In exchange transactions, both partners receive something in return for what they do, and everybody benefits to some extent. However, the feminist question about who benefits the most is still relevant here. Exchange transactions are sometimes balanced, when both parties receive the same amount of benefit, and at other times they are unbalanced. If there are young children in the home, the person who provides the services may end up with less leisure time than the person who provides the income. Such inequality is neither accidental nor random. Rather, it can be argued that it reflects major differences in the value that our society attaches to unpaid work in the home, versus paid work in the market economy.

How Are Families Connected to Other Groups?

Families do not exist in isolation. They are connected to a number of groups, because they depend upon them. Families cannot meet all of their needs unaided, in any society, and they must therefore turn to other groups for support and for resources. In a market economy, where most resources are only available if you can pay for them, that means entering into economic exchanges with people outside the family.

The connections between families and other groups are related to the level of economic development. The higher the standard of living in a society, the more resources people need and the more dependent they are on their transactions with people outside the family. In the most affluent societies, a high level of consumption can only be achieved by having a high income. That is earned by a high level of participation in the labour market. Wives and husbands are therefore both usually employed for wages in the most economically advanced countries today.

The dependence of family well-being on market transactions is one obvious way in which families are connected to other social groups. Because most families are so reliant economically on labour markets and commodity markets, they are greatly affected by economic events. A striking example of this is the impact that the Great Depression of the late 1920s and 1930s had on families in many countries. The effects of the Depression on families in the United States have been well documented by Glen Elder (1974).

Elder's important study used *longitudinal data* on children who were ages eleven or twelve in Oakland, California, in the years from 1931 to 1932. These children were studied intensively from 1932 to 1939, and they were studied again as they neared age 40. Longitudinal studies such as this, which collect information on the same individuals over long periods of time, are the most reliable way of tracing how people's family lives are affected by new situations.

The 'children of the Depression', as Elder called them, showed the effects of changes in family interactions that tended to follow from decline in the family's economic position. Average family income in the Oakland sample fell approximately 40 per cent between 1929 and 1933. Family members adapted to their financial decline by producing more goods and services themselves. The economic roles of mothers and children expanded, while the provider role of fathers shrank. These conditions weakened the father's customary role of social control, especially over sons. A high level of participation in economic activities by boys and girls strengthened their sense of autonomy, leading to early transition into adulthood. Among girls at that time, this meant early domestic responsibilities and, in deprived middle-class families, a preference for marriage over advanced education.

Studies like Glen Elder's analysis of the effects that changes in the market economy have on family patterns raise interesting questions, concerning the direction of influence between social factors. Such questions are especially important for causal theories. Is family life mainly determined by economic events, or do family events determine the nature of economic changes? Which direction of causation is most important in the long run? These questions, and the various answers to them, have been very influential in sociological accounts of family life (Seccombe, 1992, 1993).

Analyses which stress the determination of social life by economic processes are called *economic determinism*. Such accounts often seek to show how families take on distinct forms in particular economic systems such as capitalism (for example, Fine, 1992). On the other hand, there are accounts of family change, like that of Glen Elder, which suggest that family life is not completely determined by large-scale economic shifts. Rather, families are shown to create and shape their responses to change, through adaptive *family strategies*.

A family strategy is an organized attempt by the members of a family to maintain or to improve their collective situation. The most important family strategies are survival strategies. These strategies, such as how to generate an adequate income from the skills and resources of family members, are essential for the maintenance of the family as a social unit. In the industrializing society of Hong Kong in the 1970s, families with children could not survive on the low wage of an industrial worker. First-born daughters were therefore expected to find work as soon as they were physically mature, and to contribute their earnings to the family income pool (Salaff, 1995). The family could thus afford for its sons and younger daughters to stay in school longer, in order that they might earn higher wages than their older sisters when they eventually entered the labour force.

As families adapt to new situations by adopting survival strategies, they affect other groups in turn. If enough families change in the same way, then the combined impact on other groups can be considerable. For example, if a large number of families decide to economize by making their old car last longer before buying a new one then the demand for cars will drop. This will lead to falling production by automobile factories, which in turn will result in less employment for the people who work in them. In a similar way, changing patterns of marriage can affect the demand for housing. The level of demand for new homes increases if couples start getting married at younger ages. On the other hand, housing demand falls when young adults delay leaving home and continue to live with their parents for longer. Here we see that families are not just 'dependent variables' which are determined by their economic environments. Families can also collectively cause changes in markets, such as the housing market, and family change can create demands for new government policies.

In recent years, there has been a growing interest among social scientists in the potential effects that families can have upon a variety of social institutions. In particular, government economists and public pension plan administrators are often concerned about the consequences of women having fewer children, or in other words declining *fertility*. A completed fertility rate of 2.1 births per woman is defined as the 'replacement level' of fertility, at which one generation will be fully replaced by the next generation. Today, fertility rates are below the replacement level in several western countries and in Japan. This raises a number of questions about who is going to pay for the income benefits of the elderly, and how the elderly will be cared for in future when they are in poor health (Organisation for Economic Cooperation and Development, 1988). The answers that are being given to those questions will have implications for changes to income transfer programmes and health-care systems, as well as family life. It seems that in countries such as Japan, elderly spouses may have to provide each other with more in-home health care if they cannot rely upon hospitals or adult children to look after them (Ogawa and Retherford, 1997). The pace of fertility decline in Japan means that Japanese society will have to adapt very quickly to a situation in which many couples, rather than just a few, end up without a son (Mason, Tsuya and Choe, 1998). Whether that situation pushes Japanese families in the direction of the nuclear family that the West has had for several centuries, or in some other direction, is unclear.

It is important in many countries today to think about what the consequences might be of *population aging* during the first half of the twenty-first century. Throughout Europe and in North America, as well as in significant parts of Asia such as Japan, an increasing proportion of the population is being made up of people in older age groups. This major demographic change is partly due to the fact that on average people are living longer now, due to steady improvements in diet, sanitation and health care. However, the major factor in population aging is falling fertility.

We can see that in issues such as population change in Japan, family patterns are major topics of social policy now. In the past, it was sometimes suggested that family life occupied a private sphere, which was largely protected from public intervention. That is not the case today. Government legislators, the courts, and public agencies of various kinds are all constantly trying to find new ways to manage what goes on within families. There are several reasons for this. One of the main reasons is pressure on governments to balance their budgets, without raising taxes, by lowering the social expenditures that compensate for family deficiencies (Cheal, 1996a). Families are being required to meet additional responsibilities in most Anglo-American and European countries, and there has been a revival of official interest in family functioning (Sgritta, 1989). Another reason for the penetration of public policy into private life is decreased tolerance for physical and sexual abuse within families. That development is mainly due to greater awareness of the effects of power in personal relationships, raised by the feminist movement.

At the end of the twentieth century, some of the groups which are having the biggest influence on families are social movements. These movements either want to bring about accelerated family change, or they want to resist certain kinds of family changes, by mobilizing public opinion through meetings, rallies and the mass media. The feminist movement stresses female autonomy from patriarchal control. Partly in reaction to this perceived threat of increased individualism, and also in response to growing social problems, conservative pro-family movements stress a return to family values (Cohen and Katzenstein, 1988; Abbott and Wallace, 1992). In the United States and Canada, bitter conflicts over abortion, involving the rights of mothers versus the rights of the unborn, have especially divided these two groups (Luker, 1984).

One of the consequences of the recent increase in family pluralism is that family diversity has often become a major source of controversy (Jagger and Wright, 1999). As a result, clashes of opinion over sexual and relational ethics have become popular subjects of mass entertainment. In England, the intimate relationships of members of the 'royal family' have been closely scrutinized by millions of people. Inside information, or rumours, about the personal lives of royalty has helped to sell huge numbers of newspapers, magazines and books. Today, the details of family life are often public business on a grand scale.

Discussion

Sociologists of family life participate in public discussions about families in the societies in which we live, and we are therefore often involved in debating controversial subjects. Sociologists approach these topics from the perspective of an intellectual discipline which attempts to clarify the issues involved. As we do this, family sociologists also try to apply data from research to answer basic questions. In this chapter we have seen how sociological approaches to the study of family life arise from three basic questions. Those three questions are: Who are family members? What do families do? How are families connected to other groups?

Each of the three main questions about family life raises a number of subsidiary questions. Illustrative examples of specialized questions were outlined in this introductory chapter, and some of the concepts and methods used in the sociology of family life were presented. In the remainder of this book the three basic questions will be pursued in more detail. We will see how they lead into a wide array of specific enquiries, and we will learn more about the concepts and methods by which sociologists analyze the world in which we live.

2

Family Complexity

If families take many different forms, how exactly is the variation in family life to be explained? In this chapter, two main factors are considered. First, there are explanations in terms of cultural differences. These differences are often most visible by comparing family traditions in different parts of the world. Second, there are the influences of different social situations in which people live, such as their class positions. Finally, it has recently been suggested that the increased influence of individual preferences, or in other words 'individualization,' is becoming a more important factor today in deciding 'who are family members?'

CONCEPTS

family composition   joint families   arranged marriages   endogamy   matrifocal matricentric   modernization   stem family   filial piety   neolocal residence   life course   time-space distanciation   family of origin   family of orientation   family of procreation individualization   pure relationships

Belonging to a family is a very personal concern. However, the nature of family membership is also a matter of great public interest. Government statisticians spend a lot of time counting how many families there are of different types, and counting how many adults and how many children belong to them. Most governments these days prepare special reports on the number of lone-parent families (sometimes also referred to as single-parent families or sole-parent families), including whether the number is going up or going down (Lindsay, 1992). For example, in Britain the proportion of families headed by a lone parent increased from nearly 8 per cent in 1971 to 21 per cent in 1992 (Central Statistical Office, 1995).

Governments keep track of families partly because different types of families pay different amounts of taxes, and because they require different amounts and kinds of government services. Public policymakers also want to know about families of different types because of the possibility that different kinds of families produce different outcomes for their members. Knowing how different families affect children's educational performance, as well as the risk of behavioural problems, is thought to be important for policy development (Ross, Scott and Kelly, 1996b).

These are some of the reasons why one of the most basic and widely practised forms of research into families involves studying family composition. *Family composition* refers to the number and kinds of people who belong to a family. Lone-parent families and two-parent families, for example, are families with different compositions. The study of family composition is where we begin answering the question: 'who are family members?'.

The first observation to make about family composition is that it has generally become more diverse in recent decades. That is to say, more people are living in more different kinds of families than they were fifty years ago. Married couples with children, who used to comprise the majority of families in the United States, now make up less than half of all American families (Ahlburg and De Vita, 1992). In contrast, married couples without children, as well as lone parents with children (mainly sole support mothers) and other types of families have all increased in relative frequency.

To some extent, the current trend toward family diversity is remarkable only because of the contrast with a period of unusual cultural uniformity during the 1950s. There have always been families of different kinds in past times (Coontz, 1992). Earlier periods of social change, such as the Great Depression, were often accompanied by the fragmentation of families. What is unique about the present period is that there appear to be fewer legal barriers to increased complexity, and it is occurring on a global scale (Cheal, 1993a; Maclean and Eekelaar, 1997).

Family complexity takes two main forms. They will be referred to here as 'cultural diversity' and 'situational diversity'. Cultural diversity exists when different family practices are produced by people who have different ideals of family living. In contrast, situational diversity occurs when people who share the same family values engage in different family practices because they must create their lives under different conditions. Both types of family complexity will be described in this chapter.

First, we need to recognize that there are always some variations in family composition within any society, even when most people share the same basic ideas about family life. It is important to understand how this occurs. Failure to recognize the sociological processes involved in situational diversity sometimes leads to mistaken judgments about the supposed 'decline' of the family.

In culturally unified societies, there is one underlying model of the family which is considered to be a cultural ideal. The cultural ideal of family life is supported by major social institutions, such as organized religion, and it also has a preferential status in law. In western societies, the nuclear family has traditionally been the type of family that received the most public recognition. In a society in which the nuclear family is the cultural ideal, the majority of people live in a nuclear family at some point in their lives. However, not everybody lives in a nuclear family all the time, and some people may spend most of their lives in other living arrangements. That is because under certain conditions, people may be incapable of achieving the way they would really like to live. The result is a great deal of situational diversity of family composition. Such diversity does not mean that the cultural ideal of family life has disappeared, or even that the family has declined. What it does mean is that shared family values are likely to be enacted in different ways in different contexts, and at different stages of life.

In addition to situational diversity, the other form of family complexity is 'cultural diversity'. Here, more than one accepted model of family life exists, and people in different social groups follow quite different paths of family living over their lifetimes. Cultural diversity is most obvious when we compare societies having different family values that are supported by distinctive religious traditions. Societies with Judaeo-Christian religious traditions, and societies with Islamic or Hindu religious traditions, tend to have different family arrangements. Studies which compare family life in such societies are referred to as crosscultural comparisons.

Comparing the family values of people in Anglo-American societies with the Hindu ideal of family life in India is one way of seeing how important cultural influences can be. According to Steve Derné (1995), Hindu family culture consists of the following four elements. First, there is a preference for living in *joint families*. These are families which consist of the founding parents and their sons, their daughters-in-law, and their grandchildren, who are all living in one household. Second, parents prefer to choose their children's marriage partners, in *arranged marriages*. Third, activities outside the home by wives and sexually mature daughters are restricted, so as to reduce contact with members of the opposite sex. And fourth, interaction between husbands and wives is limited by gender segregation. That is, women and men tend to engage in different activities in separate places.

By comparison, family values in a society such as Australia have been described as stressing autonomy, intimacy, achievement aspiration and social acceptance (McDonald, 1995). Autonomy is the personal independence which enables people to direct their own lives, for instance by choosing who they marry. Choosing a partner often expresses a desire for closeness or intimacy with that person, which is manifested in spending time together and doing things together. The desire for interpersonal intimacy draws the members of Australian families closer together, but at the same time people do want social acceptance from the larger community. Especially, they want recognition for their economic achievements. In Australia today, the ability of a family to facilitate economic achievement by all its members is taken to be an important sign of successful family life.

McDonald (1995) points out that contemporary Australian family values are like family values in other western societies, but they are unlike those in many non-western societies since they emphasize the needs of the individual rather than the group. At the most general level, individualism is one of the strongest values in the cultures of Anglo-American societies.

In practice, no major society consists entirely of people who follow just one cultural tradition. India is culturally very diverse, and Australia today contains immigrants from many different cultural backgrounds. Population migration has occurred throughout history, as people have fled persecution or as they have sought to gain better opportunities for themselves. Intermarriage between people from different cultural groups sometimes occurs as a result (Cretser, 1990). However, intermarriage tends to be restricted by norms of *endogamy*, that is by preferential rules for marriage between partners from the same group.

Where intermarriage does occur, migrants have often adopted the practices of people in the host society and they have been assimilated into the dominant family culture. But when there has been little intermarriage, migrants have often retained very different patterns of family living from the majority of the population. In the latter instance, we can talk about the existence of family subcultures.

Subcultural comparisons of family differences within a society can be very important. In countries such as the United States, Australia and Canada, which contain the descendants of immigrants from all over the world, such comparisons are necessary in order to understand family diversity (Hartley, 1995). Subcultural comparisons are also necessary in most parts of western Europe today. These countries have become important receivers of immigrants from eastern Europe, and from the Indian subcontinent, the Caribbean, Africa, Indonesia and Turkey. Post-Second World War immigration into western Europe has brought about increased diversity, including more complex households. In Britain, multigeneration extended families living in the same household are found most often among peoples from the Indian subcontinent, that is, India, Pakistan and Bangladesh (Haskey, 1989). Here we can see the influence of cultures that favour joint families, in the higher relative frequency of households in these ethnic groups that consist of two or more families with children (Dallos and Sapsford, 1997).

In principle, cultural diversity is easy to distinguish from situational diversity. In actuality, it can be hard to tell whether the main cause of family complexity lies in cultural or material factors. Consider, for example, the family practices of African-Americans and Puerto Ricans in the United States. By comparison with non-Hispanic whites in the United States, African-American and Puerto

Rican women have more out-of-wedlock births, and they are more likely to form sole-parent families. Is that because of the relatively low economic situations of these minority groups, which make it very difficult for women to form stable marital unions? Or is it because these groups have *matrifocal* or *matricentric* (mother-centred) family subcultures, where male family roles are poorly defined and weakly supported? This question has sometimes created intense political debates about the possible influence of family subcultures on the emergence of an American 'underclass' (Moynihan, 1965; Wilson, 1987; Baca Zinn, 1989; Peterson, 1991; Hurtado, 1995). American arguments about an underclass comprised of groups with matricentric family subcultures have sometimes resonated in Britain, where West Indian households are more likely than White or Asian households to be headed by females (Diamond and Clarke, 1989).

Cultural Diversity

Sociologists are often very interested in cultural differences between western societies and non-western societies, because of questions about the impact of *modernization*. For most of the twentieth century the major western societies were the most economically developed societies. It is therefore sometimes suggested that as developing countries modernize, their cultures will inevitably become more like those of the West. This is the 'convergence thesis' of modernization and family change.

According to the convergence thesis, family practices tend to become more alike in societies which undergo modernization. Requirements of improved economic performance place common demands upon families, and benefits of greater productivity create common opportunities for individual autonomy. This idea of convergence has been very influential in crosscultural comparative studies of family change in the western societies.

Similar trends of marital and reproductive behaviour can be observed in many European countries, as well as in the United States, Canada and Australia (Caplow, 1991; Caplow and Mendras, 1995; Palomba and Moors, 1995; Teachman, Polonko and Scanzoni, 1999). Officially sanctioned marriage has tended to decline, as has the number of children to whom women give birth. On the other hand, separation and divorce have increased, as has cohabitation (Pullinger and Summerfield, 1997). The number of births out of wedlock has also risen. These trends are generally interpreted as consequences of the value attached to individual choice in western cultures within contexts of increased opportunity for freedom of expression. In particular, greater opportunities for education and employment of women are thought to have been especially important in recent family changes (Jones, Marsden and Tepperman, 1990; Burns and Scott, 1994).

The relevance of the convergence thesis to understanding contemporary family life in non-western societies is debatable. That is to say, there is evidence both for it and against it. In India, for example, there appears to be no clear and consistent trend toward the disintegration of the traditional joint family (Shah, 1998). The public perception of the decline of the joint family seems to be based on changes within a small but highly visible group. The urban professional class has adopted a flexible, mobile and career-oriented lifestyle that is tolerant toward small families. It accepts geographical separation between the generations as a price to be paid for economic success. At the same time, there are many less affluent people – perhaps the majority of the population – who see the joint family as a strategy for economic and social advancement. In this large section of Indian society, households have been increasing in size and the emphasis on the norm of joint house-holding has strengthened as a result of economic development. That is because increased life expectancy has increased the probability of individuals reaching a stage in life when they are capable of forming a joint household, and economic growth has given them the resources with which to do so. Also, increased life expectancy has increased the average length of time that joint households last, before the founders die and the household breaks up.

A further complicating factor for the convergence thesis is that rapid growth in a number of Asian countries has raised questions about the role played in economic development by culture, including family values. If Christian family values promoted individualism that was associated with western economic development in the past, then perhaps family values grounded in other religious traditions that stress harmony and respect for others may be associated with a new path of economic development in the East. This is a possibility that is of intense interest to some people in non-western societies, who are appalled by what they see as the moral failures of western family life. In countries such as Malaysia, important groups are anxious to avoid what is sometimes referred to as 'westoxification' (that is, the poisonous influence of western culture). Instead, they want to revive and strengthen Asian family values (Stivens, 1998). For this reason, the precise nature of cultural differences between eastern and western societies is of genuine sociological interest today.

In the following discussion of cultural diversity, the focus will be on certain aspects of traditional family life in selected societies in Asia. Some of these family practices have also been introduced into western societies, by migrants from places like Hong Kong and Vietnam. Asian immigrants often adapt to life in the host country in different ways, and recent migration from Asia has therefore added to the diversity of living arrangements in the West (Kanjanapan, 1989).

The major crosscultural differences in family life tend to occur on five dimensions of group interaction. First, there are different ideals of family composition. Second, there are different preferences for autonomy and dependence between family members. Third, there are different expectations about transactions within and between families. Fourth, there are different assumptions about the roles played by men and women within families, especially concerning the division of labour. And fifth, there are different expectations about the quality of interaction between family members, depending on whether the emphasis is placed upon conformity to the public form of a relationship or upon the emotional content of the relationship. Cultural influences will be illustrated in this chapter by looking at different ideals of family composition, and by examining the balance between autonomy and dependence.

Family Composition

The most visible differences between families in the East and West are often the composition of the family and resulting family size. In Chapter 1, we saw that North Americans and Europeans generally prefer to live in small family groups that have mainly taken the form of nuclear families. By comparison, eastern ideals of family living are more often expressed in preferences for extended families of various kinds. In India, for example, joint families are considered desirable, as noted earlier in this chapter. In other parts of Asia which are influenced by Confucian religious traditions, a different kind of extended family is preferred.

In Japan, the ideal type of family is the *stem family*, referred to in Japanese as the *ie* (Hendry, 1981; Kumagai, 1995). A stem family consists of a succession of males, together with their wives and dependent children, who all live in one household. The stem family, like the joint family, is an intergenerational group. But in the stem family only one representative of the male line in each generation is a permanent member. All the other descendants of the head of the household must leave when they marry, if not before, and set up their own households.

The stem family is a patriarchal family in which the eldest male is the household head. His successor is usually his eldest son. However, if there are no sons then the husband of a daughter, or failing that a male relative, is adopted into the household. By whatever method, one male is designated as the successor who will remain in the household and eventually become its next head.

The relationship between the family head and his successor is the key relationship within the stem family. It is the basis for intergenerational continuity of the household, and it also establishes who has the most say in family decision-making. The attitude traditionally expected from the eldest son toward his father is one of *filial piety*, that is great respect accompanied by a devout sense of the duty owed towards a parent by a child. In traditional Japanese culture this great respect for the preceding generation is reinforced by a general respect for all predecessors, manifested in rituals performed for the ancestors. Cultural legitimation of family continuity during ritual observances for the family ancestors has no doubt contributed to the durability of the stem family system in Japan.

The traditional family ideal of the *ie* continues to be influential among Japanese people. In Japan, as in many other parts of Asia, the majority of older people live in the same household as an adult child (Maeda and Shimizu, 1992; Chayovan, 1994). Furthermore, the probability of an eldest son co-residing with a parent is much higher in Japan than it is for other children (Kojima, 1989). The living arrangements of the elderly here are very different than they are in most western countries. In Canada, for example, three quarters of persons aged 65 and over maintained an independent household alone or with a spouse in the early 1990s (Che-Alford, Allan and Butlin, 1994). Only 15 per cent of elderly persons in Canada actually live with a child (Cheal, 1997b).

Nevertheless, it would not be accurate to conclude that Japanese family life is completely different from family life in North America. The proportion of elderly Japanese living with their adult children has been falling in recent decades, in parallel with the industrialization and urbanization of Japanese society (Maeda and Shimizu, 1992). Economic development in Japan has loosened the ties between the generations, in ways that are consistent with the convergence thesis of family change. Migration of young people from rural areas to the cities has clearly reduced intergenerational coresidence, since migrant children are likely to leave their parents behind. Also, having more disposable income enables both younger and older Japanese to live independently, if they so wish. Many of them do take advantage of this opportunity provided by economic progress (Kojima, 1989).

Are Japanese families converging toward a western style of family life? Families in Japan have clearly reduced many of their traditional ways, but family change in Japan is occurring only slowly at the present time by comparison with most western societies (Morley, 1999). On present trends, any convergence remains far off in the future, if indeed it will ever occur. For instance, disruptive effects of migration on traditional residence patterns might not last much beyond the initial period of rapid urbanization. Furthermore, there are specific economic factors in Japan, including the extremely high cost of housing, that continue to provide practical arguments in favour of intergenerational coresidence. In a difficult environment for women who want to be mothers and also have a career outside the home, living with her husband's parents can give a wife access to childcare and assistance with housework. Some wives who have adopted modern values of personal development therefore express a preference for extended family living, rather than just a sense of duty toward their in-laws (Aponte, 1999).

Autonomy vs. Dependence

In traditional extended families, such as the Japanese *ie*, individuals are encouraged to find fulfilment for their major needs within the family and to put the collective interests of the group before their own personal interests. Collective interests are especially strong in rural areas, where the family is a working group whose members cooperate to meet their economic needs. In contrast, people in urban areas often depend less upon their families since they have more independent access to jobs through extensive labour markets. Independent income-earning is often accompanied by strong desires for individual autonomy.

The balance between autonomy and dependence in family life is illustrated by the living arrangements of young adults. In traditional societies, young people usually live with their parents until they marry. When they marry, one of three things can happen. They might continue to reside in the parental home, as the eldest son does in a stem family. They might move to the parental home of their spouse, which is a common experience for brides of senior sons in stem families. Or, the new couple might establish a nuclear family with its own residence, as junior children do when they leave a stem family. (The practice of a new couple establishing their own independent household is referred to as *neolocal residence*). In all three of these possibilities, there is no room for a period of independent living in a non-family setting prior to, or outside of, marriage.

Continuous residence of unmarried adults with their parents is characteristic of all societies in which traditional family values are dominant. However, increased individualism associated with modernization is reflected in increasing numbers of people living alone. In this respect, Japanese family life has changed significantly in recent decades. The proportion of one-person households in Japan rose from 6.0 per cent in 1920 to 21.2 per cent in 1991 (Kumagai, 1995). Less dependence on family living can also be observed among contemporary Japanese residing outside Japan. Japanese immigrants living in the United States are more likely than other Asian immigrants to live in nonfamily households, consisting of one person living alone or a group of unrelated persons sharing the same dwelling (Kanjanapan, 1989).

Clearly, preferences for individual autonomy vs dependence on family vary between cultures, and they have also been changing over time. These different preferences are reflected in different living arrangements. The general trend in most countries is toward more independent living, as individuals acquire both a stronger taste for personal freedom and a greater capacity to act as autonomous agents. In countries as different as the United States, Japan and Scotland, the trend has been for more young people to leave home before marriage and to enjoy a period of living independently (Jones, 1995; Goldscheider and Goldscheider, 1999). In Canada, gaining independence rapidly replaced marriage as the main reason for leaving the parental home in the cohorts born after the Second World War (Ravanera, Rajulton and Burch, 1995).

Another consequence of increased preferences and capacities for individual autonomy is high divorce rates. Elevated divorce rates occurred in many countries in the second half of the twentieth century. In Australia, for instance, the probability of a marriage ending in divorce rose from about 10 per cent in the 1950s and early 1960s to a new plateau at about 40 per cent in the 1980s and 1990s (Carmichael, Webster and McDonald, 1997).

Situational Diversity

The number of people who live on their own is a useful indicator of cultural preferences for individual autonomy in a particular society. However, living alone can also be the result of difficult, or unusual, personal situations. (See **Box 2.1**). For most people, living alone is just a phase in life. In other phases in the past they lived in a household with other family members, or perhaps in several families at different times. Also, they may intend to resume family living at some period in the future.

Temporary separation from family members often occurs among migrants, especially when they move long distances to places which are unfamiliar to them or if they believe it may be difficult to settle in the new location. People who move from rural areas to cities, or from one part of the world to another, often do so alone. That is because migration tends to disrupt social ties, and because it is risky. If there are no guarantees of employment in the new location, and if living accommodation is uncertain, then the possibility of failure may be too serious for a whole family group to move all at once. That is especially likely to be the case if there are children involved. Initial migration often takes the form of adults moving on their own. Later, they may try to reunite their families if they are successful. When immigrants such as Haitians settle in a new location such as the United States they re-establish family groups, either by marrying someone they meet in the new place or by bringing their spouses and children – and perhaps other relatives – to join them (Stepick, 1998).

The personal lives of migrants illustrate an important point about complexity and diversity in family life. Living arrangements such as living alone do not necessarily reflect different family values. Rather, they are often the result of situational diversity. That is to say, people with the same cultural ideals of family life may live in different ways because practical circumstances affect the choices they make. Put in exactly the same situation, people who share the same family culture will probably make the same kinds of choices. But put them in different situations, such as migration versus staying in one place, and people with similar values will probably live in quite different ways.

Change Over the Life Course

The lives of migrants who move from living in a family group to living alone, and then back to living in a family group, illustrate an important type of situational diversity. People typically occupy different positions in relation to family groups at different points in their *life course*. An individual's life course

Box 2.1 Time–space distanciation

Separation of family members who live apart from one another, but who still consider themselves to belong together, is a common experience which has received more attention in a number of countries in recent years (Quddus, 1992; Hoodfar, 1997). In contemporary sociological theory, this experience is analyzed as an aspect of social order that Anthony Giddens refers to as '*time–space distanciation*'. Giddens defines this concept as 'the conditions under which time and space are organised so as to connect presence and absence' (Giddens, 1990: 14).

The conjunction of people in time and space is often taken to be a defining condition of family membership. We may talk about family members as people who 'live together' in the same household, and who 'spend a lot of time together', often because they share a 'home' to which they return at regular intervals. However, family life is not always so simple. Family life can also involve disjunctions of time and space, for example when partners have separate residences and see each other only infrequently (Gross, 1980). Such disjunctions raise a number of interesting questions about how family life is reconstituted and redefined under new social conditions.

Interest in this topic has focused mainly upon separated couples, either legally married or cohabiting, who are sometimes referred to as 'living apart together'. Although reliable evidence is hard to come by, anecdotal evidence suggests that this pattern may be increasing. Possible cultural factors that facilitate this development include social acceptance of cohabitation for couples who do not want the constraints of formal marriage, which encourages more flexible relationships in countries like the Netherlands and Sweden (Levin and Trost, 1999). Situational factors include contemporary trends of economic and technological change, such as growing migration from less developed to more developed countries, increased travel for business and leisure that raises the probability of meeting someone in a remote place, and requirements of geographic mobility for career success of both women and men. In countries like Singapore, which are currently involved in a process of rapid internationalization, these trends may lead to questions about how spouses, parents and children cope with separation over time and space (Chia, 2000).

consists of a series of social positions, through which she or he moves during the course of her or his life. Some social positions are more common at certain times of life than at others. For example, living alone in a one-person household is much more common in old age than in middle age in countries like Britain and Canada (Beaujot et al., 1995; Central Statistical Office, 1995).

In some social situations, individual life courses take the form of a predictable sequence of stages known as the 'family life cycle.' In other social environments, life's pathways are less certain and individual life courses are less predictable. In either case, we can expect that most people will live in different ways at different times of life, and that not everyone will be living in the same family situation at the same time. This point can be clearly observed in contemporary Japanese family life.

Family structure in contemporary Japan has been described as the 'modified stem family' (Kumagai, 1995). In the modified stem family, a person experiences the modern nuclear family and the traditional stem family alternately throughout the life course. This pattern of family living can be illustrated from the life course of a Japanese woman (Kumagai, 1986).

During the post-Second World War period, nuclear families became more common in Japan. Today, a Japanese female will probably be born into a nuclear family, consisting of herself, her mother and her father, and possibly a sibling. (Since this family is the family where her life begins, it is referred to as her *family of origin*). She lives in this nuclear family unit until the time when her father's parents move into the household in order to receive support in their old age. Now she is living in a stem family. She continues to live in this stem family until she marries. At that time she leaves her family of origin for her *family of orientation*. (The word 'orientation' here means preferred choice. The family of orientation therefore refers to the family members that the individual has chosen to live with, principally her or his spouse). Once she is married the young woman is living in a nuclear family again, this time with her husband and later probably with her children too. (When the first child arrives, we may refer to the family group in which she lives as her *family of procreation*). Eventually, her husband's elderly parents will move into the household, recreating a three-generational stem family once more. When her parents-in-law die, her family returns to being a nuclear family. Finally, in her old age she will move into her son's family of procreation, and she will end her days in a stem family.

Studying family change over the life course is very important for understanding the family system in Japan, and also in other countries. The majority of Japanese families now are nuclear families. It would therefore be easy to think that family life in Japan has converged upon the pattern of family life in the western societies. However, the study of the life course shows that traditional Japanese family ideals remain influential today, even though their application has been modified by later social changes. A great deal of situational diversity exists in Japanese family life, but beneath this diversity underlying intergenerational ties remain strong.

In the life courses of Japanese people, situational diversity is a result of the changing needs for autonomy of the married couple on the one hand, and for intergenerational dependence on the other hand. The practical realities of aging are interpreted as requiring intergenerational coresidence when parents are too old to look after themselves. At the same time, the closeness that exists between spouses and the bond that exists between a mother and a young child limit parental claims upon adult children, except in old age.

Situational diversity can also occur as a result of economic pressures that produce different economic interests. In Japan in the past, for example, the 'traditional' *ie* only existed in the small upper class, for whom the inheritance of property was a major concern. Most of the population followed a more flexible type of extended family system. Here, intergenerational hierarchy was less important than ability to contribute to the family economically, through leadership and hard work. The *ie* system only came into widespread use in Japan at the end of the nineteenth century. After the Meiji Restoration, it was enforced on all classes as part of a new imperial system. In other societies, that did not have such a rigid family code enforced by law and custom, class differences may be more important features of situational diversity.

Class, Race and Family

Japanese history shows that in the past the family system of the upper class tended to become publicly defined as the cultural ideal, which was then imposed upon the lower classes. Less structured family practices of the lower classes were seen as being of inferior social value. However, after the Second World War a new Civil Code was imposed on Japan by the United States. The *ie* system was officially abolished (although it did not disappear in practice), and the family unit was defined to include only husband, wife and children. With the official abolition of the position of household head, husband and wife were given equal legal rights in the family (Kumagai, 1986).

In western societies, family codes of the upper classes have been less often imposed upon the whole society by law. Yet, class differences in family composition sometimes exist that are also judged in terms of the degree of their deviation from a recommended cultural ideal. People in the lower classes, it is thought, are less likely than people in the middle or upper classes to live in intact nuclear families. Some people think that is because nuclear family living places high demands upon husbands and wives, which people in the lower classes are not always able to meet. The ability to fulfill the role of a wife or a husband may be especially difficult if class divisions overlap with racial divisions. This way of looking at family complexity was recommended by the classic American sociologist, Talcott Parsons (1902–79).

Talcott Parsons was a functionalist sociologist. He believed that the nuclear family was the type of family that was best adapted to life in a mobile society such as the United States. Parsons observed that nuclear family living in the United States was least stable among people who had relatively low incomes and low education (Parsons, 1971). That included large numbers of African-Americans, who had historically been disadvantaged by a rigid system of racial stratification. Here, the strains of struggling to make ends meet as well as to gain social approval, and the experience of sometimes failing, produced what Parsons called 'family disorganization'. By 'family disorganization' he meant the weakening and breaking of family ties, especially through marital separation and divorce.

Parsons's class analysis of American family diversity has been criticized on several grounds. He seems to have overlooked the strength of kinship networks that often link black families, and which help to sustain black family functioning (Scott and Black, 1994). Also, he did not anticipate that separation and divorce would become much more prevalent in the white middle class by the end of the twentieth century. Despite these criticisms, it remains the case that class and race differences over family practices persist in American society.

Class and race differences in the number of female lone parents, and especially births to unmarried teenagers, became a major political issue in the United States during the 1980s and 1990s. Elements of this debate linked fatherlessness, normlessness and delinquency, and this argument drew sympathetic responses in countries such as Britain (Dennis and Erdos, 1992). Growing concern about these issues led to calls for a return to traditional Christian family values. There were also new social movements to support commitments by African-American men to parenting within a family context. Researchers also became interested in the immediate causes of class and race differences in family composition, since some of those differences seem to have increased after the early 1960s (Aponte, 1999). One of the most influential, and most controversial, of the researchers into situational diversity in American family life was Charles Murray (1984).

Murray drew two main conclusions. First, he claimed that most (but not all) of the difference in family composition between the black and white populations in the United States was really due to class differences. Poor whites and blacks, as well as those with low incomes, showed similar trends between 1960 and 1980 of more households headed by solo females. Murray thought that if the increase in black households headed by solo females seemed to have been much greater than it was for whites, that was mainly because more African-Americans were poor or had low incomes.

The second claim made by Murray was that the increase in families with children headed by only one parent was largely due to reforms to the welfare system made in the 1960s and 1970s. He believed that a more generous and relaxed welfare system had undermined the family, because it provided disincentives to marry or to stay married. Under the government programme for Aid to Families with Dependent Children (AFDC), as it existed at that time, a couple could maximize their incomes if they did not marry, and if the woman kept any children she bore. Murray therefore concluded that from an economic point of view, getting married is 'dumb' (Murray, 1984). He and his followers in the United States and Britain thought this was a simple economic explanation for much of the family disorganization which they observed in the lower classes between 1960 and 1980.

Murray's analysis of racial differences in family composition, as being mainly due to class factors, was initially well received in sociology. However, many sociologists were at the same time unconvinced by his hypothesis that welfare dependency among the poor is a significant factor in causing unmarried motherhood. Rather, they tended to see this line of argument as another example of 'blaming the victim' (Blaikie, 1996). Instead, sociologists who study social stratification argued that the major influence on family patterns in the lower classes is a narrowing of occupational opportunities. There are fewer jobs for people with little education in a period of rapid economic change.

William Julius Wilson (1987) has argued that it was the rise in male joblessness in inner-city areas which was the major situational factor behind growing female headship in African-American families. He believes there is no evidence to show that the welfare system is a major factor in the rise of childbearing outside marriage. Rather, he concludes that what he calls the 'fading of the inner-city family' (Wilson, 1996) is mainly due to the falling capacity of many young males, especially young black men, to act as family breadwinners (Wilson, 1993). Increased joblessness among African-American males, caused by the restructuring of labour markets in an era of globalization, led many inner-city black women to expect less from black men. It also led many African-American men living in the inner cities to expect less from themselves. Faced with limited job prospects, many young black men concluded they have limited prospects for gaining social status via the traditional male route of supporting a family. They are therefore more likely to seek social recognition and support through activities that are disconnected from nuclear family life (Anderson, 1993).

Wilson (1996) has subsequently recognized that economic factors alone cannot account for the extremely low commitment to husband–wife families in inner-city African-American communities today, especially by comparison with Mexican immigrants. He has therefore outlined a complex explanatory model, that combines both situational and cultural factors. Increased joblessness in an entire community erodes community norms of work and family discipline, he believes. In turn, a decline in community norms that would otherwise legitimate and sanction marriage means that relationship decisions are increasingly made on personal criteria of sexual attraction and economic interests. It is in this social environment that a relative fall in earnings among young men is most likely to lead to calculations which favour individual gratification outside marriage.

Individualization

Changing norms of family formation are not limited to inner-city African-American communities, nor are they found only in the United States. As William Julius Wilson has noted, the intact nuclear family is less of a cultural ideal in America than it once was. Today, there is less stigma attached to out-of-wedlock births, marital separation and divorce in most communities. Increasingly, decisions about the formation and dissolution of families are made as a result of personal preferences, rather than in response to communal or societal expectations. One result of this is that in the United States there are more people living on their own now than ever before.

The likelihood that unmarried individuals of any age will live alone is positively associated with income, and the historical increase in single-person households at all ages is largely attributable to increasing affluence. This finding is consistent with the thesis that personal privacy and independence are strong values in the United States, which many individuals act upon whenever they have the resources to do so (White, 1994).

The growth of a style of decision-making in which individuals respond only to their own immediate situation is referred to as *individualization*. Discussions of the effects of individualization on family life today have been prominent in countries such as Germany and the Netherlands, where it is argued that inherited class positions are less important than they once were (Beck, 1992; Peters, 1995). If it is true that class divisions are no longer passed on from one generation to the next, because of increased education, greater occupational mobility and intensified competition at all levels, then the choices individuals make will reflect their unique preferences as well as the demands and opportunities of their particular social positions. Individual life courses have thus become more variable in most countries.

One idea which has emerged out of discussions of individualization is a suggestion that increased complexity of the life course is associated with subjective changes in how people think about themselves, and how they think about family life. In an individualized world, people self-consciously reflect upon their own needs and their plans for the future as the bases for social action. Goals of realizing the inner self become prominent. Personal relationships are looked at either as opportunities for, or as obstacles to, certain kinds of self-development.

Individualization, which is a result of increased social complexity, adds to the complexity of family life. That is because more people have more short-term relationships in order to satisfy changing needs and desires. A belief that continuing to live with a particular person has become a barrier to self-fulfilment is often a basis for breaking off a relationship. On the other hand, being with a person who creates unique conditions for self-development can provide the basis for forming a new relationship.

There is another important social change that follows from individualization. Formal structures of family ties become less important than the subjective contents of personal relationships. Young adults, for example, are often less concerned about getting married than they are about having 'relationships'. Anthony Giddens (1992) argues that more and more people are seeking what he calls '*pure relationships*'. These are intimate relationships, in which the participants take little or no account of community norms or the expectations of others. Each person enters into a pure relationship for the benefits that it is expected to bring, and they stay in it only insofar as it continues to provide enough satisfactions for both partners. Pure relationships may be sexual or non-sexual, they may involve living together or living separately, and they may involve either marriage or cohabitation.

Individuals' preferences for pure relationships erode cultural ideals of fixed family structures. This does not necessarily mean that cultural influences on family life are in decline. Rather, contemporary individuals are participating in the emergence of a flexible culture, which emphasizes the psychology of personal relationships instead of inherited traditions. Ideals about pure relationships are basic features of post-traditional cultures (Beck, Giddens and Lash, 1994). Nevertheless, in the practical world of everyday family life it is debatable how many people actually realize those ideals (Bittman and Pixley, 1997; Jamieson, 1999; Langford, 1999; Smart and Neale, 1999).

Discussion

In this chapter we have seen that the diversity of family groups is due to three main causes. First, there is the cultural diversity which is produced by people following different ideals of family organization. Most societies have a collective preference for one type of family organization rather than another. Collective preferences for nuclear families, joint families or stem families shape the everyday choices that people make about family relationships. The result is a great deal of crosscultural diversity between families in different societies, and subcultural diversity between families in the same society.

Second, there is the situational diversity that occurs when people who follow the same family values must apply them in different circumstances. Inequalities in economic resources between classes, and social segregation between races, are often important situational influences. The situational diversity produced here sometimes takes the form of a contrast between more family organization in more privileged groups, and less family organization or even family disorganization in underprivileged groups. In the latter groups, unsuccessful attempts to be economically self-sufficient and to gain social esteem may lead some people to give up on conventional goals. When they do, the result can be a fall in commitment to conventional family structures, including looser family ties.

Third, there is the expanded emphasis on individual autonomy, which is referred to as 'individualization' (Beck and Beck-Gernsheim, 1995). This way of life is increasingly characteristic of populations in contemporary western societies. However, it is debatable whether or not all non-western peoples will converge on this pattern in the near future. In those places where a high level of individualization exists, people act in ways that they think are most useful to themselves in their immediate situation. Cultural traditions, including religious codes of conduct, are accorded less importance than ideas about personal relationships. Among other developments, cohabitation tends to replace legal marriage here.

Today, popular culture contains a variety of ideas about personal relationships, concerning how they work and how they can be improved. When particular relationships do not work as well as expected, the resulting disappointments often lead to a search for intimacy in a new relationship. Intimate relationships in a highly individualized society therefore tend to be unstable. Under these conditions, more people enter into more new relationships over their lifetimes, and individual life courses become more complex and more diverse. All of this complexity and diversity leads to increased questioning about the future of family structures (Beck-Gernsheim, 1999).

3

Family Priorities

The question, 'who are family members?' is further examined through the choices that people make about particular individuals in particular situations. Choices express systems of priorities about relationships that are judged to be more or less important. In Chapter 3 we consider the extent to which these priorities reflect a set of cultural rules, or 'normative guidelines', and to what extent they are influenced by other factors such as the history of family interaction and the negotiation of responsibilities. How people make their choices, and why, takes on a new importance as relationships change due to divorce or separation, and as the shape of family structures changes due to population aging.

CONCEPTS

conjugal relationship   conjugal family   marital status   normative guidelines   commitment demography   longevity   bridge generation

Contemporary social life is highly individualized, but we all need help and support in times of difficulty and almost all of us feel strong needs for intimate, human contact. Family members are, of course, not the only people we can turn to for help in meeting our needs. Each of us has a personal network that is made up of a mixture of family members, friends and acquaintances (Cheal, 1988; Allan, 1996). Nevertheless, family members often lie at, or near, the centre of our personal networks. Data from Britain clearly show that family members are seen as overwhelmingly more important than friends by a margin of around eleven to one (McGlone, Park and Roberts, 1996). Similarly, by a margin of around four to one, people would rather spend their time with other family members than with their friends.

The significance of family life for most people is clearly demonstrated in the British Household Panel Survey, in answers to an open-ended question about what recent events people personally regarded as important (Scott and Perren, 1994). Family events were mentioned by respondents more often than any other kind of event. Not all of these events were positive, since they included family problems (2 per cent) and the deaths of family members (16 per cent). However, positive events involving family members, such as births (26 per cent) and weddings (19 per cent), were the most likely to be stressed. Women and older people were more likely than men and younger people to mention family events involving others, but the importance of family events crosses gender and generational boundaries (Scott, 1997). Adults living alone are almost as likely to mention other family members as those living in married households.

Family members are people to whom we feel especially close, and they are also people to whom we are expected to feel close. In some families, this expectation is expressed in the belief that 'the family comes first'. A good example of putting the family first can be seen in an Australian study of who helps when people are unable to cope on their own (d'Abbs, 1991). Most people expressed a strong preference for 'keeping it all in the family' when they have been seriously ill or following surgery. They wanted to be cared for by family members, and not by outsiders. People outside the family are seen as less reliable and therefore as potentially threatening, especially if they have access to the family home and the lives of all the people in it. Furthermore, it is thought that outsiders will not have the same level of personal interest in the individual. This sense of a sharp division between the inside world of the family, and the outside world of society is accentuated where people are distrustful of their neighbours, and when they have a dislike for using publicly funded social services.

'Keeping it all in the family' can mean different things to different people. For some people, it means being prepared to accept help from within an extended family. The preference here is usually for receiving personal care from a close relative, such as one's mother or a daughter, who can come and live with a sick person temporarily while help is needed. For other people, 'keeping it in the family' means accepting personal services only from someone who normally lives in the same household. Practically speaking, this involves relying upon a spouse in most cases. In Peter d'Abbs' study of who provides personal care at home in Australia, spouses were the most common caregivers (d'Abbs, 1991).

The Structure of Family Relationships

The notion that there exists a system of priorities in people's relationships is not new. One influential example is found in the functionalist sociology of Talcott Parsons (1943). As we shall see in a moment, Parsons's ideas have to be modified in a number of ways. Nevertheless, his work constitutes a useful starting point for discussing the standard theory of family systems, especially in Anglo-American societies. (See **Box 3.1**).

Talcott Parsons observed that certain key family relationships lie at the centre of most people's lives. He elaborated this idea in what he called the 'onion' principle of family structure. Like an onion, family relationships can be looked at as a series of layers. Each successive layer is more distant from the person who is at the centre. Increasing social distance is expressed in weaker ties between the individual at the centre and persons in the outer layers of the 'onion' structure. For example, contact is less frequent, and giving is less generous (Cheal, 1986). Outside the 'onion', there is the larger society which does not allow or encourage personal relationships.

According to Parsons, the heart of the 'onion' structure is made up of two family groups. First, there is the group consisting of the individual, plus her or

---

Box 3.1   Standard model of family life

According to the standard model of family life, the family is a task-performing unit which mediates between the individual and society (Hill, 1971). Families are described as adaptive systems that respond to the stresses produced by unmet needs. Standard accounts of family life therefore usually emphasize the positive features of family relationships. The family is seen as helping individuals to meet their needs, by redistributing resources from those family members who have more to those who have less, and by providing emotional and social support to family members in times of difficulty. The family also shields its members from some of the pressures exerted by powerful external groups. In modern industrial societies, it may provide a 'haven in a heartless world'.

Assumptions of standard family theory are notably influential in studies of coping in old age, within the discipline of gerontology and in the sociology of aging (Chappell, 1989). Families are thought to be important because they help older people adjust when they have to deal with impersonal, bureaucratic organizations, such as hospitals. Also, family members may provide intimate personal care to elderly people who can no longer look after all of their own physical needs. Social gerontologists therefore often visualize families as 'informal support systems' which support and protect their members and help them to live long and healthy lives (Keating et al., 1999).

Standard family theory has had many detractors as well as supporters. For example, it has been criticized for paying insufficient attention to negative aspects of family life, such as domestic violence and sexual abuse, as well as for failing to recognize that inequality and conflict are endemic in family relationships.

his mother and father, and any brothers and sisters (that is, the individual's family of origin). Second, there is the group which most people form at some point in their life, consisting of the individual plus his or her spouse, and perhaps some sons or daughters (that is, the individual's family of orientation). Although both of these groups are extremely important to most Americans, Parsons claimed that the latter group has the highest priority in adulthood and therefore during the longest part of the life course. Anglo-American culture tends to emphasize the long-term value of a *conjugal relationship* (that is, a heterosexual marriage) over descent ties to parents and grandparents.

As stated by Parsons, it follows logically from the priority given to the conjugal relationship that all other relatives, such as aunts, uncles and cousins, as well as in-laws acquired through marriage, form the outer layers of the onion structure. People in the outer layers receive less attention, and they are not given as much help on a regular basis. In return, less is expected from them, except on the major ritual occasions such as weddings and funerals that every family member is expected to attend.

Thinking about the model of family priorities as an onion structure is a useful starting point for analyzing family responsibilities and family obligations. However, Parsons's model needs to be qualified in several ways if we are to understand the choices that people actually make.

To begin with, family priorities are often gendered. That is to say, women and men tend to interpret their family obligations in different ways (Maclean and Eekelaar, 1997). This pattern is shown in a study of higher-income couples in England, in the early 1990s (Jordan, Redley and James, 1994). The couples in this study had strong commitments to maintaining the independence of the family, by ensuring that all of the family's needs were met through their joint efforts. However, 'putting the family first' often meant different things for wives than for husbands. Husbands, for example, might decide to move to a different, and less desirable, place in order to get a promotion that would mean more money for the family. Wives, on the other hand, were more likely to forego opportunities to take a better job, in order to avoid working longer hours that would result in less time spent with their children. Clearly, feelings about priorities in the family are heavily influenced by gender roles. We shall have much more to say about gender later in this book.

The second main point to keep in mind when modifying Parsons's thesis about family structure is that ideas about 'putting the family first' are always affected by cultural and situational factors. We turn to these two issues next.

Cultural Factors

Cultural differences in defining who is included within the circle of family life are expressed in different rules about how people should make decisions involving other people. These decision rules provide guidelines for how people should make choices about their relationship priorities when resources such as time and money are scarce. It is impossible to do everything that we would like to do in the limited time that is available to us. So, we have to make choices. We allocate more of our time, as well as money and other resources, to some people rather than to other people. People in different cultures tend to make those choices in different ways because they are following different decision rules.

Families in the East and West often differ in the kinds of family rules that their members are expected to follow. For example, different priorities may be assigned to people in different generations. This can be seen in a comparative study of Japanese and American perspectives on family and the life course, conducted by Akiko Hashimoto (1996).

It will be recalled that Talcott Parsons thought the heart of the family structure consists of two family groups. First, there is the family into which we are born. Then, there is the family that we form when we enter into a partnership that we hope will be long lasting. When choices have to be made, which of these families takes priority? Parsons claimed that in the United States priority is generally given to the *conjugal family*, due to the strong cultural preference that Americans have for marriage as an expression of important social values. People in other countries, with different preferences, may have other priorities.

Japan is one country where we can find somewhat different preferences from the United States. Although traditional family care of the elderly in Japan has been declining due to industrialization, parents still tend to have a high priority in Japanese family life and they are therefore more likely to receive care from their children (Maeda and Nakatani, 1992). In the United States, husband–wife households are the most common type of household in early old age. With the death of a spouse, these households usually shrink to single-person households. In Japan, in contrast, many elderly people live in three-generation households where they have easier access to family supports.

The cultural differences that underlie the contrasting American and Japanese systems of family priorities are interesting. When examined in detail, as they are in Hashimoto's (1996) comparison of Odawara, in Japan, and West Haven, in the United States, they reveal some important features of how family responsibilities are socially constructed.

Americans living in a place like West Haven are more likely than Japanese people in Odawara to believe that when they need help in old age they can draw upon a wide pool of goodwill from among their family members, other relatives, friends, neighbours and even strangers living in their community. This belief is realistically based upon a relatively high level of community involvement in West Haven. It is also based on a widespread tendency to form close bonds with one's generational peers such as one's spouse, and friends of the same age, rather than with one's parents or children who belong to different generations. People in Odawara, Japan, on the other hand, tend to see their community as less likely to support them. They also tend to prefer that their adult children should be their personal confidants, rather than confiding in people outside the family.

Although it is necessary to be cautious in drawing conclusions about two large societies from a comparison based on only two cities, it seems that in Japan social support for the aged is more certain than it is in the United States. Receiving support in the United States depends, first, upon demonstrating a clear need for it. Support-giving by many Americans, therefore, tends to take the form of crisis intervention, being offered only when problems arise that the elderly cannot handle on their own. In contrast, three-generation Japanese families are more likely to protect their elderly members so that they do not get into crisis situations in the first place.

Support-giving by Americans tends to be contingent in another, and sociologically more important, sense. In American cities it is often not immediately clear who should provide what support, from within a wide circle of family members, friends and community organizations that are potentially accessible. Provision of support is therefore usually negotiated among the various support givers, and between the potential support givers and the receivers themselves. Such negotiations take into account people's understandings about the nature of family responsibilities (Gubrium and Holstein, 1990). They also take into account who has what kinds of resources available at the time.

The above description of families and old people in Japan and the US reveals some very basic differences between cultures. It is important to add here that neither of these family systems is necessarily superior to the other. They reflect different values, and they therefore produce different outcomes. In Japanese society, historically, an important family value has been security of support in the face of a difficult, and sometimes hostile, social environment. The United States, on the other hand, has historically placed more emphasis upon individual autonomy and the independence of conjugal families. As a result, elderly Americans tend to enjoy more personal freedoms, and they often derive a sense of pride from not having to rely upon their children. However, it is almost inevitable that with advancing age personal problems will arise that are beyond their control. In crisis situations, external interventions may be needed by the individuals' support networks, or by public agencies.

Situational Factors

Changed circumstances create changed needs, and they are frequently accompanied by shifts in obligations as well as by changes in the ways that obligations are fulfilled. Changes in individuals' situations are therefore highly visible causes of different family priorities. We shall begin looking at this issue by focusing upon the problems that occur when someone stops fulfilling their customary family obligations. This event often precipitates a crisis for other family members. In response, attempts may be made to redefine family obligations in order to maintain family priorities, albeit at a reduced level. For example, Finch and Mason (1990a) report that when a couple is separated their children may nevertheless persuade them to support one another, despite great individual reluctance to do so. Apparently, children sometimes believe in the continued existence of family obligations even when their parents do not.

In a society like the United States, where there is a strong emphasis upon personal autonomy, and the giving and receiving of support is heavily contingent upon individual circumstances, the actual priority given to particular persons is very likely to change with changing circumstances. When change occurs suddenly, and the magnitude of change is large, then the displacement of people who until recently had a high priority in someone's life is usually experienced as disruptive. That is very often the case following separation and divorce. Marriage breakdown has therefore come to be seen as a cause of social problems in a number of western countries, especially in its effects on women and children.

We noted earlier that Talcott Parsons's model of the American family as an 'onion structure', with the conjugal family at the centre, is a useful starting point for studying family life. However, it is a static model. It needs to be complemented by a dynamic analysis of family change.

If the conjugal tie is truly fundamental in the system of priorities in American families, then what happens when that tie is broken? The answer to this question, of course, is that when people learn they are no longer at the centre of their partner's social world there is often a great deal of unhappiness and disappointment. That experience may be accompanied as well by a loss of economic security. For some people, that means a greater risk of falling into poverty (Cheal, 1996a).

The economic consequences of dramatic shifts in priorities following separation and divorce are well known. Ex-spouses no longer share the expenses of a common household, and so each of them must meet the costs of living on their own. For higher-earning spouses, the new arrangement can mean that they are actually better off than before. These fortunate individuals are no longer obligated to support a partner at the same standard of living as themselves. Thus, they have more disposable income. On the other hand, the economic consequences of divorce for lower-earning spouses are usually negative. When they must rely largely, or entirely, upon their own resources, the inevitable result is a lower standard of living.

Husbands tend to earn more than wives in every society, even after several decades of increased earnings for women (Arber, 1999). Ex-husbands are therefore more likely to be better off after a divorce, and ex-wives are likely to be worse off. In addition to the effect of low earnings, the main reason why wives are often worse off after a divorce is that women who are not living with a husband are much more likely than men who are not living with a wife to be caring for dependent children. These women must share their personal incomes with their children, and in the United States this often pushes the family's standard of living below the poverty level (Farley, 1995).

In Canada, too, children are often plunged into poverty when their parents divorce. In fact, a change in the parents' *marital status* from married to separated or divorced has a bigger impact on the probability of a child entering a situation of low family income than does a change in the parents' employ-ment or the level of their wages (Picot, Zyblock and Pyper, 1999). When there was no marital separation, only 13 per cent of Canadian children from middle-income families entered into a new situation of low family income between 1993 and 1994. But when the parents separated, the proportion of children entering into a low-income situation jumped by almost five times to 61 per cent.

Many children suffer economically from their parents' divorce, and attempts are therefore made to ensure that children's needs are not ignored when parents' priorities change. The custodial parent who keeps the children with her (usually the mother) may make moral appeals to the ex-spouse for help in raising the children. Such appeals are effective in persuading some ex-husbands to help, but not all of them. As a result, the number of children growing up in the United States without regular financial or emotional support from their fathers grew from the 1960s onward (Gerson, 1993). Collective efforts were therefore made through government legislation and through enforcement by public agencies to ensure that fathers pay for their children's upkeep. Those efforts have been only partially successful.

In a large study of the consequences of divorce in California during the second half of the 1980s, Maccoby and Mnookin (1992) found that on average fathers paid between two-thirds and three-quarters of the amount of child support awarded by the courts. Reasons for non-compliance or partial compliance varied, but several factors stand out in this study.

First, the amount of contact that fathers have with their children after separating from the mother affects the amount of support they are willing to pay. The more contact between father and child, the more reliable fathers are at paying. As a result, courts and social agencies in a number of places have tried to find ways of sustaining post-divorce contact between fathers and children. This can be done, for example, by making joint custody arrangements easier. It is thought that children will have a higher priority in their fathers' financial decision-making if the fathers can see how their children are growing up.

The second major factor affecting fathers' support payments for children is the fathers' ability to pay. Income level on its own is not a good predictor of whether or not payments are kept up, but loss of employment is. In Maccoby and Mnookin's California study, unemployed fathers were three times more likely than employed fathers to pay no child support.

Finally, the amount of support payments actually paid is influenced by judgements about what is considered to be fair under the circumstances. When the day-to-day care arrangements for a child of divorce change significantly after a court order has been made, the parents often revise the payments accordingly, usually without bothering to seek legal approval. If the mother was awarded custody of the child, but the children actually end up living with the father most of the time, then the father seldom pays any child support that had been ordered. In the California study, more than 80 per cent of these modifications were negotiated and adopted informally rather than through the legal system.

Later survey research in the United States has shown that both women and men are prepared to agree to child support amounts that are below official guidelines, especially when the father's financial status changed or the mother remarried (Coleman et al., 1999). The guiding principle behind popular ideas about child support payments is some notion of fairness to the particular individuals involved, under their particular circumstances. However, there is little agreement in practice about how much money fathers should pay. Marilyn Coleman and her colleagues point out that as a result there is little agreement on how important it is for divorced parents to actually comply with court-ordered support awards. Divorced fathers who do not keep up their child support payments may have significant support from their social networks for not doing so.

When governments attempt to impose a version of family responsibilities which is regarded as unreasonable, some people will respond by developing avoidance strategies that are tolerated by others in their social networks (Finch, 1989). Attempts by lawmakers to standardize behaviour are therefore not always successful when faced with a range of attitudes about the nature and extent of family obligations. People's ideas about family priorities are usually an important part of how they see themselves, and how they see their place in the community. In the case of marriage and divorce, especially, these ideas often reflect deep feelings about love and fairness. They also reflect community standards about what behaviour is appropriate or acceptable, which are used as guidelines for individual decision-making.

Normative Guidelines

Social rules about family obligations are loosely defined in the Anglo-American countries. Although they provide guidelines for appropriate conduct, they do not state precisely what actions are required by whom. Furthermore, the appropriate behaviour is rarely regarded as compulsory, whatever the law may say. These open-ended rules, or *normative guidelines* as Janet Finch (1989) refers to them, must therefore be interpreted by family members when they are applied to particular people in particular situations. Finch suggests that there are five main normative guidelines about family obligations in Britain. She expresses them in the form of positive recommendations, as follows:

1. Consider who the other person is, and especially what their relationship is to you in genealogical terms.
2. Consider whether you get on particularly well with this person.
3. Consider the pattern of exchanges in which you and they have been involved in the past.
4. Consider whether receiving assistance from you would disturb the balance between dependence and independence in this person's family relationships.
5. Consider whether this is the proper time in both your lives for you to give this type of assistance to this particular person.

Evidently, some individuals will have a higher priority than others according to these guidelines. However, it is not always easy to tell in advance exactly who will have the highest priority. In a country like Britain there are often substantial differences in opinion about how much priority should be assigned to elderly parents, for example. A survey conducted in the Greater Manchester area in the mid-1980s found that although the majority of respondents (57 per cent) rejected the idea that children have no obligation to look after their parents, a sizeable minority (39 per cent) in fact agreed with this position (Finch and Mason, 1990a).

Despite the variation that exists in the sense of obligation to care for the elderly, Hazel Qureshi and Ken Simons (1987) have suggested that a systematic set of rules exists in England for deciding who has the greatest obligation to assist when help with household tasks is needed. Help should be given; first, by a spouse; second, by a daughter; third, by a daughter-in-law; fourth, by a son; fifth, by other relatives; and sixth, by non-relatives. This set of family priorities is very similar to the onion structure described by Talcott Parsons for the United States, with an additional gender criterion. Where domestic tasks are concerned, and especially when they involve personal care for an elderly woman, it is usually preferred that a daughter or daughter-in-law should be the caregiver if a spouse is not available (Qureshi and Walker, 1989). Sons are rarely chosen as the people who should provide care for an elderly woman. On the other hand, daughters are rarely chosen as appropriate people to provide money (Finch and Mason, 1990a).

Thinking about family priorities as a system of rules helps to clarify the existence of a hierarchy of obligations in family life. However, there are so many individual circumstances which must be taken into account that very few people actually follow these rules precisely. For example, if an unmarried adult son is still living at home he may be expected to help his parents with more practical tasks around the home than a married daughter who lives some distance away.

The system of family priorities in England is in fact very flexible. Because of this, Janet Finch and Jennifer Mason (1993) have concluded that family responsibilities operate in a way which is much more complex than simply following obligatory rules. People do have an understanding of what would generally be regarded as the 'proper thing to do'. However, instead of following fixed rules they use this understanding as a guideline in negotiating particular allocations of responsibilities between particular individuals.

In a country like England family obligations have to be negotiated between family members, rather than being imposed upon them, because in most cases there is no patriarchal authority figure whose decisions are binding upon an entire extended family. Instead, people who define themselves as having family ties cooperate with one another to the extent that they voluntarily agree with what is being proposed. Family priorities are interpreted in individual ways, and they are inevitably influenced by the individualism of the surrounding culture.

In an individualistic society, people are believed to have the right not to do things that they do not want. At least, that is a right which is generally accorded to adults, although the rights of children are less clear. The individual's right to refuse to do what is not wanted means that family priorities cannot be expressed in legitimate demands for people to do things. Family members cannot simply assume that they will receive community backing for whatever demands they choose to make upon each other. Furthermore, individuals who are clearly in need of help may be careful not to expect it, in case it is not forthcoming (Finch and Mason, 1993). In practice, help is often given within the family after some acknowledgment that it was not required ('you didn't have to do that'). This kind of voluntary support is understood to be part of an individual's *commitment* to a relationship.

The concept of commitment has come to be very important in the sociology of family life. That is largely because many men today are said to be in a 'flight from commitment' (Gerson, 1993). As more men apparently avoid the long-term obligations that were traditionally associated with legal marriage and legitimate fatherhood, new questions are being raised about the nature and origins of commitment.

Commitments are obligations that individuals feel to perform certain acts for other people, due to the fact that they have accepted and fulfilled similar obligations in the past. Sometimes, commitments begin with a conscious act such as a marriage vow. More often, they develop gradually over time as individuals learn how other people rely on them and the value they attach to their contributions. Exactly what the valued contributions are, and how much one person can rely upon another, are matters that the individuals involved negotiate between themselves as their relationship deepens over time.

Interpersonal commitments modify the onion structure of family obligations. Because people typically have multiple commitments they have to find some way of managing them, so that they do not become overburdened with responsibilities. One way of doing this is to provide 'legitimate excuses' for why people are unable to respond to all of the needs that arise (Finch and Mason, 1993). For instance, people who have several young children to look after are not expected to be the first to offer help in a family crisis. Family members usually look for help first from someone who is not heavily burdened with existing commitments. Otherwise, an obligation overload could undermine a person's ability to meet the needs of their dependents. It could also lead to feelings of unfairness if some family members have much greater obligations than others, and that can put a strain on family relationships.

Family History

Avoiding difficult situations which create bad feelings is an important feature of interaction in many families, though not all. If pushed too far, repeated family difficulties might cause some people to leave the family altogether. It is for this reason that the allocation of responsibilities between particular individuals usually takes into account the quality of the relationships between them. There is no point in requiring one person to help another if the result is going to be tension, conflict and a worsening of relationships. Family responsibilities therefore tend to operate on a basis of maximizing cooperation and positive feelings between family members, in order that they will want to continue interacting with each other. The overwhelming priority in most family interactions is simply to keep the interaction going, even if this means that not everyone is believed to be following the rules.

The easiest relationships to maintain are those that have been working well for some time. The history of the relationships between particular individuals therefore emerges here as a factor of great importance in family life. The relevance of family history can be seen when people are forced to re-evaluate their relationships with each other, after there has been a divorce in the family. A divorce not only affects the couple's own relationship, but it can also affect relationships within a larger set of people who had previously considered themselves to be 'in-laws'. Following a divorce, there is no longer any formal link between the people who previously had in-law relationships with each other. This is confirmed by the fact that there is no conventional kinship terminology with which these people can describe one another. They must therefore decide for themselves how, or if, they want to continue interacting.

After a divorce, family obligations are more likely to be maintained for biological ties such as grandmother and grandchild, than they are for ties between in-laws such as an ex-mother-in-law and an ex-daughter-in-law (Coleman, Ganong and Cable, 1997). Whenever links through marriage are broken, biological ties of descent take priority. The obligation of a grandmother to a grandchild persists more strongly than the grandmother's obligation to her ex-daughter-in-law. Nevertheless, biological ties are not the only basis for maintaining relationships after divorce. In some cases, people may choose to disregard formal ties as much as possible, by focusing instead on the quality of their informal relationship. According to Janet Finch and Jennifer Mason (1990b), in England 'the evidence seems to point to the history of interpersonal relationships as the key element in understanding why some people sustain close and supportive relationships after divorce, others remain friendly but do not expect to offer each other support, and others cut off contact completely'.

Relationships between in-laws are usually not very close, but where close relationships do develop they are often seen as worth continuing even if the marriage ends. Such relationships between in-laws are built partly on feelings of affection, and partly on exchanges of practical assistance that are mutually rewarding. Women seem more likely than men to develop and maintain these relationships over time, mainly in their roles as mothers-in-law, daughters-in-law and sisters-in-law. Women in these roles frequently have a shared interest in child rearing, which is the context for practical assistance back and forth over the years. In a minority of cases, these relationships may be so valuable that they ultimately have a higher priority than the original marriage tie which was the basis for the first contact between them.

Structural Change in Family Relationships

Increased prevalence of divorce in the western societies in recent decades is one factor that has changed the structure of family relationships, and it has therefore changed family priorities. The outer layers of the onion structure of family relationships have had to expand, to include growing numbers of people who maintain continuing relationships despite the breaking of marriage ties which originally brought them together.

Increased divorce is not the only social change with implications for family priorities. In the long run, some of the most profound shifts follow from changes in two aspects of *demography*, namely fertility and *longevity* (that is, the length of the individual lifespan).

In practically all of the western societies women have been having fewer children on average, and average family size has fallen as a result. At the same time, the probability of dying at any given age has declined in most countries and longevity has therefore increased. The combination of people living longer and having fewer children is slowly changing the structure of family relationships. As the structure of family relationships changes, so too does the relative priority of different kinds of family members.

The changing structure of family relationships is sometimes envisaged as a change in the shape of families. Instead of an onion structure, it is suggested that what we are seeing is the emergence of a 'bean-pole' family. Families are becoming smaller, and thus are growing 'thinner'. Also, more families are being 'stretched out', as the elderly live longer and more families grow from three generations to include four generations, and even five generations.

A study of people aged 55 and over in the Netherlands illustrates the shape of family life today (Dykstra and Knipscheer, 1995). More than seven out of ten older Dutch people belong to multigenerational families. Three-generation families are the most common, as 54.6 per cent of older persons belong to this type of family. Here, the oldest person is a grandparent, who has surviving children and grandchildren. In four-generation families the oldest person is a great-grandparent, with surviving children and grandchildren, and great-grandchildren as well. More than one in six (17.8 per cent) of older people in the Netherlands belong to this type of family structure. By comparison, five-generation families are still extremely rare, at less than half a percent (0.4 per cent) of the sample in the Dutch study. In these unusual five-generation families, the oldest person is a great-great-grandparent, with surviving children, grandchildren, great-grandchildren and great-great-grandchildren.

Dykstra and Knipscheer (1995) refer to the growing proportion of multi-generational families in the Netherlands as the 'verticalization' of family life. In the population pyramid that was characteristic of traditional societies, there were few generations alive at the same time, and the younger generations clearly outnumbered the older generations. This traditional form has changed into a vertical structure, with several generations of similar sizes coexisting, plus a small capstone generation. The authors suggest that the verticalization of the multigenerational family affects the pattern of interactions among family members. Interactions within generations have decreased in frequency and intensity, as people have fewer brothers and sisters, and fewer cousins. However, interactions across the generations have increased as descent ties have been extended. Does this mean that descent ties will have a higher priority in the family structures of the twenty-first century?

David Reher (1997) has speculated about this point concerning the future of family life in Spain. Family life has traditionally been very important in Spain, but profound changes have occurred in the past three decades. Due to very low fertility and mortality in recent years, families in Spain are following an unmistakable path of reduction in size and extension of generational depth. Children and young people in Spain today have fewer family members of the same generation as themselves than ever before. Conversely, the percentage of children and young people with living grandparents and great-grandparents is higher than it has ever been.

Reher suggests that these changes affect the lives of children and young people in two main ways. First, he thinks that older generations will play an increasing role in the upbringing and education of the young, especially since more Spanish mothers are now working outside the home. Second, David Reher believes that the traditional flow of wealth down the generations, especially in the form of inheritance, is being disrupted. Because older people are living longer they will need to use more of their economic assets to support themselves in old age, and they will have less wealth to pass on when they eventually die. More importantly, there is a change in the timing of the intergenerational transfer of wealth. In the past, when people tended to die at younger ages than they do now, their children often inherited property in early adulthood, at a time in their lives when it could make a major difference to the children's economic position in society. But now, by the time most parents die, their children are probably in their fifties or even older and inheritance of wealth must have less of an impact upon their economic position. If intergenerational ties of economic support for young families are to continue to have a high priority in the twenty-first century, new normative guidelines for transferring wealth may have to be invented. Intergenerational transfers of property may have to skip the child generation, and wealth may have to be passed directly from grandparents to grandchildren. That would be an interesting modification of the classic onion structure of family obligations.

Discussion

Family obligations always reflect some system of priorities in family relation-ships, simply because it is impossible to do everything for everyone all at the same time. Choices must be made about who will be given more time or who will get more money, and who will receive less attention and who will get less money. The choices that are made can vary enormously, based on individuals' unique preferences and circumstances. Nevertheless, family priorities are not random. There is typically a structure to them, and they are also influenced by the particular family history as well as by the history of demographic and social changes in a particular society.

One of the main conclusions to be drawn about family priorities is that they are related to physical closeness, and especially to living in the same residence. Most of the informal caring for people who are sick or handicapped is provided by people who live in the same residence. In a country like Britain, this means that spouses are the most common caregivers in nuclear families and husbands are as likely to provide care as wives (Arber and Ginn, 1999).

When people share the same dwelling their lives are interlinked in many ways, and they tend to share many other resources including their incomes. In Japan, where three-generation households continue to be more common than in most western societies, this means that elderly parents have a relatively high priority and they have a higher level of social protection.

Relationships between family members living in separate households tend to have a lower priority in general. The actual level of priority here is influenced by ideas about biological descent, and therefore by genealogical closeness, and also by ideas about connectedness through marriage. Qureshi and Walker (1989) claim that caring relationships exhibit a hierarchy of preferences, which they refer to as the 'traditional Western normative preference structure'.

The rules for this structure are: close relatives are preferred to more distant ones; any relative is preferred to a non-relative; and female relatives are preferred to male relatives.

The rule on gender preference highlights the importance of the mother-in-law/daughter-in-law relationship in family caring, as well as the more obvious mother/daughter tie. However, in societies where divorce is fairly prevalent, ties with in-laws are clearly vulnerable to disruption. In contrast, we may see a strengthening of descent ties in multigenerational families, which are becoming increasingly common. Within multigenerational families in modern societies, intergenerational flows of resources between family members generally give higher priority to helping younger family members. In countries like Canada, resources tend to flow from older generations down to younger generations (Cheal, 1983).

Intergenerational ties between children and grandparents, as well as great-grandparents, may become more important in the future, especially when there is a history of physical proximity and frequent contact between the generations. If so, then the mediating influence of the generation in the middle, or *bridge generation*, will probably receive more attention. Research in the United States suggests that adults who have frequent contact with their parents are also more likely to be in frequent contact with their grandparents, especially if the parents and grandparents have a close relationship (Hodgson, 1995).

Clearly, family obligations are not limited only to people living in the same household. Nevertheless, when people leave a household their priorities often change dramatically. This sequence of events is most obvious when the reason for leaving is marital separation or divorce. In societies like Britain and the United States, where high priority is given to a conjugal relationship as the principal basis for material support of children, separation and divorce have a notable impact on children's lives.

4

Entries, Exits, and Voices Off-stage

So far, we have looked at the question of who are family members mainly in static terms (that is, as if family relationships were fixed at a given point in time). In Chapter 4 we take a look at the dynamics of family membership. Members join families in various ways, for example through birth or marriage. They also leave families in a variety of ways, for example through divorce or death. And then there are the 'voices off-stage'. These are people who have left a family, but whose presence is still felt within it, or who wish that they still had a part to play in family life. How do people adjust to these ambiguous relationships? And how do social institutions respond when ambiguity becomes an arena for conflict?

CONCEPTS

family dynamics   family life cycle   cohort
transitions   trajectories   rites of passage   family
formation   role conflict   stepfamily   symbolic
interactionism   joint actions   custodial parent   role
differentiation   surrogate mother   marriage work

Changes in family life are heavily influenced by entries into family roles and by exits from them. They are also influenced by interactions between family members and other people outside the family who have a strong interest in its members. Some of those interested outsiders are people who used to be insiders, but who have since separated from the family unit.

Family groups sometimes give the appearance of stability, when a family lives in the same place for a number of years and puts down roots in the community. But families are not static. They are constantly changing as some individuals leave and other individuals join. The British Household Panel Survey found that people referred to the most important family events as changes in family composition (Scott and Perren, 1994). In particular, births (26 per cent), weddings (19 per cent), and deaths (16 per cent) were mentioned most often. Other important family events included separation and divorce (6 per cent), leaving home (3 per cent) and family visits (7 per cent).

Some family changes are related to biological developments. When individuals become sexually mature and have children, they bring new members into the group. When someone dies, on the other hand, the process of change is reversed since the family loses one of its members. Other changes, such as marital separation, are related to lifestyle choices made by individuals, perhaps concerning the different opportunities provided by new relationships. Sometimes people act on conscious choices to break with family tradition and create alternative forms of social relationships.

From a perspective of *family dynamics*, the connections between individuals and their families consist of a series of entries and exits. Entering into a family, and exiting from it, are basic experiences of family life. One way of thinking about the dynamics of entries and exits is to imagine a typical set of changes that occurs over an individual's lifespan. This typical set of changes is referred to as the *family life cycle* (Cuisenier, 1977; Murphy, 1987; Falicov, 1988).

The concept of the family life cycle is rooted in the idea that family life goes through a cycle of birth, growth and decay. The cycle begins with the joining together of two persons of the opposite sex in marriage, and it ends with the dissolution of their union when one of them dies. In between, the family expands and contracts as children are born and leave home.

For many years, the concept of a family life cycle provided the main way of thinking about family dynamics. One reason is that it can be a useful way of analyzing housing careers, or in other words trajectories of housing demand, in a country like Australia, because people have different housing needs at different stages in the family life cycle (Kendig, 1984). A young married couple begin with modest housing demands, which can be met by renting an apartment or a small house. Then, if they have children, their need for space increases, and they will probably prefer to buy a larger house if they can afford it. Later, after the children have left home, and especially in old age when a large home is physically harder to maintain, most people opt for a smaller dwelling once more.

The main difficulty with the concept of the family life cycle is that not everyone follows the supposedly 'typical' pattern. Marriage does not necessarily initiate the family cycle, as growing numbers of people cohabit before, or instead of, getting married. Also, some women have children outside of marriage, and other women become sole parents when they separate from their partners. Furthermore, housing careers are not entirely predictable from the family life cycle because they are heavily affected by experiences of employment and unemployment. A young couple who cannot afford a place of their own may continue living at home with their parents, either together or separately (Wallace, 1987).

The recent history of family change in Britain, the United States and many other countries is one of increasing life course diversity (Ahlburg and De Vita, 1992). Greater life course diversity is confirmed in a study of different cohorts born in Canada between 1910 and 1970 (Ravanera, Rajulton and Burch, 1994). A *cohort* is defined by social scientists as a group of people who were all born in the same period of time. In the study by Ravanera and his colleagues, six birth cohorts were identified at ten-year intervals. The researchers then focused attention on a sequence of three events in the traditional family life cycle. The three life-cycle stages studied were:

1. leaving home (that is, leaving the family of origin);
2. getting married; and
3. having a first child.

It was found that the probability of Canadians completing all three events in the expected order was highest for people born between 1931 and 1940. Most of the people in the 1931–40 birth cohort reached adulthood in the 1950s, when the cultural idealization of the nuclear family was at its peak. In contrast, the expected sequence of the family life cycle occurred least often in the youngest cohort, born between 1961 and 1970. In this cohort, cohabitation after leaving home rivaled the traditional life-cycle sequence, to the extent that cohabitation was actually slightly more common than marriage. Evidently, the classic sequence of life-cycle stages is no longer adequate to understand the lives of younger cohorts in Canada.

Cultural ideals of a predictable family life cycle are less relevant now than they used to be. Instead of describing the family life cycle, therefore, many researchers today focus on analyzing *transitions* in the life course (Beaujot, et al., 1995). A transition is simply a change from one condition to another, for example from that of being unmarried to being married. Every transition (except death) is eventually followed by some other transition. We can therefore study sequences of family transitions, which are referred to as life-course *trajectories* (Elder, 1985). An example of a life-course trajectory might include a first marriage, which is followed by a divorce, and then a second marriage.

Role Entries

The study of family transitions begins by describing the roles into and out of which people move (George, 1993). According to classical sociological role theory, cultural expectations exist about the nature of role behaviour and the timing of role transitions. In theory, these expectations regulate when people choose to enter and when they leave specific family roles, and the manner by which they do so. However, the influence of cultural expectations upon family roles is not as strong as it once was. An important trend in a number of countries today is the 'decline in conventions', as the American sociologist Martin King Whyte (1990) calls it.

Family Formation

Transitions into family roles do not seem to be as strongly affected by cultural influences as they once were. Whyte's detailed analysis of data from the Detroit Area Study, in the mid-1980s, led him to conclude that such predictors of Americans' cultural background as social status, religion, ethnicity and rural-urban residence no longer have much effect on patterns of premarital behaviour, choice of marriage partner, or the quality of the marriage relationship itself. Rather, he concluded that Americans have shifted from a situation in which there was once a 'right way' and a 'wrong way' to conduct premarital and marital relations, to a situation in which there are alternative ways of behaving that have ambiguous cultural meanings. Concerning a range of issues such as retaining virginity until marriage or marrying someone of the same faith, there is a declining consensus among Americans about what is acceptable and what is unacceptable.

This trend does not mean that conventions have disappeared entirely, or that the transition into marriage is no longer of any consequence. On the contrary, weddings remain important *rites of passage* for many people. Furthermore, there is some evidence to suggest, as Whyte observed, that overall there is greater ritual elaboration in, and larger expenditure on, weddings today compared with the first half of the twentieth century. Paradoxically, a study of mothers in long-term cohabiting relationships in Britain found that a quarter of them cited the cost of a big wedding as a reason for not getting married (McRae, 1993).

The continued importance of wedding ceremonies for many people is evidently not the result of strong cultural traditions based in community solidarity. Ritual practices today are freely borrowed from different cultural repertoires and they are combined in unique ways, especially in ethnically diverse cities (Cheal, 1988). This mixing of cultural elements is widely accepted now, because 'it is their day' to decide as the partners wish. Despite the increased prevalence of cohabitation, weddings remain important to many people in many places because they provide the opportunity to publicly demonstrate a private commitment to a long-term relationship. Weddings today may not always formally initiate the process of two people living together, but they do symbolize the passing of a relationship into a different state that is intended to be more long lasting.

Today, cultural expectations have less influence upon family choices than they did in the past, and transitions are less standardized (Peters, 1995). That is clearly so with respect to *family formation*. The term 'family formation' refers to transitions that create a new family group. Traditionally, a new family was understood to be created by marriage. Subsequently, alternative transitions, such as beginning to cohabit or unattached childbirth, have also been recognized as types of family formation (Rowland, 1991).

Family roles that are created with family formation are usually well defined and well known within a local system of meanings. However, new types of transitions sometimes result in ambiguity about family roles and family boundaries. Becoming a spouse (husband or wife) is very obvious if the transition is brought about by a socially recognized ritual such as a legal marriage ceremony. But if two people start living together without going through a public ceremony, then the question of whether or not a new family has been formed is initially not so clear. That ambiguity is partly because the cultural meaning of cohabitation has changed over time. In countries like the Netherlands, cohabitation started as an alternative way of living, then it evolved into a temporary phase before marriage, and finally it became a strategy for moving into a union gradually (Manting, 1994). Cohabiting couples may or may not have any intention to marry. And they may, or may not, marry eventually depending upon the individual circumstances that affect the transition from cohabitation to marriage.

A cohabiting couple are unlikely to think of themselves as wife and husband at first, and they will therefore talk about themselves differently and be identified differently by others. Substitute terms, such as 'partner' or 'significant other,' or 'live-in boyfriend' may be used instead. These alternative ways of describing their roles are sometimes meant to imply the formation of a new family, and sometimes not. Often, people are not really sure if a cohabiting couple constitutes a family unit until they have a child.

Having a first child is almost always regarded as important evidence of family formation. That is partly because childbearing is conventionally understood (or hoped) to indicate some degree of stability in a relationship. Furthermore, it initiates at least one dramatically new family role, namely that of 'mother', and usually that of 'father' as well. This has important consequences. Although the arrival of a child affects both men and women, it often does so in different ways (Walzer, 1998).

Parenthood

Bonnie Fox (1997) claims that parenthood is the major experience that produces gender differences in Canada today. Even egalitarian partners who become parents inevitably face difficult choices. Those choices often force differences in women's and men's lives. In her interviews of mothers in Toronto, conducted before and after the birth of a baby, Fox found that couples who had not previously divided the housework did so as soon as the child was born. Mothers became the primary caregivers for their babies, and by extension they gradually assumed more responsibility for other domestic tasks. The most influential decision here was that the mother should be the one to stay home with the baby.

Fox observed that an important consequence of mothers staying home with their babies was that these women also began to do more of the household tasks, such as cleaning. In other words, the new responsibilities of 'mother-work' led to intensified responsibilities for housework.

The biggest source of stress for new fathers in Fox's study was the feeling of being pulled in two directions at once, between the demands of their paid work and their responsibilities at home. Sociologists refer to this experience of struggling to meet the demands of two roles that are difficult to satisfy simultaneously as *role conflict*. New fathers were expected to give their wives more support, both practical and emotional, but at the same time they were expected to meet their families' needs for increased income through active employment. Most of the new fathers in the Toronto study became noticeably more serious, even aggressive, about their jobs and careers. In most cases they had been earning more than their wives before the baby was born, and so it was usually taken for granted that they would now take on the extra financial responsibilities appropriate to being the primary breadwinner. That could mean taking on more overtime work for extra pay, or pursuing opportunities for promotion. Either way, they usually ended up working longer hours.

Following the birth of a first child, men are more likely to increase their hours of employment whereas women are more likely to decrease their hours of paid work. Having children has a notably large effect in reducing the proportion of wives who are employed full-time (Cheal, 1999; Beaujot, 2000). Women who live in a family with children are less likely to be working full-time than men who are living in a family with children. Also, the younger the children are, the more likely it is that men will be working full-time and the less likely it is that women will be working full-time (Beaujot et al., 1995). This has obvious effects upon the average incomes of fathers and mothers. Partly because mothers often have fewer hours of paid employment than fathers, and partly because the wages of women who do work full-time tend to be lower than men's wages, women in general earn less than men, and the gender earnings gap is even larger between fathers and mothers (Logan and Belliveau, 1995). Unlike the situation among mothers, fathers' earnings do not appear to be negatively affected by having and raising children. On the contrary, average annual earnings of men with children at home are slightly higher than those of all men.

The gendered effect of children upon parents' employment also has impli-cations for wives' economic position within the family, including the balance of power and influence in marriage. Financially-dependent wives may have less control over the family's resources and therefore have less influence on major decisions affecting the well-being of all family members. Data from the National Child Development Study confirm the strong relationship between having children and income dependency among married women in Britain (Ward, Dale and Joshi, 1996). Wives with children are much less likely (only 17 per cent) to contribute as much or more as their partners to the combined family income compared with childless wives of the same age (48 per cent of whom are not financially dependent).

Economic and social consequences of becoming a mother or father are usually very clear to the participants. However, that is not always the case. The role of mother or father may itself be in dispute. That sometimes happens when divorced parents remarry. If one partner in a couple has a child from a previous relationship, then it may not be agreed by everyone that the child now has a new father or mother. The child may resist the imposition of a new parental role, or the new partner of a child's natural parent may be reluctant to take on additional responsibilities involved in becoming a step-parent. In such situations, new family roles have to be negotiated, sometimes over a considerable period of time, before a new *stepfamily* is created. Under these conditions, it may be more useful to think about family construction rather than family formation. This way of thinking about families is especially emphasized by the theoretical approach in sociology known as *symbolic interactionism*. (See **Box 4.1**).

The symbolic interactionist sociologist Herbert Blumer (1969) recommended that sociologists should study social acts as *joint actions* which involve fitting together the individual lines of behaviour of all the participants. Fitting individual acts into joint acts is made possible through shared definitions of the situation. These shared definitions of the situation provide the participants with images of the interaction and its effects.

Following this approach, Irene Levin (1997) has described the creation of new stepfamilies as 'projects' in which the individuals involved construct family life according to some shared idea about the meaning of their relationships. On the basis of her research in Oslo, Norway, she claims that family members act according to three main ideas about life in stepfamilies. First, there are those who idealize the model of the nuclear family and who set out to reconstruct a new nuclear family to replace the one that was disrupted by marital separation or divorce. Here, the step-parent attempts to meet all of the social expectations that were previously held about the biological parent. Also, the children are encouraged to think of the new step-parent as their father or mother. These stepmothers and stepfathers subsequently judge their success by the extent to which they are accepted in their chosen role.

Second, stepfamily members may consciously strive not to follow the model of the nuclear family, since they believe it has failed or they think it is impossible to imitate. In these families, the role of step-parent is clearly distinguished from

Box 4.1 Symbolic interactionism

Symbolic Interactionism is a theoretical approach that is concerned with the ways in which individuals define the meanings of their situations, as well as themselves, in relation to other people with whom they engage in joint actions. Special attention is paid to the ways in which individuals' images of themselves are shaped in their interactions with others. Each person's sense of herself or himself as a family member is thought to be derived from the communications that take place in everyday life.

Symbolic interactionist studies sometimes examine the shared meanings held by family members as a group, and sometimes they examine the different definitions of situations held by particular individuals. In either case, the emphasis is more likely to be upon family unity rather than conflict within the family. For example, one of the classic topics for symbolic interactionist studies of family life has been 'marital adjustment' (Burgess and Cottrell, 1939; Adams, 1988). It is assumed that during the course of extended interaction over time individuals will tend to adjust their meanings, and therefore their behaviour, to ensure cooperative relations with one another.

Symbolic interactionist studies do not usually presume that there is only one way of conducting family life. There may be multiple meanings which can support effective cooperation in different groups of people, and in the same group of people at different points in time. Symbolic interactionist studies of family life therefore include descriptions of the ways in which behaviour is negotiated, and re-negotiated, among family members in shifting patterns of interaction (Backett, 1987; Finch, 1987).

Symbolic interactionism has been criticized for its micro-sociological approach, which is said to understate the long-term influence of macro-structures such as market economies and the inequalities which they generate.

that of the biological parent. In this case there are powers that the step-parent may not exercise, such as disciplining a stepchild, and there are obligations that the step-parent is not expected to meet, such as providing for a stepchild's education.

Finally, there is a mixed approach to life in a stepfamily that is followed by people who uphold the nuclear family as an ideal, but who are uncertain about whether they can achieve it in practice. Here, family members wait and see how things will work out between them. There can be considerable ambiguity about family boundaries in this kind of situation. Step-parents are sometimes inside the family, and sometimes they are outside. For example, a stepmother may be the caregiver at home who prepares food for the children and washes their clothes, but she may not be included in special occasions such as high-school or university graduation celebrations for her stepchildren.

Stepfamilies have become more common in recent years, as long-term trends in marriage and divorce have had a major impact on changing family structures. Divorce rates increased substantially in most western societies between the 1960s and the end of the 1980s. This trend was accompanied by more remar-riages among divorced people. Although first marriages continue to be the most common means of family formation, second or subsequent marriages are also important. It has been estimated that in the United States today about 4 out of 10 people who marry are entering into a marriage in which at least one of the spouses has been married before (Ihinger-Tallman and Pasley, 1997). In other words, entering into marriage often follows after an exit from an earlier married relationship.

Role Exits

Exits from family roles are very hard to predict, perhaps because they occur in so many different ways. Take, for example, 'leaving home'. Some children run away from home in their teens, while others remain in the family home until they are well into adulthood. When adult children do leave home, they may nevertheless return to live with their parents if their marriage breaks up suddenly. Sociological analysis is complicated by the fact that contradictory trends are sometimes found. Paradoxically, in Britain during the 1980s, teen-age males became more likely to live away from their parental home, whereas the opposite was true for men in their mid-to late twenties. Above age 21, more British men were living with their parents at the end of the 1980s than were doing so at the beginning of the decade (Berrington and Murphy, 1994).

Leaving Home

Despite some uncertainty about current trends, there are some clear patterns in home leaving that are connected to issues introduced earlier. One of these is gender. Women tend to leave the parental home earlier than men, and they are less likely to return (Mitchell, Wister and Burch, 1989; Aquilino, 1991; White, 1994; Zhao, Rajulton and Ravanera, 1995). The main reason for this is an age difference between women and men in the timing of first marriage. Women have a younger age at leaving home than men for almost all reasons for leaving, but particularly when they leave for marriage (Young, 1987). Furthermore, young women are more likely to leave home in order to marry than are young men (Aquilino, 1991; Ravanera, Rajulton and Burch, 1995). This can be illustrated with data from the Survey of Labour and Income Dynamics in Canada (Cheal, 1997b). In 1993, only 7.7 per cent of young men aged 19–23 were living with a partner, but 18.9 per cent of young women were doing so. Conversely, 70.5 per cent of young men were still living at home with a parent, whereas just 57.4 per cent of young women were living in the parental home.

Another consistent finding in Canada and the United States is that the type of family structure makes a difference to the probability of teenagers leaving home. Children from stepfamilies tend to leave home earlier than other children, especially by comparison with children from intact two-parent families (Mitchell, Wister and Burch, 1989; Aquilino, 1991; Boyd and Norris, 1995; Zhao, Rajulton and Ravanera, 1995). This finding has been replicated in the Netherlands (Spruijt, 1995) and also in Scotland, where it was found that young people with a step-parent were more likely than other young people to leave home by the age of 19 years (Jones, 1995). Children in single-parent families are also likely to leave home earlier than those raised in families with both biological parents. However, the effect of living in a stepfamily is consistently stronger in this regard than the effect of living with a single parent.

Data from the Canadian Youth Foundation Survey help to specify the reasons for these patterns (Mitchell, 1994). Detailed data analysis shows the complex interplay of economic and symbolic factors. On average, children in stepfamilies and single-parent families are more likely to experience economic deprivations than are children living with both of their biological parents. As a result, they are more likely to stay at home because they do not have the money to leave. However, if children in stepfamilies and single-parent families do have the money to leave, then they are more likely to want to live independently because they report having more conflict at home.

Children in stepfamilies tend to report having more difficulty at home than do other children. This includes greater difficulties with their biological mothers, with whom most children in stepfamilies in fact live (Solomon, 1995). This points to an important characteristic of stepfamilies, namely the existence of a very large gender imbalance in step-parenting. This feature of stepfamilies is the result of a sociologically interesting pattern of role exiting, which we will look at next.

The overwhelming majority of stepchildren (about four out of five in Canada) live with their biological mother and a stepfather. Contrary to widespread myths about stepmothers, very few stepchildren actually live with their biological father and a stepmother (Cheal, 1996b). The underlying reason for this is that in contemporary societies, where stepfamilies are largely formed as a result of divorce and remarriage, the children remain with the mother in most cases. That is usually the preference of the mothers themselves. It has also generally been the preference of judges when making decisions on child custody throughout Europe, as well as in Canada and the United States (Bawin-Legros, 1992; Stamps, Kunen and Rock-Faucheux, 1997). It is thought that the parent with whom the child resides, or in other words the *custodial parent*, should normally be the child's mother. The noteworthy consequence of this pattern is that role exiting by parents is a highly gendered process.

Divorcing

Among women, marriage and motherhood are often experienced as distinct, and separable, family ties (Seltzer, 1994). The children that a woman bears almost always live with her and remain her responsibility, regardless of whether she is married or single, separated or divorced, remarried or cohabiting. For most men, on the other hand, marriage and coresidence seem to be what mainly define their responsibilities to children. Regardless of their biological ties to children, men share resources with the children of their current wives or other females who live with them. When marriages dissolve, many men disengage from their biological children at the same time as they disengage from their former wives. These men may then form attachments to different children, through new wives or female partners.

Remarriage following divorce, either by the self or by the ex-partner, tends to be accompanied by a lower level of involvement in the lives of non-resident children, among both men and women (Christensen and Rettig, 1995). However, since women are much more likely to keep their children with them after a marital disruption, this tendency has little practical effect on mothers in most cases. Men, in contrast, are unlikely to be living with their children after a separation or divorce, and if they remarry they are likely to withdraw from post-divorce parenting of their biological children.

Not all divorced fathers accept being estranged from their children, however. They are especially likely to remain in contact with the children if their ex-partner does not remarry. Some divorced fathers even seek and obtain sole custody of their children. In this reversal of what is often regarded as the 'normal' situation, the gendered character of role exiting is nevertheless still apparent.

Most non-custodial fathers give up their children because they believe that the mother's role is especially important for a child. It is thought that the children should naturally stay with the mother. Non-custodial mothers who have given up their children are aware of these cultural assumptions, and they share them to some degree. When non-custodial mothers give up their children, it is usually due to an overwhelming pressure of personal desires and/or practical circumstances that makes it impossible for them to achieve the cultural ideal. One of the most important of these practical circumstances is financial inequality between ex-spouses.

In an American study of non-custodial mothers (Greif and Pabst, 1988), it was found that the most common reason cited by women for giving up their children was 'money'. Specific problems arising from relative lack of money included: 'I could not afford to raise them'; 'He could provide for them better financially than I could'; 'He threatened me with not paying alimony or child support if I took custody'; and, 'I could not afford a good lawyer'. Clearly, economic inequalities between women and men can affect the process of disengagement from marriage, just as they can affect power relationships within marriage itself.

Women who relinquish all rights of day-to-day care for their children often have to struggle with the stigma attached to acting in a way that is thought to be unnatural (Babcock, 1997). Because mothers leaving children reverses what most people think of as the natural order of role exiting, people may ask 'How could a mother do that?'. They may then go on to suspect that there is something wrong with a non-custodial mother, such as drug or alcohol abuse. Consequently, non-custodial mothers may try to hide the existence of their non-resident child from employers or co-workers. In the study by Greif and Pabst, non-custodial mothers who gave up their children unwillingly as a result of losing a divorce-court battle found it hardest to live with the stigma of not being a normal mother.

Divorce-court battles became increasingly common in the latter part of the twentieth century, as divorce rates increased. Conflicts over child custody grew, and some of these had to be resolved by the courts. As a result, during the 1980s and 1990s vociferous claims were made in the courts and elsewhere for 'fathers' rights' of access to children (Bertoia and Drakich, 1995). Some of those claims included demands for shared custody of the children by both parents. These demands were politicized when they were supported by influential groups concerned about the psychological and financial consequences for children of separation from their fathers. Problems of role exit due to marriage breakdown have therefore received a great deal of attention.

Role entries and role exits can both give rise to difficulties and interpersonal conflicts during periods of social change, when accepted ways of managing new transitions from one role to another have not yet been worked out. In practice, problems associated with role exits tend to be seen as more threatening than the difficulties of role entries. That is partly because premature exit from a family role disrupts expectations of relationship continuity that are a defining characteristic of families. For example, fathers who are physically separated from their children after divorce often experience a sense of loss that is only partly compensated for by contact over the telephone. This can precipitate feelings of grief, guilt and anger (Lund, 1987).

Sudden role exits may also expose social and economic inequalities between different family members, that were previously compensated inside the family (Kurz, 1995). In particular, women leaving marriage often experience significant declines in income and increased rates of poverty (Morgan, 1991). In general, women do not fare as well economically as men do after the dissolution of a marriage, especially if they have children (Holden and Smock, 1991; Galarneau and Sturrock, 1997).

A great deal of confusion inevitably arises when individuals suddenly find that they must find new ways of living on their own, especially if they must do so at a lower standard of living. Difficult decisions have to be made about many issues, including what to do with the things that were accumulated as common interests within the family. Somehow, joint property such as a house, the household equipment and furniture, intangible assets such as pension rights, and the children, must all be divided up and shared between the ex-spouses (Voegeli and Willenbacher, 1992; Weitzman, 1992). Among the difficulties encountered at this point is reluctance to give up customary rights and privileges of family roles, such as those which parents exercise over children and that husbands may have exercised over wives. Sudden loss of power in the family can be very disturbing, notably to men whose wives choose to leave patriarchal relationships. As Carol Smart argues (1989), claims for fathers' rights can be seen as one way for men to regain some of that power.

Public solutions to problems of divorce have been difficult to reach, and when reached they have often been unstable. That is because two conflicting points of view exist concerning post-divorce family life and its effects on children. These two points of view have been described by Irene Thèry (1989) in France, and similar patterns can also be found elsewhere. On one hand, Thèry says, there is the 'substitution model' of the post-divorce family. According to this approach, the best interest of a child after divorce is seen to lie in the speedy and complete creation of a new nuclear family to replace the old one. A divorce is therefore seen as entailing a complete split between the former spouses, and the emphasis is on recreating a 'normal family' to provide stability for the child. It follows from this point of view that all of the familial rights of the non-custodial parent should be transferred to the custodial parent's new spouse. That person now becomes the child's new father or mother. This point of view is reflected in the expectation that a step-parent should fulfill all of the responsibilities previously performed by the biological parent (see Levin, 1997).

The point of view described above is contradicted in practice by a second way of thinking about post-divorce family life, which has become more influential in recent years. From the perspective of the 'durability model', it is believed to be important that both biological parents should be in frequent contact with the child, during and after marriage. As seen in Levin's study of stepfamilies in Norway, those families that strive to follow this model must create distinctions between the role of the step-parent and the role of the biological parent. Therefore, divorce is not seen as a total split but as a process of *role differentiation* that creates new, and more specialized, roles. For example, the social responsibilities of fatherhood may be divided between two fathers, namely a child's biological father and stepfather.

The important point to emphasize from the perspective of the durability model is that divorce does not necessarily bring an end to the family (Thompson and Amato, 1999). Family relationships often continue after divorce, especially where children are involved. This sometimes comes as a surprise to people who hoped they would be completely free from their ex-partner. Nevertheless, government agencies, legislators, lawyers and family counsellors have all exerted growing pressure upon divorcing couples to continue selected aspects of their family roles in the post-divorce situation. In this sense it is possible to talk, as Elisabeth Beck-Gernsheim (1999) does, about the 'post-familial family'. The nuclear family consisting of a couple and their children who all lived in one household may have come to an end, and with it the traditional roles of husband and wife. But some of the previous obligations of those roles now continue in the new roles of ex-wife and ex-husband, along with new expectations and new responsibilities arising from separate residences and separate household budgets.

The durability model of family life has tended to replace the substitution model in many divorce-court decisions, as well as in policies for reforming family law. There are several reasons for this shift. First, as the number of divorced fathers has grown, so there has been a corresponding growth in demands from them to have more access to their children. Second, these demands have resonated with some public decision-makers, who believe the best way to ensure that divorced fathers support their children financially and in other ways is for them to be in continuous contact with the children. Fathers who watch their child grow up, it is thought, are more likely to take an interest in supporting and facilitating the child's development. This claim is supported by research showing that frequency of visits by non-custodial fathers is associated with positive outcomes for children, such as higher academic achievement (Kissman, 1997). Finally, there is a third reason for the increased popularity of the durability model of post-divorce family life, which is probably most important of all. The substitution model simply no longer works very well as a blanket prescription for public policy.

The substitution model for reconstructing post-divorce family life only works well in a society with high marriage rates and low divorce rates. Here, most divorces are followed by remarriages and nuclear families are quickly reconstituted. Change either of those factors, as has happened in a number of countries recently, and the substitution model runs into several difficulties. If substitute nuclear families are not created soon after divorce by mothers' early remarriage, then it becomes harder to resist demands that divorced fathers should play an expanded role in post-divorce family life.

In Britain, the Children Act of 1989 responded to demands for an increased post-divorce role for fathers by requiring that divorce does not alter the legal relationship of parents to their children (Smart, 1999). The courts therefore no longer make orders about child custody in Britain, and in theory parents retain the parental responsibility that they enjoyed while the marriage was still intact. In practice, significant differences remain in many cases between the daily routines of residential parents (mainly mothers) who live in the same house as the child, and non-residential parents who have only limited contact with the child (mainly fathers) (Neale and Smart, 1997).

Voices Off-stage

Fathers who no longer live with the mothers of their children have tended to become disgruntled 'voices off-stage' in a number of countries. In Iceland, for instance, fathers without custody of their children suffer more emotional stress than other parents. They are frequently discontented with the child custody arrangements which they see as unfairly favouring their ex-wives (Júlíusdóttir, 1997). Non-residential fathers express frustration over seeing the children within imposed time limits, and they tend to see themselves as losers because of their restricted possibilities for participation and influence in the children's daily lives. In Canada and Britain, too, some non-residential fathers find it difficult to adapt to a 'visiting' relationship if they had been highly involved in their children's lives while the marriage was intact. They may be unable to construct an effective new role as a 'part-time father' after divorce (Kruk, 1993).

In addition to part-time fathers, families are surrounded by the off-stage voices of many other people whose relationship to the family unit is ambiguous. These individuals sometimes possess intimate knowledge about family members, and their actions can induce changes in families. Ambiguity about their position may be due to unresolved conflicts (for example, after divorce); or to confusion about roles that are not well defined in law or in custom (for example, ex-sisters-in-law). Role ambiguity may also exist because the relationship contradicts official definitions of family ties (for example, romantic friendships between women), or because the individuals involved are engaged in illegitimate activities about which knowledge must be suppressed (for example, secret lovers). This diffuse category of persons also includes deceased loved ones, who remain a subjective reality to those who remember them and who therefore continue to influence the living as symbolic representations (Grinwald and Shabat, 1997). Whatever their various characteristics may be, these insider/outsiders are all outside the frame of the family residence or household.

People have always had relatives outside the household, of course, and we discussed earlier how these kinship ties are structured as a set of family priorities. It was noted that relationships between family members who live in different households tend to have a lower priority than relationships between coresident family members. Typically, degrees of genealogical closeness are expected to be matched by residential closeness, and both are expected to be associated with relationship priority. But that is not always the case. For example, when a couple adopts a genetically unrelated child they may have to deal with the fact that family members who live together do not resemble one another physically.

Adoptive family life is further complicated by the fact that it is increasingly common for birth mothers who gave up their children for adoption when the children were infants to want to renew the parenting role in later life. They therefore ask to be given access to the records of the adoptive families in which their children were placed. The ultimate goal is usually to arrange reunions with their biological children who do not live with them (Modell, 1997). The off-stage voices of these birth mothers add to the complexity of kinship structures today (Hoffmann-Riem, 1990; Bartholet, 1993; Modell, 1994; March, 1995).

Another emerging factor in the complexity of kinship structures in some technologically advanced societies is the ability to become a *surrogate mother* (Ragoné, 1994). Here, one woman gives birth to a child with the explicit intention of giving it up to another woman, who then takes it home with her.

In the past, the only option for an infertile woman who wanted a baby was to adopt a child that had been orphaned, or whose mother was separating from it. Today, in those legal jurisdictions where it is permitted, it is also possible to arrange for another woman to conceive and give birth to a baby for the intended mother. In these surrogacy arrangements, the two women reach an agreement in advance of the birth about the birth mother's future relationship with the child. Both women intend that the child will live with its social mother, and not with its birth mother. The more difficult question is whether or not the birth mother will ever see the child again, or be informed about its progress. Surrogacy programmes offered by clinics often recommend complete separation between the surrogate mother and the family which receives the child. But that advice is not always followed in practice. Some couples consider the surrogate mother to be a kind of appendage to their family, whose interest in the child should be recognized by sending photographs as well as letters describing the child's achievements. Less often, occasional visits may be arranged that allow limited physical proximity between birth mother and child.

Conventional images of family life are strongly associated with shared experiences of physical proximity, especially through living in the same household. That is what is normally expected for relations between biological parents and children, and also for the bond between husband and wife. The preservation of marital ties, it is thought, depends heavily upon common residence and it is threatened when that condition does not exist. Nevertheless, there are many circumstances in which people must construct their relationships on grounds other than coresidence. Such people are likely to feel that they have a somewhat lower priority in family life, and family life often has a lower priority for them.

People who leave a residential family unit sometimes disappear completely, but that is rare. More often they retain some connection with the family, which is maintained by telephoning, writing letters, sending gifts and paying occasional visits. This is how non-residential fathers frequently maintain contact with their children. It is also how adult children tend to keep up ties with their parents after leaving home. In some situations, this 'emotional support at a distance' can be an important part of marriage too (Gerstel and Gross, 1984).

In the case of male military personnel, for example, geographical separations may be so frequent that family life is structured around the husband's absence (Harrison and Laliberté, 1994).

Military organizations are described in sociology as 'total institutions'. That is to say, they make extreme demands upon their members and these are impressed upon the individual by a rigid power structure. In the case of combat personnel in the military, these demands include being prepared to leave home at a moment's notice in order to serve in any location in the world. The demands also include valuing one's combat team above any other social group, including the family. That is because absolute team loyalty is believed to be essential to survival in combat. It is understood by everyone that while they are on a tour of duty military personnel should not be distracted by the mundane worries of their wives and children, who they have temporarily left behind. Furthermore, when they are back at their home base, team bonding remains a high priority, in order to maintain the mental preparedness for a quick military response to whatever emergencies may occur.

In most military organizations combat personnel continue to be men, and male bonding lies at the basis of military social organization. Wives of military personnel must therefore adapt to a situation in which tightly structured male groups have the power to remove their husbands at any time. This involves learning to cope with loneliness and lack of support from their husbands. Military wives are expected to be very self-reliant. However, they can also turn to the informal support network of other wives who are in the same situation. Especially in military quarters for families, the male bonding of combat teams is paralleled by female support networks within which strong friendships can develop.

Throughout history, women have depended upon close female friends to help them meet needs that were not being met by men. Those needs have changed over time, and so have the patterns of female friendships. From the sixteenth century through to the nineteenth century, romantic friendships were very important to middle-class women as a way of meeting their needs for personal support and understanding. In a context of gender segregation which meant that wives and husbands lived separate lives to some extent, significant emotional needs for intimacy and companionship remained unsatisfied in marriage. Romantic friendships between women were thus alternative relationships outside marriage, through which emotional needs could be met.

Subsequently, according to Stacey Oliker (1989), friendship patterns of American women changed during the twentieth century. By mid-century, husbands and wives of all classes were expected to have close relationships and to be more like companions rather than business partners. Wives' friendships therefore evolved to meet a new requirement, namely that of providing support for *marriage work* (Oliker, 1989).

Women interviewed by Oliker in California, in the 1980s, spent a lot of time talking with their best friends about their relationships. For the majority of women who were married, this meant primarily their relationships with their husbands. In conversations with their best friends, wives could talk through their personal problems and identify solutions, or they could come to accept things that they could not change. Women talked about marriage problems with their close friends for a number of reasons: in order to be able to think out loud, to let off steam, to reassess their perceptions and dissatisfactions with their husbands, to plan how to communicate with their spouses, in order to re-establish empathy and appreciation for neglectful husbands, and to figure out how to change them. From the accounts that Oliker heard, it seems that these women engaged in marriage work more to solidify and reinforce their own commitments to their marriages, rather than to learn how to change them.

Unlike male friendships among military personnel, which tend to draw husbands away from their wives, Oliker stresses that female friendships in modern America have the principal effect of helping wives to mentally adjust to their marriages. However, it is not the case that every voice off-stage has the effect of supporting marital stability. There are also other partners who have a role to play in the dynamics of family life, in the interplay between intimacy inside marriage and intimacy outside marriage.

Discussion

In this chapter we have examined some of the ways in which role entries and role exits can change the composition of a family. We have also seen that transitions of entering and exiting roles are connected, when leaving one family is followed by joining or creating a different family. After a role exit, earlier family ties are rarely given up completely. Many people therefore accumulate multiple family ties, in their 'old' families as well as in their 'new' families. As a result, social networks of ex-partners and new partners, and all their children, may emerge that resemble traditional extended families (Ambert, 1989).

Role entries, role exits, and multiple ties produced by sequences of role transitions, have all become more diverse in western societies over recent decades. The result has been increased pluralism in family life, accompanied by challenges to pluralism. There has also been a great deal of confusion over acceptable and feasible family norms (Mason, Skolnick and Sugarman, 1998). Notable trends include increased cohabitation, more divorce and remarriage, as well as changes in family law and its interpretation by the courts. Those changes have not always occurred smoothly. Role exits frequently create practical and emotional problems, and they can sometimes provoke intense conflicts (Faust and McKibben, 1999). Children may be at risk of becoming pawns in these struggles between their parents.

The number and intensity of legal disputes over disposition of marital property and over access to children following divorce have provoked great public debate. Many people have wondered whether there is some better way of dealing with the problems created by role exits than through court cases. Separating and divorcing couples are therefore increasingly encouraged to negotiate a post-marriage settlement, if necessary with the help of counselling or mediation services. The emphasis today is less on working out some final and irrevocable division of everything that was once contained within the marriage, including the children, and more on redefining a relationship that is now entering a new phase. That shift in thinking is consistent with an important long-term trend in family life, which is reshaping how lawmakers and policymakers in many countries think about family issues. Family ties are ultimately not fixed in place by social institutions such as churches, legislative bodies, or law courts. Rather, they are constantly being created and recreated in social interaction.

Intimate Relationships

Turning to the question of, 'what do families do'? Chapter 5 begins by examining the modern ideology of companionate marriage, and its causes and effects. Heterosexual and same-sex relationships are discussed, with an emphasis on the similarities in recent social developments. Changes within, and outside, marriage are described in relation to processes of modernization that are occurring on a world scale. Not all developments are positive, however, and special attention is paid to patterns of violence and abuse in families. These patterns, like many others described in this book, are highly gendered.

CONCEPTS

ideology   companionate marriage   urbanization
industrialization   home   emotion work
families of choice   economy of pleasure   cultural
alternative   negotiated marriage   cultural
contradiction   violence   abuse   sexual abuse
heteronormative   legitimation   romantic fusion
encapsulation   dependence   illusion of control
moral panic   normal violence   private sphere

In the last few chapters we have studied a variety of issues concerning the nature of family membership, and how family membership has changed over time. In this chapter we are going to take up a different theme. The next major question to be explored is: what do families do? Here we are concerned with acts of emotional intimacy, caring and economic exchange.

In Chapter 1 we saw that debates over family functioning in sociology quickly led to the examination of particular activities engaged in by particular family members. These issues in turn have led to questions such as who benefits the most, and who benefits the least, from particular family transactions. We shall see in the next few chapters that such questions involve studying classic sociological topics about equality and inequality in social life. But first, we need to look at how families are held together by certain kinds of interactions, and how people think about those interactions. Without certain kinds of interactions and their associated meanings, modern families might not exist at all.

Family Ties

When a couple gets divorced, lawyers and other observers are often most interested in the economic consequences of divorce, concerning who gets what and what the separate individuals' incomes and assets will be. However, the most painful divorces are not necessarily the ones that leave people the worst-off financially. The most traumatic divorces are often ones that were precipitated by adultery, leaving one partner with deep feelings of betrayal, loss of trust, and emotional distress (Ambert, 1989). That is because non-consensual adultery contradicts an ideal relationship of 'true love' between husband and wife. It therefore breaks the modern social order of marriage, based on special feelings of one person for another person (Lawson, 1988),

The balance between emotion and economic interest in family life has always exerted a profound influence upon the dynamics of family life, although it has varied at different times and in different places. The particular balance preferred at a particular time and in a particular place is usually expressed in a set of ideas known as an ideology. An *ideology* provides collective definitions of what a 'normal' family is thought to be, what is a 'proper' marriage, and what it means to be a 'good mother' or a 'good father.' Family ideologies are held out as ideal ways of living, although it is often unclear how many people are actually able to achieve those ideals in practice (Morgan, 1991).

From the late nineteenth century through to the last third of the twentieth century, the western middle classes developed an ideology of 'companionship' which has dominated how we think about families in general, and marriage in particular (Finch and Summerfield, 1991). The modern ideology of *companionate marriage* places feelings of love at the centre of family life, as the main reason and ultimate justification for everything that family members do. This was not always so, and it is not the only way of thinking about family life even today. For example, differences remain between western and Chinese views of what constitutes a 'good' versus a 'bad' marriage. Compared with the United States, there is less emphasis on togetherness of spouses and more emphasis on parental approval in China (Pimentel, 2000). In the ideology of the companionship family, an acceptable marriage is not based on parental approval of the choice of marriage partner, but rather upon continuous approval of their ongoing interactions by the partners themselves. This feature is very visible at the beginning of married life in the process of family formation.

Companionship Family I: Heterosexual

A good illustration of the effects of the ideology of companionship in modern western marriage is found in the honeymoon as a rite of passage that follows a wedding. A honeymoon is organized as a private retreat by the new couple, who leave behind their co-workers and friends in order to engage in a relationship of romance, pleasure and passion before returning to everyday life (Bulcroft, Smeins and Bulcroft, 1999). Honeymoons do not teach the bride and groom how to run a home together, nor do they prepare the couple for the even more difficult task of raising children. Rather, honeymoons are removed as far as possible from these mundane facts of life. Honeymoons are held, by preference, in a 'tropical paradise' or some other exotic location in a far-off place, or in the fantasy world of a theme park like Disneyland or the West Edmonton Mall.

The focus of a honeymoon is the intimate relationship that a husband and wife are constructing between themselves, and for themselves, to the exclusion of the outside world. In historical terms, this is a relatively new idea of what marriage is all about. Although most people think of a honeymoon as a normal accompaniment to a 'traditional' marriage, honeymoons have existed on a large scale for little more than a century. Honeymoons were introduced during the last few decades of the nineteenth century at a time when the emerging urban middle class was defining a new ideology of family life.

The ideology of companionate marriage assumes that a wife and a husband will spend a lot of time together because they choose to do so. From the viewpoint of this ideology, the existence of marriage is ultimately justified only by the relationship itself. Marriage is not justified in most cases by religious or social obligation, as may have been the case in earlier times. Married life today is therefore not confined to housework and childcare, but it includes joint recreational activities that are engaged in because they are pleasurable and because they reinforce positive feelings between the partners. It is important that both partners should enjoy their time together, otherwise they will not want to spend much time together in the future. It is therefore considered to be essential that each spouse should be sensitive to the other's needs and feelings. Finally, marriage partners are recommended to learn communication skills which can help them to avoid arguments and conflicts, and they should look for ways to make their partner's enjoyment of their interaction more pleasurable.

This way of thinking about marriage developed gradually in the United States and in other countries in response to a common set of challenges produced by urbanization and industrialization. Urbanization and industrialization are two major forces of social change that often have the effect of weakening traditional social ties, including family ties. People in modern societies have therefore faced a series of challenges to redefine the means by which families are held together.

Over the past century, individuals gained greater autonomy from the extended families and communities that previously exercised control over them. This change occurred mainly during the process of *urbanization* when large numbers of people moved into cities. During mass migration, migrants tend to become separated from restrictive local ties. Later, cultural changes that began in large cities initiated a greater tolerance of lifestyle diversity. As a result, individuals' preferences about who to spend time with, and for how long, have become more influential than social norms. For example, in a country like Britain today there are few sanctions of any kind against cohabitation outside legal marriage. This lack of social control has made it easier for people to introduce a great deal of flexibility into their relationships, according to their changing feelings for each other (McRae, 1993).

Some of the results of this process of change, such as extensive heterosexual cohabitation, are relatively new. But the underlying process of change itself has been going on for a long time. In the United States, the decade of the 1920s was particularly important in this respect. It was during this decade that a famous American sociologist of the family, Ernest Burgess, began to write about the emergence of a new image of the family as 'a unity of interacting persons' (Burgess, 1926). Later, he described the changes that were occurring in American family life as a shift 'from institution to companionship' (Burgess and Locke, 1945).

In the past, Burgess thought, a stable and secure family life was guaranteed by external pressures of law, custom and public opinion. Those external controls were reinforced inside the family by socially approved authority of the male family head, rigid discipline exercised by parents over children, and by religious and other rituals. Burgess argued that this system of control had broken down in the United States. However, he thought it was being replaced by voluntary relationships of mutual affection and understanding, or in other words by the companionship family. Burgess (1973) thought it was unlikely that individuals could construct stable patterns of family life entirely by their own efforts. Individuals' attempts at self-understanding and relationship development would therefore have to be guided by the results of scientific experts. Child guidance specialists, marriage counsellors, psychiatrists and clinical psychologists would all be needed to help manage the adjustment problems of family members, Burgess believed.

The changes described by Burgess were accompanied by another set of changes that received less attention at the time, but which we recognize as being of great importance today. In the early decades of the twentieth century America underwent rapid *industrialization*. By the middle of the century technologies of mass production had spread to other countries such as Canada, with similar social effects in the period following the Second World War.

In the factories of industrial society, and in the offices where industrial managers and their staff were employed, new forms of work were developed that separated industrial employment from home and family life. In most cases men were employed in the factories and offices, and women occupied a separate existence as 'housewives' or 'homemakers', especially in the growing urban middle class. This new pattern of life that accompanied the shift from an agricultural to an industrial economy had several consequences for families. There was a new emphasis on the *home* as a private place in which family members could construct a shared existence away from the workplace (Allan and Crow, 1989). The modern desire for the private expression of intimacy came to be particularly anchored in the home, especially in countries with northern climates. A great deal of effort was therefore expended on making the home the right kind of place in which to feel a sense of togetherness, comfort and security (Gullestad, 1995). This responsibility fell mainly upon women.

In an industrial society, husbands and wives are separated for most of the day. During the second half of the nineteenth century, and the first half of the twentieth century, this took the form of a sharp division of labour between them as husbands worked in the factories and wives worked at home. Gender differences were strongly reinforced by a wife's dependence upon the 'family wage' earned by her husband. This gendered economic dependence created many possibilities for conflict between spouses as they adjusted to a new type of family economy (Zelizer, 1997). Finding workable solutions to family problems in order to reduce conflict in marriage therefore became a subject of urgent public debate between the two World Wars. By the middle of the twentieth century acceptable solutions to family problems came to be identified with the ideals of companionate marriage.

The classic study from this period is Seeley, Sim and Loosley's (1956) report on the affluent Canadian suburb of Crestwood Heights. In places such as this, a new style of life was being developed in the 1950s, that was based on increased education, better communication, and a dedication to progress and improvement in personal life. The newly affluent middle-class families, created by the post-war boom, realized that they needed a business-like plan to manage their shared resources. Husbands and wives were encouraged to negotiate a shared financial plan according to the norms of a democratic society, and joint decision-making by couples was therefore recommended. Husbands were expected to make a special effort to set aside time from their busy schedules to talk to their wives.

In practice, much of the burden for adjustment in companionate marriage tends to fall upon the shoulders of wives rather than husbands. Although companionate marriage is conceived of as a partnership between equals, financially dependent wives usually have more at stake in marriage than husbands. That is because the latter tend to be more oriented toward the labour market (Duncombe and Marsden, 1995). To the extent that men's role as breadwinner becomes their central life interest, women are left with the primary responsibility for family life, including the marriage work that is necessary to maintain a couple's relationship. Wives who are dissatisfied with the emotional quality of their relationship may perform *emotion work* upon themselves, by convincing themselves that marital troubles are really only minor annoyances and that they are truly happy in their marriage.

Beginning in the 1960s, ideals of companionate marriage began to be affected by a new set of changes that led many women to re-evaluate their place in marriage. Increased employment led to more economic independence for many women. At the same time, divorce became more readily available due to changes in family law. Subsequently, divorce has become more socially acceptable as a means of dissolving marriages that do not meet the needs of one or both partners. In today's 'divorce culture', divorce is regarded as an optional way out of any marriage which fails to meet either partner's goals (Hackstaff, 1999). Expectations have therefore risen among women and men, but especially among women, that marriages should be relationships between equals. The continuation of a marriage is now thought to depend upon that goal being achieved.

Although the initial effects of these changes were most visible in increased divorce rates, individuals' desires to preserve their marriages have once again led many people to reinvent the terms of marriage. By the 1970s, in the United States, anxieties about divorce led many new couples into an intensified commitment to communicate and cooperate in a relationship of equals. Companionate marriage was modified during this period by new ideas about gender equality, although many women were left with the feeling that their ideas were changing faster than men's ideas. Nevertheless, by the end of the 1970s, the ideology of companionate marriage had been deepened in many sections of the population as a way of making marriage more democratic and more rewarding for both wives and husbands.

Happiness in marriage is increasingly seen to be an outcome of the ways in which situations are jointly managed by husbands and wives. This includes managing sexual relations, in which the right kinds of emotions must be elicited at the right times and places (Duncombe and Marsden, 1996). From the 1960s onwards, ideas about companionate marriage paid increasing attention to questions of sexual responsiveness and enjoyment of sex, by both women and men. This development occurred in a more liberal culture that saw sexual relations as not only a source of sexual release for men and biological reproduction by women, but also as a means for self-fulfilment by both sexes (Pilcher, 1999). Contemporary liberalized cultures also include the possibility of homosexual relations between men, and between women.

Companionship Family II: Homosexual

Struggles over the pursuit of innovation in intimate relationships are especially evident today in some of the debates about *families of choice* (Weeks, Heaphy and Donovan, 1999). Families of choice, or 'families we choose', are social structures constructed by lesbians and gays who want a sense of belonging to a group, and who value social support in long-term relationships (Weston, 1991; Weeks, Donovan and Heaphy, 1999). The discourse of the companionship family is often used to describe these relationships, because it implies continuity of intimacy over the life course. A discourse of enduring intimacy in gay couples sometimes includes expectations of sexual exclusivity, or in other words being faithful to one sexual partner as a sign of total commitment and mutual satisfaction (Yip, 1997).

In order to ensure that the enduring nature of a partnership is understood by everyone, some same-sex couples would like to have equivalent recognition in law to that enjoyed by heterosexual couples. It is further argued by some gays and lesbians in long-term relationships that this should include the right to marry (Allen, 1997). However, other homosexual couples are afraid that full legal recognition might destroy the flexible and egalitarian nature of their relationships. They want to avoid becoming entangled in the legal system, which they fear could create the same kinds of power struggles that exist in heterosexual relationships. Conflicts over property, for instance, can turn into battles between lawyers in which the original meaning of a relationship gets lost. Idealistic same-sex couples may prefer to trust in a cooperative, democratic approach to freely chosen relationships, without trying to create legal weapons that might later be used by one partner against another.

Contemporary accounts by lesbians and gays of their relationships as unions between equals often contain elements of the ideology of companionate marriage (Heaphy, Donovan and Weeks, 1999). Love, friendship, sharing, communication and negotiation are all specially valued for being combined in one unique relationship. The contemporary discourses of gay and lesbian relationships show that the ideology of companionate marriage has been enormously successful, and it continues to evolve today in interesting and unexpected ways. Nevertheless, companionate marriage is not the answer for everyone, nor is it the preferred way of living at every stage of life. Sexual relations are not easily fitted into one ideological straitjacket.

Sexual Relations: Beyond Companionship?

In the companionship family, sexuality is incorporated into marriage in the form of an *economy of pleasure* which deepens and intensifies the bonds between partners (Foucault, 1978; Cheal, 1993a). An economy of pleasure is an exchange of gratifications, including sexual gratifications, that stimulate emotions and heighten each individual's sense of well-being. In the ideology of companionate marriage the ideal of sexuality as an ongoing exchange of gratifications which strengthens a relationship is thought to be most capable of achievement via sexual exclusiveness. A mutually sexually exclusive relationship focuses and intensifies the partners' love for each other. It also reinforces the sense of a uniquely important relationship, and it supports the idea that this relationship will last. Thus, sex is equated with love within the enduring emotional bonds of marriage.

In many countries this way of thinking about sexuality is less prevalent now than it used to be. Some of the largest changes in attitudes have occurred in the ideas of women. Ideas about enjoying many forms of pleasure have increased, and sexual pleasure is less often confined to established relationships. This important cultural shift, which has been underway since at least the 1960s, can be illustrated from two surveys of sex life in Finland. These surveys were conducted twenty years apart, first in 1971 and again in 1992 (Kontula and Haavio-Mannila, 1995). In 1971, most Finnish women still believed that sex life should be connected to a permanent couple relationship, though men's ideas were more permissive. Almost 3 in 5 women (58 per cent) thought that sexual intercourse between young people was acceptable only when they were going steady and planning to get married; and 64 per cent regarded sexual intercourse without love as wrong. In 1992, less than half (43 per cent) of women thought that sexual intercourse without love was wrong, and only 13 per cent of women under age 55 still believed that intention to marry should be a prerequisite for sexual relations.

Casual sexual relations clearly became more acceptable in Finland during the latter part of the twentieth century. Nevertheless, the majority of people still want to live with a sexual partner and to be sexually faithful to him or her. Generally, sex life is still based on one established relationship, even if that is not true for everyone at every stage in the life course. (The notable exception is young men). In Finland in 1992, 62 per cent of all men and 67 per cent of all women stated a preference, at that time in their life, for marriage or cohabitation with no other sexual partners. This opinion was most common among women around age 30, of whom about 80 per cent held this opinion.

In a country like Finland we can see that the preference for companionate marriage remains strong, at the same time as more people are open to alternative possibilities for expressing individual desires, especially when they are young. Perhaps what is happening here is that companionate marriage is becoming recognized as just one possibility among many alternative forms of relationship that are culturally available. As a *cultural alternative* companionate marriage probably has a specialized appeal to couples who are making a family in which to raise children. It may therefore be on its way to becoming a specialized social institution. If so, that would be consistent with the historic process of social change known as modernization.

Modernizing Marriage

Increased capacity for pleasure and happiness is claimed to be one of the great achievements of modernization. Modernization is a complex process of change that involves raising human productivity and giving people more freedoms. In the long run, it is thought to benefit large numbers of men and women all over the world. We see this belief in many countries when people draw a distinction between the 'bad' customs of the past that restricted women, and the 'good' practices of the present which enable women to have more control over their lives. It is widely believed that marriage practices have become more favorable towards women as a result of all the changes that have occurred. What evidence is there for this claim?

The strongest evidence in support of the beneficial effects of modernization upon women's lives is increasing average age at first marriage. Because marriage is often followed closely by childbearing and related domestic responsibilities, age at marriage has a determining influence on the subsequent life course of women. Early entry into marriage for women tends to be associated with having many children, little or no independent employment after marriage, gender segregation and exclusion of women from public life, and a domestic and subordinate role for women in family life. Furthermore, very early age at marriage is often associated with parental control through arranged marriages, and little personal influence over the choice of marriage partner. It is therefore especially noteworthy that the number of females who get married before the age of eighteen has declined almost everywhere.

In the second half of the twentieth century, women's average age at marriage rose in many places, including notably the Islamic societies where early marriage by girls has a strong cultural basis. In countries as widely separated as Jordan, Egypt, Indonesia and Malaysia, women's average age at marriage has risen sharply (Jones, 1994; Heaton, 1996). For example, in Egypt 53 per cent of women born before 1950 were married by age 18, but less than 20 per cent of women born after 1970 were married that young.

The major factor associated with change in the timing of marriage is female education. The longer that girls stay in school, the less likely they are to marry young. That is because the time demands of marriage would conflict with their educational achievement. In the modern world most parents want their daughters to be educated. A good education is seen as the best route to success in life, and parents in almost every country now want their daughters to gain the benefits of education in the form of earning a higher income. In many places they also want their daughters to be educated in order for them to marry more educated and upwardly mobile young men, who otherwise might not be interested in them.

Many women have clearly benefited from modernization through its effect on increased age of marriage. However, it is not so clear what the trends have been in the quality of marriage, or if women everywhere have benefited from those trends. To examine these issues we need to look at accounts of how marriage partners are selected, and how husbands treat their wives.

In the past, in many parts of Asia, marriages were arranged by parents because marriage was thought to be too important for inexperienced children to decide for themselves. Family stories describe the unhappy wife who did not see her husband until the wedding day, and then disliked him on sight. In parts of Africa where polygyny was widely practised, stories about traditional practices include accounts of the patriarchal power exercised by men over multiple wives, following a strategy of 'divide and conquer'. Many of these things have changed now. Nevertheless, modernization does not always produce more equality and greater social harmony. It can also produce new social divisions and new forms of inequality.

In many parts of Asia today the social institution of arranged marriage has evolved into *negotiated marriage*, in which the wishes of the prospective bride and groom as well as the parents are taken into account. Parents may still use matchmakers to identify suitable wives and husbands for their children, but then the prospective bride and groom are allowed to express their opinion of the person selected through an 'arranged meeting'. As described by Laurel Kendall (1996) in Korea, an arranged meeting introduces an element of choice into family formation. However, it does not necessarily promote greater mutual understanding.

In negotiated marriages the limited nature of the arranged meeting can lead to an emphasis upon physical appearance and conventional attractiveness, such as the importance of a young woman having a slim waist. Women who do not meet contemporary standards of physical beauty are therefore at a new disadvantage in modern Korea. Furthermore, young women as a whole may have benefited less than young men from the shift toward negotiated marriages. The initiative in arranged meetings is presumed to lie with well-educated young men with good prospects of earning a high income, who are highly desirable as marriage partners. According to Kendall, Korean brides in the 1980s and 1990s were 'less than equal players in a marital enterprise constructed on the premise that women attract and men choose' (Kendall, 1996: 110).

The re-introduction of revised forms of gender and class divisions during the modernization of marriage can also be seen in the recent history of polygyny in Africa (Pitshandenge, 1994). In areas subject to heavy Christian influence, multiple marriages came to be defined as 'backward' and therefore as culturally incompatible with higher education and other aspects of participation in a modern society. Nevertheless, many African men have continued to be attracted to polygyny. Also, many less educated women have seen in it advantages for themselves as a means of gaining access to the superior economic resources of higher status men. It is financially successful men who can most easily afford multiple wives. These men are mostly well educated, and at some level they tend to accept the modern identification of monogamous marriage with the idea of progress. The *cultural contradiction* in which they are caught is handled, as most such contradictions are, by having one set of rules for public display and another set of rules for private use.

Throughout Africa, modernizing elites have engaged in a variety of attempts to define the status of polygynous unions and the children who stem from them. One solution to this problem, found in western Nigeria, is the division between a formally monogamous marriage contracted according to statutory law, and 'outside marriages' which are based on custom and tacit acceptance (Karanja, 1994; Mann, 1994).

In elite circles, a legally married woman or 'inside wife' is usually well educated and can command the respect appropriate to her social status. A man's marriage to his 'inside wife' is therefore publicly recognized, and she and her children have clear legal rights to inherit his property after death. An 'outside wife', on the other hand, receives economic support for herself and her children only as long as her husband is alive. She has no right to share in his property after death. Importantly, 'outside marriages' are considered to be private matters about which little is said outside of a man's circle of friends. The existence of an 'outside marriage' may be known to an 'inside wife', but she does not publicly acknowledge it or accept it since it is a source of competition that may eventually result in divorce. Unlike the situation in traditional polygyny, then, an 'outside wife' must maintain a separate residence from her husband. Furthermore, although the children of multiple marriages may be encouraged to interact, this does not usually extend to interaction among the wives. It would appear that the benefits of the modernization of marriage in this case are very mixed.

The example of 'outside marriages' in West Africa, described above, illustrates a disjunction between ideology and practice that has been found in many ex-colonial societies. Of course, disjunctions between ideology and practice can occur in many places, for a variety of reasons. An especially important example is the contradiction found in some marriages between an ideology of love between equal partners, and practices of violence that enable one partner to dominate the other.

Intimate Violence and Abuse

For purposes of sociological discussion, *violence* can be defined as any act which is intended to cause physical pain or injury to another person. *Abuse*, on the other hand, is any act which has a high probability of causing long-term harm to the person on whom it is inflicted. Forms of abuse include physical violence that is dangerous because it has the potential for serious injury (this is called 'abusive violence'). Abuse also includes non-violent acts that cause long-term emotional problems, such as *sexual abuse*.

Concepts of violence and abuse have been highly controversial, for a number of reasons. For one, it is not always clear what are the long-term effects of interactions between children and adults. To what extent do events in childhood in fact shape our emotional well-being in adult life, compared with later events? This issue is particularly difficult to resolve since adult memories of childhood may be unreliable, and because professional theories of child psychology may lack supporting evidence. It is possible that the intentions of family members, the nature of their acts, and the consequences of their acts can all be misinterpreted by outsiders who adopt a rigid image of what they think family life should be like.

On the other hand, sociologists need to be aware that claims that estimates of family violence and abuse are exaggerated can just be ways of avoiding having to take women's fears seriously. Denying the evidence that any serious problem exists in the exercise of social power is a classic means by which the powerful have always deflected criticism and resisted calls for change. In this context, research by Dobash et al. (1998) in Scotland found that male perpetrators of violence against women tend to under-report the severity of their actions. By comparison with their women partners, men who had been sanctioned by the justice system for an offence involving violence against a partner reported fewer and less frequent incidents of serious violence. The greatest discrepancy in reporting occurred with respect to choking, demanding sex, and threatening to kill the partner. Very few men in this study admitted to forcing their partners to have sex (only 6 per cent), whereas just over a quarter of women reported at least one instance of being forced to have sex with their partner. Similar differences existed in reporting the consequences of violence. Men reported inflicting far fewer injuries than women reported receiving. For example, about 40 per cent of women, but only 14 per cent of the men, reported that the women were knocked unconscious at least once during their relationship. And about 10–25 per cent of women, but only 5–12 per cent of men, reported broken teeth and fractures of bones in the face or limbs as a result of the violence. Dobash et al. conclude that in the gendered context of family life, men's accounts of their own violent behaviour cannot be used uncritically and without reference to women's accounts of men's violence.

Violence Between Partners

The nature and extent of family violence and abuse have been the subject of intense debates in recent decades (Sadler, 1996). One thing is clear, there has been growing recognition of intimate violence and abuse as problems for social research from the 1970s onwards (Breines and Gordon, 1983; Gelles and Conte, 1990). Feminists, in particular, drew attention to issues of wife abuse. (See **Box 5.1**). Violence as a means of getting one's own way in marriage is not consistent with the companionate ideal of decision-making through democratic communication, and this is one reason why claims about intimate violence and abuse have been taken increasingly seriously.

The companionship model of family life is based on certain widely held beliefs, including beliefs that marriage is based on love and that a close family is the most secure environment in which to raise a child. The evidence on family violence is not entirely consistent with this point of view. In the United States between 1977 and 1992 there were 337,747 reported homicide victims, of

Box 5.1   Feminism

The study of family violence is an important issue in feminist critiques of family life. Wife beating exemplifies the oppression of women within traditional family structures. Also, the fact that wife beating received so little public attention for so long illustrates how powerless many women have been to improve their lives.

Feminism is an approach that seeks to improve women's lives by challenging an oppressive social order (Barrett, 1980). Feminist studies therefore describe the various inequalities that women have faced, and they provide critiques of the social conditions that are responsible for those inequalities. The central contribution of feminist theory to family studies has been to describe women's oppression in marriage as the result of a system of patriarchal gender relations.

Monolithic concepts of 'the family' as a unified social group are thought to be ideological barriers to understanding the real causes of women's oppression in gender relationships (Eichler, 1981). The analysis of gender, or in other words the analysis of the social construction and social organization of marked attitudinal and behavioural differences between women and men, is the basis for most feminist studies of family life (Thorne, 1982; Potuchek, 1992; 1997).

Men and women often have different social experiences as a result of childhood socialization into traditional sex roles, and they therefore acquire different interests and skills. Those differences may then be rationalized into sexist ideologies which claim that there are many natural differences between women and men. A notable characteristic of such ideologies is that heterosexual relationships are believed to be the natural and inevitable basis for family life. Alternatives to heterosexuality are unlikely to be tolerated, and they will often be labelled as deviant. Contemporary feminist studies are therefore specially interested in challenges to the dominant *heteronormative* and patriarchal social order posed by gay and lesbian relationships (Dalton and Bielby, 2000). Donovan (2000), for example, has described how lesbian self-insemination families challenge three assumptions associated with traditional family life: that biological fathers should be involved as parents; that parenting involves gendered assumptions about mothering and fathering; and that fathers and mothers should share a household with their children.

On the other hand, feminist views on family life are sometimes resisted. In particular, they have been criticized for underestimating the prevalence of domestic violence and abuse in which women are the perpetrators and men are the victims.

whom 66,018 (19.5 per cent) were killed by relatives (Ewing, 1997). Wives are the most common victims of intrafamilial killings, followed by husbands, sons, daughters, fathers, brothers, mothers, and sisters. In recent years, more than a third of all female homicide victims in the United States were killed by a family member, most often their husband.

Patriarchal ideas still influence how some men think about 'their' women and how they should be treated when they do not do as expected. For example, it appears that a substantial minority of Arab husbands living in Israel believe that it is justifiable to beat a wife who is sexually unfaithful or who causes trouble in other ways (Haj-Yahia, 1998). That includes if she constantly refuses to have sex with her husband. Forced sex continues to be a major issue for women in many countries (Kelly, 1988; Hester, Kelly and Radford, 1996; Wood and Jewkes, 1997; Ouattara, Sen and Thomson, 1998). Also, disclosing sexual abuse of women under conditions of patriarchal domination is often both difficult and risky. That is because the emphasis of patriarchal males tends to be upon silencing the abuse of family members in order to preserve the family's 'honour' and reputation. In extreme cases, silencing is achieved by the death of the victim (Shalhoub-Kevorkian, 1999).

Violence and sexual abuse of women in family relationships often occurs in an ideological context that stresses women's complete dependence upon their families, and upon men. For example, traditional patriarchal ideologies in a number of societies have considered women to be inherently unreliable and deceitful (Dhruvarajan, 1989). Viewed in that context, it is believed to be important for husbands to control their wives even against their will. Such beliefs justify, or in other words legitimate, acts against women that might otherwise not be acceptable. The *legitimation* of power relationships is one of the most fundamental ideological processes in family life, as well as in larger social structures.

Most people do not like to think of families as contexts for serious violence and oppression, since that image clashes with the idealized image of the companionship family as a source of love and support. Instead of the idealistic modern viewpoint which sees marriage as an egalitarian relationship, we see evidence of power struggles in marriage with dominance and control as the rewards for successful violence. Violence can indeed be found in companionship families. In fact, intimate violence among couples in western societies is facilitated by certain features of the companionship family.

The interpersonal dynamics of intimate violence in companionship families begin during the process of partnership formation, usually well before the couple get married or move in together (Rosen, 1996). Individuals in couples – especially girlfriends and wives – become vulnerable to repeat abuse by violent partners, when they believe that there is no alternative to the relationship that they are in. The beginning of this process of entrapment in the companionship family is an emotional state of *romantic fusion*.

Popular culture contains many images of people whose lives were miraculously transformed by a romantic relationship with a new partner. Finding the right person, or being lucky enough to meet the right person at the right time, is often believed to be crucial to achieving real happiness. Romantic fantasies about 'the one for me' are fuelled by movies and magazines which prepare people to experience a 'magic moment' with that very special person. Actual fulfilment of romantic fantasies may not match the performed experiences of tabloid celebrities. However, most people come close enough to be satisfied with their own piece of the romantic dream.

An important aspect of the romantic dream is the imaginary fusing of two people into one. There is a fusion of identities, as a result of which the partners cannot bear to be separated. The positive side of this romantic fusion is that it establishes the basis for companionate marriage. But it can also produce extreme possessiveness by people who then turn to abuse as a means of control, as well as reluctance among their victims to give up and leave a partner who no longer treats them well. In a relationship in which one person develops severe problems, such as excessive drinking, romantic fusion therefore makes repeat abuse possible. Unwanted actions are tolerated and violence is interpreted as a painful episode which must be endured, in order to maintain the only relationship that makes life meaningful (Velleman, Copello and Maslin, 1998).

If abusive relationships usually begin with the romantic fusion of the couple, a secondary feature is very often *encapsulation*. People who fall in love, and who develop a strong commitment to each other, usually want to spend a lot of time together. They are willing to spend less time with their friends and acquaintances, in order to spend more time with the person they truly love. This sociological process of giving up a wider set of social ties is known as 'encapsulation'. At first, the relinquishing or weakening of other social ties may not even be noticed, because it is not experienced as a loss. Later, a lack of alternative relationships may make it difficult for someone who is being abused to get advice or support to end the relationship.

Leaving a relationship is especially difficult for someone who depends heavily upon her partner for the basic necessities of everyday living. Encapsulation of any kind greatly increases someone's *dependence* upon specific individuals, and perhaps ultimately upon only one person. Dependence in marriage is usually emotional or psychological to begin with, but subsequently it may be extended to material dependence. Access to housing, and money for food and clothing, may all depend upon remaining in a particular relationship. This extension of dependence in companionate marriage is due to the fact that life partners share their resources. Since women have had fewer financial resources than men on average, this means that wives are more likely to depend financially upon their husbands. That is especially likely to be the case among wives who have several young children. Wives who believe that they have no option but to stay in their present marriage are especially vulnerable to repeat incidents of violence and other forms of abuse.

Finally, the ideology of companionate marriage is also involved in the production of family violence insofar as it provides partners, especially wives, with beliefs that justify their remaining in the relationship. These beliefs provide partners with the *illusion of control* (Rosen, 1996). The ideology of the companionship family assumes that family members will communicate and cooperate with one another, in order to work out arrangements that will be gratifying to everyone. The assumption is made that someone who loves another person will listen to what that other person has to say. It is also assumed that they will try to meet the other's needs and help them to achieve their goals. Believing that the partner will respond to one's wishes is crucial to the ideological justification for companionate marriage as a voluntary relationship. In some cases, however, this belief is an illusion that is rationalized by selective memories of the 'good times' in the relationship. Illusions of control make it possible for trapped individuals to believe that more effort on their part to make the marriage work will eventually encourage their partner to stop the violence.

Public Responses to Family Violence

Individuals who are subject to repeated violence in their most intimate relationship cannot always do much about it on their own. Some activists have therefore reacted to family violence by trying to find better ways to control it or prevent it. Policy changes that have been made include new police and court procedures, new legal remedies, and setting up women's refuges or shelters where battered wives can go for help (Turner, 1995; Ursel, 1995; Duffy and Momirov, 1997). Some people, on the other hand, have reacted to claims of family violence with denial and disbelief. They have tried to avoid seeing it, or doing anything about it, because they find it impossible to understand.

Women who have been abused in lesbian relationships seem to find it particularly difficult to elicit much attention or understanding for their predicament (Miller and Knudsen, 1999). There is a lack of reporting about it, which is partly due to disbelief that same-sex violence can occur. Straight and lesbian groups both tend to equate battering with heterosexual marriage, and members of the lesbian community are likely to think of batterers as men. Intimate violence in lesbian couples contradicts feminist ideologies that equate men with patriarchy, and patriarchy with violence. It therefore tends to be ignored by other lesbians, because it challenges the ideological belief that a lesbian community must be egalitarian and nonviolent.

Claire Renzetti (1992) studied 100 women in the Philadelphia area who had been in lesbian relationships, and who had been abused. She found that factors correlated with abuse in lesbian relationships were similar to those reported for heterosexual relationships. A lesbian batterer was likely to be someone who was emotionally highly dependent on her partner, and who attempted to monopolize her time. She was also prone to jealousy. These similarities to the situations of many wives who have been assaulted by their husbands might have elicited understanding for lesbian victims of violence. In practice, lesbian victims expressed concerns about responses by police and workers in shelters. Because they were not in 'normal' relationships, they perceived their problems as being ignored or trivialized.

Public responses to family violence are profoundly influenced by the prevailing ideas in society about what is 'deviant', compared with what is 'normal' and therefore 'acceptable'. When ideas about what is acceptable and unacceptable behaviour change, this sometimes sets in motion a 'moral panic.' A *moral panic* is an intense, collective fear that the moral failures of a deviant group of people are having harmful effects on society (Goode and Ben-Yehuda, 1994). In the 1980s and 1990s, moral panics about intimate violence against women and sexual abuse of children occurred in several western societies (Atmore, 1999). This heightened concern did not necessarily reflect any real increase in actual family violence or abuse, although it may have reflected a greater willingness of women to report as confidence in official action grew. Public impressions about the amount of violence and abuse depended upon the amount of information that was available, especially in the mass media. In turn, the amount of available information often resulted from the degree of attention that public organizations gave to the problem. For example, in the mid-1990s only the United States, Canada and Australia had specific legislation that required the reporting of child abuse to official agencies (Gelles, 1997). Official data on child abuse have not been as readily available in most other countries.

Data collection in official studies, as well as in social science research, rests upon the way in which key concepts are defined. That is why it is always important to pay careful attention to the definitions that are being used in research on family issues, including studies of family violence (Johnson, 1995; Nazroo, 1999). For instance, is parents' spanking of children really violence, or is it an effective means of child discipline? Deep differences of opinion exist over this question. They reflect cultural differences between countries, and sometimes between ethnic groups within a country, as well as political differences between people who hold different ideologies. Among sociologists, the tendency is to define violence in a way that identifies spanking as *normal violence*, that is violence which is socially accepted within a given culture.

In the past, 'normal violence' between husbands and wives tended to be treated by police as 'family disputes' which were best left to the individuals involved to settle on their own. That attitude existed partly because the rights and wrongs of a case can be hard to establish when a wife and her husband are the only witnesses present. Furthermore, most people would like to believe that we can do whatever we want in the privacy of our own homes.

The latter idea of domestic privacy has been very important historically. It is based on the principle that a society consists of two quite different areas of life, namely a public sphere and a *private sphere*. The public sphere consists of government, business, education and organized religion. The private sphere consists of family, kinship and friendship relationships that take place in and between people's homes. In early modern societies the idea developed that the private sphere was a kind of refuge, a 'haven in a heartless world', into which people could retreat from the pressures of work in industry and in bureaucracies. People could thus 'be themselves' at home, without risk of interference, because there were strong legal and social barriers to public institutions invading their privacy. The problem that many feminists recognized, especially from the 1970s onwards, was that privacy of family life and the reluctance of police to intervene also protected men who battered their wives (Edwards, 1991).

Today, feminist activists have been relatively successful in ensuring that the need is widely understood for legal and social restrictions on men's use of intimate violence toward women. Nevertheless, the tendency persists to exclude people in close relationships from the full force of public protection. Claims that all children need to maintain contact with their father, for instance, sometimes put the safety of children, and their mothers, at risk. Changes to laws and policies concerning access to children after divorce or separation, as well as family reunification/family preservation programmes, have therefore all given rise to new controversies about the social distribution of risks of violence and abuse (Gelles, 1993; Hester and Radford, 1996).

It has been even more difficult to reach social consensus about limiting the use of physical punishment by parents as an everyday means of disciplining their children (Straus, 1998). Agreement has also been difficult to reach about what constitutes satisfactory evidence on sexual abuse of children and how it should be handled. In Britain, a notorious example of this in the late 1980s was the 'Cleveland affair', which was named after the area where the events took place (La Fontaine, 1990; Rodger, 1996).

Child Abuse

In 1987, 125 children from 57 families in the County of Cleveland, in England, were referred to medical experts who diagnosed them as having been sexually abused. Twenty-seven children were removed from their parents into the care of municipal services, and a further 67 children were taken under the protection of the state as wards of court. The unprecedented number of sexual abuse cases for an English county at that time provoked great public concern. Public opinion was divided between horrified acceptance of the magnitude of sexual abuse that needed to be treated, and rejection of the medical evidence on most of the cases combined with outrage against misuse of power by the state. The latter reaction, which dominated in many media reports over the next two years, focused on the rights of parents and the freedom of the family from state interference. An irreconcilable conflict developed between claims for freedom of the family within an autonomous private sphere, and demands for the state to intervene as the agent for public protection of children. The 'Cleveland affair' also revealed gender divisions in British society. Women were more likely to believe that sexual abuse had occurred, and to put public care for children above the rights of parents. Men, on the other hand, were more likely to deny the existence of sexual abuse and to stress parental authority over children.

Public attention to the vulnerability of children within families tends to fluctuate between periods of intense interest and almost total lack of interest. Today, it is recognized that intimate violence is an especially important cause of violent deaths among children. When children are killed, their killers are usually relatives, most often their parents. Children of all ages are killed by abusive parents, but the problem is greatest for very young children who are more likely to die when exposed to severe physical abuse. While accurate figures on abuse as a cause of death in children are hard to come by, it is estimated that parents are responsible for the majority of violent deaths among young children in the United States. When a parent kills a child, mothers are as likely to be the perpetrators as fathers (Ewing, 1997).

Discussion

In this chapter we have begun to take up the second of the basic questions that were asked about family life at the beginning of this book. That question is: 'What do families do?'. We began by focusing on the idea that relational intimacy is central to family life. We have seen that this is a cultural ideal which emerged in western societies mainly during the past century, and that is associated notably with the ideal of companionate marriage.

The ideology of companionate marriage has flourished because it gives meaning to intimate relationships that are no longer defined mainly in religious terms. Especially in an era when cohabitation is replacing legal marriage for many people, the ideal of companionship provides a recognized meaning for relationships which the participants construct without reference to any formal authority. Family life is defined mainly as an arena of personal freedom, in which people create whatever kinds of relationships they think will meet their needs for companionship.

Despite its ubiquity, the ideology of the companionship family has certain limitations that have been questioned in recent years. When spouses share everything, and they are close in all aspects of their daily lives, what rights does each of them have as an individual? And, should there be any limits to inter- actions between husbands and wives when a couple are together in the privacy of their own home? In recent decades the legal answers to those questions have tended to come down on the side of expanding individual rights against family members, and in favour of public prohibitions against socially unacceptable behaviour. This has been done mainly for the protection of wives and children. The cause for greatest concern here has been family violence.

Violence within families contradicts ideals of companionship, except in rare cases of sado-masochism, because it is not mutually enjoyable and it does not equally respect the wishes of both parties. In one sense, the wave of public criticism of family violence in many countries at the end of the twentieth century was simply a late extension of the ideology of the companionship family. But it was also much more than that. It was an attempt, led mainly by feminists, to redefine the rights of individuals within families in the direction of greater individualization. A good example of this kind of issue is the debate that occurred over 'wife rape' (Bergen, 1996; Kelly and Radford, 1996).

According to English legal tradition, which was followed in other countries such as the United States, a husband who forced his wife to have sex could not be convicted of raping her. The thinking behind this was the idea that a married couple constitute a single legal entity which cannot be divided. It followed from this idea of matrimonial unity that one spouse could not reliably testify against the other in court, and a husband could not be accused of violating 'himself'. Furthermore, it was held that upon entering into marriage each individual grants the other access to all of his or her resources, including sexual access. Therefore, a married woman was considered to have irrevocably consented to sexual intercourse with her husband as a condition of the marriage relationship. Given this construction of reality, married women found it impossible to claim that they had 'really' been raped by their husbands.

Changes to the law have been slow and incomplete, and convictions have been hard to achieve, but the long-term trend is nevertheless clear. Wife rape is increasingly considered to be an affront against individual rights for protection of the person. Although this is a relatively minor issue in terms of the number of court cases, it does illustrate a fundamental change that is taking place in the balance between individual rights and family obligations. Family life is slowly being modified by struggles over rights of women, in opposition to an ancient patriarchal order that has maintained and defended male dominance (Peacock, 1998).

In western societies, power struggles over the rights and responsibilities of women and men are often most visible during divorce, and during the post-divorce construction of new family roles. At this point, hidden inequalities and divisions between men and women within many supposedly egalitarian companionship families come into the open. In the United States, wives often report anticipating the end of marriage long before they talk about it with their husbands, and they initiate divorce more often than men (Thompson and Amato, 1999). Of course, some wives remain in an unhappy marriage and convince themselves that it is working, due to financial worries or concerns about the effects of divorce on children. But, by the time the divorce process begins, they are often ready to move on with their lives. Men, in contrast, more often experience divorce as an unexpected and unwelcome step, and they are more likely to worry about losing contact with their children. Like the tip of the iceberg, these gender differences in divorce are merely the visible outcomes of underlying gender differences in childcare that existed within marriage. Patterns of childcare and caregiving are considered in more detail in the next chapter.

6

Childcare and Caregiving

The social organization of childcare and caregiving activities, and consequences such as time stress, are studied in Chapter 6. Attention is paid to
social inequalities in the effects of gender, age and class differences,
especially gender. The influence of the symbolic order of childcare is also
investigated, in family roles, social identities and self concepts. Modern
ideas of parenting, such as 'intensive mothering,' are described as
having profound, and sometimes contradictory, effects upon the lives
of many women today.

CONCEPTS

transactions   caregiving   intrahousehold transactions
interhousehold transactions   filial responsibility
social distribution of work   childcare
pseudomutuality   stereotypes   anomie
anticipatory socialization   time stress   dual-career
couples   symmetrical families   role segregation
social identity   self concepts   caring about
taking care of   intensive mothering   care deficit

An expression of emotion felt toward a loved one, an act of caring for him or
her, or an exchange of goods and services that helps each person to meet their
needs of daily living, are all examples of transactions between individuals.
Transactions are interactions in which an object such as money is transferred
from one person to another, or a service such as washing clothes is performed
by one person for another person. It is in the study of transactions that
questions raised by feminist sociologists often become most important. Who
does what, for whom? And who gives what to whom?

The care that family members provide for one another is one of the most important activities carried on within families (Waerness, 1989). Families can provide an intimate and comprehensive caring environment that is rarely available in any other social group. In fact, the existence of an intimate, caring relationship is regarded by many social policymakers as the defining characteristic of 'the family'.

Caregiving is actually not just one activity, but it consists of a whole set of tasks that involve one person helping another person to meet their needs for daily living. It includes food preparation and clean-up, house cleaning, laundry and sewing, as well as house maintenance and repairs, shopping for groceries and other necessities, providing transportation to and from activities outside the home, doing the banking and bill-paying, and personal care such as bathing or dressing someone, and assistance with using the toilet. This diverse set of activities is carried out in many different ways, in many different kinds of relationship. For instance, there are important differences in the kinds of care provided by people who consider themselves to be close family members, compared with people whose relationship is more distant. Intimate personal care, such as getting dressed or using the bathroom, is usually carried out by a close family member. On the other hand, help with shopping or transportation can be provided by a much wider range of people (Cranswick, 1997).

Most caregiving, and almost all intimate personal care, is provided by someone living in the same household in the form of *intrahousehold transactions*. This is usually most convenient, because people who live together have the easiest access to helping one another. Indeed, having access to caregiving can be one reason why people choose to live in the same home. This happens, for example, when elderly parents and their adult children live together so that the senior generation can receive better care. In many cases, however, people in need of care are either unable to live in the same home as their caregivers, or else they choose not do so in order to maintain their independence.

A Canadian study of individuals who care for others with long-term health problems or physical limitations found that only six per cent had actually moved in with the person they were assisting (Cranswick, 1997). In the majority of these cases, then, caregiving takes the form of *interhousehold transactions* between people who live apart. In western societies, like Canada, interhousehold caregiving is the main way in which elderly parents receive help from their adult children. Obviously, living separately makes daily caregiving more difficult. Non-resident caregivers may have to relocate their homes in order to be within reasonable travelling distance, and they may have to juggle their work schedules and vacation plans in order to make time for caregiving.

Whether a person in need of assistance receives it from someone living in the same household, or from someone living in a different household, depends in part on the marital status of the care recipient. Married recipients are more likely to receive care from someone living in their own home. The US National Long-Term Care Survey of older people who had problems performing at least one task of daily living showed three distinct patterns of receiving care. Receiving care differed between the currently married, the formerly married (that is, the separated, divorced or widowed), and the never married (Coward, Horne and Dwyer, 1992). Older people in need of assistance, and who were currently married, were highly dependent on their spouses. For these people, help received from children was a distant second in relative frequency. The formerly married, on the other hand, were more likely to be receiving help from an adult child (especially daughters), and other female relatives, hired help and social service agencies as secondary supports. Finally, the never married relied heavily upon their siblings (especially sisters), and upon other female relatives. They also made more use than people in other marital statuses of hired help and people from social service agencies.

Studies of caregiving for the elderly raise a number of interesting questions for sociologists and for social policymakers. For example, what will the implications be of increased divorce rates when the current generation of middle-aged adults enter old age? Current cohorts of the elderly raised their families at a time when divorce in middle age was relatively uncommon. But that is not the case today. Future cohorts of older people will contain more divorced and separated persons. If there are more formerly married older people in the future who do not have a spouse to look after them, then on present evidence they are likely to turn first to their children to provide care when they develop a disability. However, future cohorts of older people will also have fewer children than earlier cohorts, and it is unclear how their adult children will respond to increased demands upon their time.

The balance of opinion among researchers in North America is cautiously optimistic about future care for the elderly. It seems that the impact of increased divorce rates upon availability of adult children as caregivers for the elderly is unlikely to be large (see for example, Montgomery, 1992). The majority of caregivers do not describe providing care for elderly parents as a burden, despite the extra work and lifestyle adjustments that are often involved. *Filial responsibility*, in the western form of a sense of obligation to respond to emerging needs of elderly parents, has remained fairly strong in many families even though patterns of family living have changed (Blieszner and Hamon, 1992). Also, caregiving is often a negotiated responsibility, which is influenced by feelings, comparative commitments and physical closeness or distance. There is a great deal of flexibility in assigning caregiving responsibilities in most families, which ensures that the needs of elderly parents are usually met by someone.

Social Distribution of Childcare and Caregiving

The last issue draws attention to the *social distribution of work*, or in other words who does the work. It is necessary to pay careful attention to the unequal ways in which *childcare* and caregiving, as well as other kinds of work, are distributed between people in different categories and who occupy different roles.

Family groups are composed of two or more individuals who play different roles, and they do not all engage in exactly the same kinds of activities. In practice, different family members provide different amounts and kinds of care. Those differences are important because they affect how families work. They also affect what happens when families break up.

Many divorced fathers are less involved in post-divorce parenting than divorced mothers. That is partly because fathers have usually spent less time at home caring for children and doing related housework prior to divorce (Smart, 1999). Fathers who have not had much involvement in childcare are likely to be distrusted by the children's mothers after divorce. Also, men may lack confidence in themselves when faced with the challenge of independent parenting.

The apparent contrast between gender inequality in childcare, and the ideology of marital equality in the companionship family, has inspired two Australian sociologists to describe contemporary marriage as a system of *pseudomutuality*. Pseudomutuality is a social situation in which two people who claim to treat each other as equals in fact do not give and receive in equal amounts, and they hide this fact from each other. Michael Bittman and Jocelyn Pixley (1997) believe that there is a hidden contradiction between attitudes and behaviour within most companionate marriages. This potential threat to family order is suppressed by ignoring the question of how much work each partner does. As long as both partners want the marriage to last, the emphasis is on cooperation and peaceful coexistence in order to keep the relationship going. The existing division of labour between spouses is allowed to go unchallenged for long periods of time, and negotiations over the allocation of tasks are avoided because they might lead to open conflict. Nevertheless, there is always the possibility that resentment at perceived injustices may build up over time, and eventually lead to divorce. Bittman and Pixley suggest that this may be a contributing factor to increased divorce rates in Australia.

In Britain, it is widely believed that most fathers do more for their children now than used to be the case. However, significant differences remain in both the quantity and type of childcare carried out by men and women (Pilcher, 1999). Gender differences in providing care tend to be accentuated in post-divorce families, since a non-resident parent (usually the father) does not contribute as much to the care of a child as the resident parent does (Smart, 1999; Smart and Neale, 1999). Similar conclusions emerge from comparable studies in the United States (Walker, 1999). In general, women still tend to perform more childcare and caregiving than men. Nevertheless, it is important to note that gender differences decline with advancing age, as children leave home and as husbands provide more care for elderly wives.

Age is an important factor in both caregiving and childcare. For example, the people who are most likely to be caring for young children are young adults. These young parents are also likely to be heavily involved in the labour market, and juggling childcare and paid employment is especially difficult for this age group.

In contrast, caring for ill or disabled parents is a responsibility that usually falls upon people who are considerably older. The length of the average life span is steadily increasing, and people often stay healthy until well into old age. By the time older people need a great deal of care their children are likely to be in middle age, or even entering old age themselves. That is why the age group which is most involved in providing care for people with long-term health problems in Canada is between 45 and 64 years of age (Cranswick, 1997).

Sara Arber and Jay Ginn report from Britain that in addition to age differences there are gender differences in caregiving. This affects the relative importance of intrahousehold caregiving compared with interhousehold caregiving. Men and women are equally likely to provide care for someone living in the same household, but a higher proportion of women than men provide care for someone living in another household (Arber and Ginn, 1999). British women are about one third more likely than men to provide care to someone who is not living with them. Married women are the most likely to provide care to someone living in another household, and single men are the least likely to do so. It is primarily when their wives require care, mainly in old age, that men take on a major caregiving role in the family.

Support from a spouse is often a critical factor in enabling the elderly to retain the independence of living in their own homes. The living arrangements of older people have a large influence on whether informal care is provided by another household member, or by someone living in another household, or whether they rely upon formal care in a residential institution such as a nursing home (Arber and Ginn, 1993). Single men in Britain who are in their late seventies have a 17 times greater chance of being in residential care than married men of the same age, and widowed men have a six times greater chance.

Research by Arber and Ginn suggests that prior to old age there are large class differences in intrahousehold caregiving, but not in interhousehold caregiving (Arber and Ginn, 1992). The lower the class position of an individual, the more likely it is that he or she will be providing care for someone who lives in the same household. This pattern is stronger for men than it is for women. Below the age of 45, men in unskilled occupations are five times more likely to be coresident caregivers than men in upper middle-class occupations. Women under age 45 with an unskilled class background are two-and-a-half times more likely to be coresident caregivers than upper-middle-class women.

The precise reasons for this class gradient in intrahousehold caregiving are not entirely clear. Part of the explanation is almost certainly that people from lower-class backgrounds tend to have poorer health. That may be due to the harmful effects of some of their occupations, or to consequences of managing on a low income, or to lifestyle differences such as smoking. Also, when members of upper-middle-class families do get sick they are more likely to be able to afford alternative forms of care. They may be able to hire health care workers to come into the home to replace them, or they may use more expensive formal care services such as nursing homes. Either way, the greater financial resources of members of upper-middle-class families can be used to reduce the burden of intrahousehold caregiving, thus giving them more time in which to do other things. Notably, they have more time available for paid employment outside the home. This increases their comparative financial advantage over working-class families. Nevertheless, it is important to keep in mind that on average less than ten per cent of working-class families are providing care to someone who is living in the household. The impact of this factor upon time use is therefore weaker overall than that of gender.

Time Use

Men generally spend more time on paid work than women, but women generally spend more time than men on unpaid work such as childcare, caregiving and volunteer work (Devereaux, 1993; Frederick, 1995; Haas, 1999; Walker, 1999). Women and men also tend to differ in the kinds of activities which they carry out on behalf of their families. Women in the United States, for example, spend almost half of their family-work time on the core housework activities of cooking, cleaning and laundry, while men spend only about one-quarter of their family-work time doing housework (Robinson and Godbey, 1997). Women also spend proportionally more time on childcare than men. Men, on the other hand, spend proportionally more of their family-work time on household repairs, home-management activities and obtaining services for the family.

Time use studies in the United States suggest that gender differences in time allocation are minimal or non-existent among children. However, as children mature they tend to conform more and more to the prevailing *stereotypes* about gender roles. Gender stereotypes have had an enormous influence upon family life, as well as upon theories of family life. (See **Box 6.1**). It appears that images of men as breadwinners, and women as homemakers, still have a surprising amount of influence upon child development in the USA. In ninth grade, (ages 14–15), American girls and boys spend about equal amounts of time on household chores (Call, 1996). Interestingly, the amount of time spent performing these tasks falls between the ninth and twelfth grades (ages 14–18) for both genders. However, the reduction in time spent on household tasks is greater adolescent boys than it is for adolescent girls. By twelfth grade (ages 17–18), boys are spending approximately 60 per cent of the time that girls spend on household tasks.

Adolescence is a crucial period in the life course when individuals begin preparing themselves for the adult roles which they expect to enter. During this phase of *anticipatory socialization* they seek out experiences which help them to develop attitudes and skills that they believe they will need in later life. It is therefore striking to find that American boys and girls between the ninth and

Box 6.1 Suicide: Family and gender issues

Sociologists have long been interested in gender differences in family life, and the reasons for them. They have offered a variety of explanations over the years. Some of the early explanations were evidently influenced by gender stereotypes when male sociologists speculated about the reasons for women's behaviour. Caution is always necessary when comparing our own group with another group, perhaps especially in gender issues.

One of the most notorious examples of the influence of gender stereotypes was the discussion of suicide patterns by the classical sociologist Emile Durkheim (1858–1917) (1951[1897]). Durkheim observed that in late nineteenth-century Europe there were systematic connections between marital status, gender and the incidence of suicide. He concluded that 'the family is a powerful safeguard against suicide' (Durkheim, 1951: 202). However, he also noted that the protective benefit of the family for women was less than that for men.

Similar results have subsequently been found in a number of countries, including Canada and Australia, and the overall patterns have been remarkably consistent over time (Trovato, 1991; Cantor and Slater, 1995). The married generally have lower suicide rates than the unmarried, and the change from a nonmarried state to married produces a greater reduction in the risk of suicide for men than for women. Furthermore, any protective effect of family life for women seems to be associated more with having children rather than marriage *per se*.

The difficulty with Durkheim's work on suicide lies not so much in his analysis of data as in his explanation for the differential effects of marriage upon women and men. This he attributed to men's greater need for protection from a state of moral confusion that he referred to as *anomie*. Durkhem claimed that women were less susceptible to this condition because their 'mental life is less developed' since a woman is 'a more instinctive creature than man' (Durkheim, 1951: 272).

Feminist scholars have criticized Durkheim's stereotypical views on women (Sydie, 1987; Lehmann, 1990; 1991). It is further pointed out that his questionable interpretation enabled him to gloss over the potentially explosive implications of his findings for a feminist critique of the effects of marriage upon women.

twelfth grades have already adopted a division of labour which conforms to stereotypical notions of masculine and feminine work. Boys spend much more time than girls taking out the garbage and doing yardwork, including shovelling snow in the winter. Girls, on the other hand, spend significantly more hours per week than boys on cleaning, cooking, and doing dishes and laundry.

Furthermore, throughout their high-school years, girls spend more time caring for other family members, especially younger children. In the eleventh and twelfth grades (ages 16–18) girls spend more than twice the number of hours caring for younger children than boys do.

Gendered attitudes towards housework are developed early in life, and they are later reinforced by adult experiences in work organizations and in family relationships. Most employers expect that men will devote themselves fully to their jobs, including being available for overtime work at short notice. Having a reputation for putting family commitments before an employers' needs usually results in lost opportunities for promotion. Partly for this reason, and partly due to gender stereotypes about caring, most men expect that women will take on the primary responsibility for housework when difficult choices have to be made.

Women consistently spend more time on housework than men. Even women who have never been married spend more time on housework than men, whether they are still living with their parents or living independently (South and Spitze, 1994). When members of the opposite sex begin living together the amount of time each devotes to housework is also affected by an emergent division of labour. As they carry out the tasks of a new household, gender differences in time spent on housework increase. Gender differences occur when men and women cohabit, and they are even larger among those who get married.

The amount of time that American men spend on housework does not change very much when they marry or start cohabiting. Indeed, it may even decline slightly. However, cohabiting women and married women increase the time they spend on housework. As a result, wives allocate much more of their time to housework than do their partners, especially if they have children.

Mothers in the United States carry out almost 80 per cent of the family childcare. In particular, they do most of the 'custodial' childcare such as cleaning and feeding children. Fathers' time with children is more often spent in interactive activities, such as play or helping with homework. American men are now participating in more childcare than they used to do, but the trend toward greater equality within marriage has been counteracted to some extent by the fact that more women are raising children on their own. In post-divorce families, the existing division of labour over caring for children is often intensified. That is because mothers usually have the sole responsibility for everyday childcare, whereas the father's role is often limited to providing economic support.

Discussions about the gender division of labour in families have led to questions about who experiences the most *time stress*. Time stress is the feeling that there is too much work to do, and too little time in which to do it. There are many causes of time stress, and different people respond to it in different ways. People who work away from home for many hours each day may worry that they don't have enough time to spend with the ones they love. In contrast, people who are overwhelmed by the demands of others, including family members, may wish to have more time alone. Studies conducted by Statistics Canada show that about one-third of the adult population worries that they do not spend enough time with family and friends, and about one-quarter would like to spend more time alone (Frederick, 1993). Men and women are equally likely to be concerned about lack of time with family and friends. However, women (26 per cent) are more likely than men (19 per cent) to want to spend more time alone.

The total amount of leisure time enjoyed by people in western societies has increased over the past half-century, due to a combination of legislative changes, union agreements and earlier retirement from paid employment among men. As well, falling fertility rates mean that women today have fewer children on average to look after. Nevertheless, time stress has become an important issue in countries such as Britain, Canada and the United States. That has occurred because work pressures are distributed unequally in the population, and because more people now have to juggle multiple responsibilities to different groups in different places. In Canada, for example, policies on work developed by employers, governments and unions have had little impact overall on the nature and distribution of childcare and caregiving. The effect of increased employment by mothers has therefore been felt mainly in adjustments within families, especially by mothers themselves. Conflicting responsibilities arising from multiple roles, and competing demands for time, have tended to become a bigger factor in mothers' lives than they were in the past.

The biggest factor in the incidence of time stress in Canada is responsibility for children. Most parents start having children when they are young adults, and this has major effects on the age distribution of time stress. Time stress is highest among those aged 25–44, who are in their prime childbearing and childrearing years. It is lowest among those over age 55, whose main responsibilities for children have been completed and who are also beginning to exit from paid employment. In families with children, the age of the child and the gender of the primary caregiver also have a large effect on the social distribution of time stress. In particular, mothers with infants report feeling exceptionally stressed for time as they attempt to cope with the unrelenting demands of a new baby.

There are also significant variations in time stress between different types of families. Couples in which both partners are working full-time (sometimes referred to as *dual-career couples*) are among the most time stressed members of Canadian society. Obviously the adults in these families carry heavy workloads, but there are also inequalities in workloads within these families.

Thirty years ago in Britain, Michael Young and Peter Willmott predicted a trend toward *symmetrical families*. They envisaged that in the families of the future both husband and wife would be employed full time, and they would also share the housework and childcare equally (Young and Willmott, 1973). In other words, there would be no *role segregation* in the family. Young and

Willmott expected that marriage partners would not only spend the same amount of time on housework and childcare as each other, but they would also be doing the same kinds of tasks according to who was most available when the work needed to be done. This line of argument emphasizes situational influences upon behaviour, as discussed earlier in this book. Influenced by their economic situation, couples who are very involved in the workforce are expected to adjust the internal allocation of tasks within the family so that both partners can maximize their hours of employment. How realistic is that hypothesis, in fact? Over the last thirty years there has been a large increase in employment among married women, both in terms of the number of wives who participate in the labour force and in terms of the number of hours that employed wives work. To what extent has this trend in work practices brought about a shift towards more symmetrical families?

Thirty years later, we can see that symmetrical families are more common now than they used to be, but they are still infrequent. Roles of husbands and wives are less segregated now than they once were. Nevertheless, they are far from identical in most cases. That is partly because wives who are employed often work less than full time, whereas most husbands continue to seek full-time employment. It is also because housework and childcare are not distributed equally, even in most dual career couples. Dual-career couples may give the appearance of gender symmetry, but appearances can be deceptive.

Australian time-use surveys from 1974 to 1992 show that the trend toward symmetrical families is slow and uncertain, and it may have stalled recently (Bittman and Pixley, 1997). Like women in other countries, Australian women have responded to increased employment outside the home by reducing the amount of time they spend on housework, especially cooking. However, there has been little change in the domestic duties of Australian men, although they are spending slightly more time with children now than they did in the past.

In Canada, the extent of wives' responsibility for housework declines as their involvement in the workforce increases, and husbands' responsibility for housework grows, as predicted by Young and Willmott. However, the increase in husbands' contributions is small on average, and it is not large enough to approach equality with their wives (Marshall, 1993). Husbands are more involved in meal preparation when their wives work full-time, but wives are nevertheless responsible for most meal preparation in the majority of couples. The 1990 General Social Survey in Canada shows that in families where husbands are employed full time, 89 per cent of wives who are not in the labour force have the primary responsibility for meal preparation, as do 86 per cent of wives who are employed part time and 72 per cent of wives who are themselves employed full-time. Equal responsibility for meal preparation is found in only 12 per cent of dual career couples (Marshall, 1993).

Not surprisingly, more than 28 per cent of wives in dual-career couples in Canada have been found to be severely time stressed, compared with less than

16 per cent of husbands (Frederick, 1993). This gender difference in time stress within dual-career couples is principally due to unequal responsibilities for childcare, as it occurs only in younger couples. Mothers in some of these families evidently have the primary responsibility for childcare, as well as the extra housework that children create, at the same time as they struggle to meet the demands of full-time employment.

Research in the United States suggests that family role expectations of wives and husbands have a significant influence upon the allocation of responsibility for housework in couples (Vannoy-Hiller and Philliber, 1989; Shelton and John, 1996). The importance of cultural – or, more accurately, subcultural – influences upon the division of labour in contemporary families is confirmed by the particular social factors that do make a difference to the allocation of housework. Dual-career couples in Canada with the most flexible allocation of housework are those who are most exposed to non-traditional influences, and who prefer non-traditional lifestyles. This includes people who cohabit instead of getting married, as well as those who have higher educational attainment, and younger generations of Canadians (Marshall, 1993). Cohabiting does not seem to be associated with a more equal gender distribution of the total amount of time spent on housework, however it is associated with less role segregation. In Canada in 1990, 40.1 per cent of married women had sole responsibility for meal preparation, but 28.9 per cent of women in cohabiting couples did all of the meal preparation (Wu, 2000). Sole responsibility of wives for housework is more common among those who are legally married, older Canadians, and less educated women.

Cultural and situational factors both influence the allocation of household tasks, but it is hard to avoid the conclusion that the biggest influence on this aspect of family life is the gendered experience of having children living at home (Horrell, 1994; Cheal, 1999). Analysis of British Social Attitudes Surveys shows that liberal attitudes among cohabiting couples concerning family roles only affect their behaviour when they are childless (Kiernan and Estaugh, 1993). Childless cohabiting couples are more likely to share domestic responsibilities than their married counterparts. However, among couples with children there is little difference in the proportions sharing domestic duties according to marital status. Regardless of marital status, most women continue to have the main responsibility for childcare. This means that domestic activity in the home continues to have a special importance for many women.

Family Roles, Social Identities and Self Concepts

Women make up the overwhelming majority of people who consider their main activity to be homemaking, or keeping house. Although the breadwinner/homemaker type of family is in a distinct minority in Canada today, women who identify homemaking as their primary activity nevertheless comprised 30 per cent of the adult female population in the early 1990s (Dever-eaux, 1993). The manner in which women and men use their time is not only connected to their roles in the family, but it is also related to how they see themselves and how they are seen by others. In other words, the social distribution of family time is connected to people's self concepts and their social identities.

A *social identity* is a set of personal characteristics that are believed to be typical of someone who occupies a particular social role, or who belongs to a particular social category. For example, 'mothering' is a gendered identity which has profound effects on the lives of women (Glenn, 1994). Mothering as a social identity is much more than just bearing and raising a child. Mothering is being in a relationship of nurturing and caring for a child so that it will flourish and grow. Women who are mothering are expected to offer warm, uncritical support and to pay close attention to the needs of children, as well as putting the needs of children ahead of their own needs whenever a conflict arises.

Significant differences often exist between the social identities and *self concepts* of men and women in families. It is important to note that men do not usually think of themselves as caring about their children any less than women do, if by *caring about* we mean having feelings of interest and concern which motivate awareness and attention. However, fathers and mothers tend to think about caring in different ways, and they often express different meanings when they talk about their caring responsibilities. Women and men tend to resolve time pressures and conflicts between paid employment and caregiving by emphasizing different priorities. Mothers are more likely than fathers to limit their labour force participation, and fathers are more likely than mothers to reduce their caregiving responsibilities. That is because women are more likely than men to think about caring for children in the practical sense of *taking care of* them by watching over them and responding to their immediate needs (Fisher and Tronto, 1990). Men, on the other hand, tend to have a more diffuse sense of caring for children. Men's sense of caring is more likely to involve some sort of ongoing responsibility and commitment, which is not necessarily connected to practical childcare activities but includes being a good economic provider (van Dongen, 1995).

Family roles, social identities and self concepts about childcare and caregiving are connected in many ways that tend to reinforce established commitments to raise children and help close family members. However, that is not always the case. In certain respects, connections between structural components of family life are becoming looser than they were in the recent past. The structural elements of roles, identities and selves are sometimes separated, altered and re-combined in ways that add to the complexity of contemporary family life. We will consider an example of this phenomenon next, in the lives of family daycare providers.

Family daycare providers are individuals such as childminders in Britain (almost always women) who provide paid daycare for other people's children in their homes. Often, family daycare providers have children of their own whom they care for at the same time as they care for other children. Being a family daycare worker can be a convenient way of being a stay-at-home mother and earning a modest income at the same time. While there are many reasons for becoming a family daycare worker, including lack of alternative job opportunities, it tends to be an attractive option for women who occupy the role of mother and who are strongly committed to the social identity of mothering. The self concept of these women is primarily that of a motherly woman who loves children and who wants to spend as much time with them as possible. With respect to their own children, the family role, social identity and self concept of these mothers are all positively reinforcing. However, the situation is more complex with respect to the other children they care for.

Mothers who are family daycare providers care for children who are not their own under a variety of short-term contracts that involve the 'commodification of caring' (Crompton, 1997). Here, the social identity of mothering and the self concept of being a motherly person are not consistent with the family role. Family daycare providers are not in fact the mothers of the children in their care, although they are expected to act like their mothers in most respects and they may have some of the same feelings towards them as their mothers do. This structural dissonance creates a number of difficulties for family daycare workers, which can produce negative experiences for them (Nelson, 1994).

Family daycare providers find themselves involved in three kinds of contradictions that are due to the separation of motherhood from mothering and motherly identity. First, those women who choose to be family daycare providers because they believe that all children need the constant love and attention of a mother work at home because it enables them to look after their own children. At the same time, their participation in daycare work enables other women to be employed in jobs which keep them apart from their children. Such family daycare workers face an ideological dilemma. Their beliefs about providing loving care for children cause them to be involved in an activity which cannot provide other women's children with a mother's love that they are thought to need most.

Many family daycare workers do try to give children in their care the love that they believe each child needs. In so doing, they sometimes develop personal attachments to the children that are similar to the feelings they have for their own children. Nevertheless, these women are not in fact the mothers of the children in their care, and they therefore have no rights over them. Sooner or later, family daycare providers will be separated from the children, which may be followed by feelings of loss. It is a common experience of many stay-at-home mothers that they have a sense of loss when their children start school. This feeling can also arise among family daycare providers who may never see the children they cared for after the children leave their care. In addition, family daycare providers are vulnerable to sudden and unexpected losses of the children in their care when a mother's job changes, or she changes residence, or she simply decides that she does not like how the family daycare provider is looking after her child.

The final difficulty experienced by many family daycare providers is that women who choose to look after other children at home, in order to spend more time with their own children, inevitably find the standard of care for their children is compromised. They are unable to spend as much time with their own children as they would like, because their attention must now be divided among a larger number of children. Also, a family daycare provider's children must learn to share their domestic space, their toys, and their mother, with the other children present in the home. Sometimes children resent doing that. Tensions can therefore arise between mothers and their children, which may be followed by feelings of guilt if the mother doubts the value of what she is doing. In sum, being a family daycare provider is a contradictory activity in which the separation of motherhood from mothering, and being motherly, inevitably gives rise to emotional and practical problems.

Intensive Mothering

One potential problem in family daycare is that mothers who employ family daycare workers may expect them to provide intellectual stimulation for their children, whereas childcare providers may define their role simply as one of providing a safe and comforting environment for children. This clash of perspectives arises from modern attitudes towards children's education and the importance of early child development. Modern mothers are usually not content to just let a child grow up until it is old enough to attend school. Rather, they believe that they should nurture the physical, social and intellectual development of the child so that each child can realize its innate potential. Sharon Hays (1996) identifies this particular belief as part of a system of ideas that she refers to as the 'ideology of intensive mothering'.

Intensive mothering is a self-sacrificing commitment made by a mother to focus most of her time and energy upon managing every aspect of the child's relationship with its environment. This is done in order that her children will emerge from childhood with superior physical, emotional, social, cultural and educational advantages. Specific features of intensive mothering, according to Hays, are that it is child-centred, emotionally absorbing, expert-guided, labour-intensive, and financially expensive.

In an intensive pattern of childrearing, the needs of the child are given priority over the needs of adults in general, and the mother in particular. Every effort is made to ensure that the child does not cry, or in any other way express pain or discomfort. This means that there is a practical prohibition on physical punishment for children, which is extended to any adult who comes into contact with a child. Harsh punishment of any kind for children tends to be avoided whenever possible. Instead, emphasis is placed upon frequent expressions of love and attention. The child is expected to respond to this by forming a close attachment to the mother.

Mothers who follow an intensive approach to childrearing often look to child experts for guidance, at least at first, rather than relying upon their own limited experience as new mothers. Child experts have strongly reinforced an intensive style of mothering in the past half-century. The main message of the child experts is that children can always be improved by better parenting. Special emphasis is placed on the role of the mother, since she is in a unique position to influence the development of the child at every stage, beginning with the child's experience in the womb. In order to be sure of influencing the development of the child in the right direction, it is thought that the mother should be in constant contact with the child and observe its development closely. The mother also believes that she must give the child whatever it needs, whenever the child demonstrates a need for it. Of course, the needs of children are always changing, and the needs of young children in particular change rapidly. Intensive mothering involves providing a steady flow of new goods and experiences with which to enrich the child's world. This style of childrearing is very expensive. In the United States, intensive childrearing ideas therefore exist alongside the idea that mothers should also be workers and providers.

The ideology of intensive mothering described above is an international ideology. It is found in any society where the dominant culture stresses collective progress based on individual effort and achievement. Prominent examples include the United States and Japan, two of the largest and economically most advanced countries in the world. Within these countries there are local variations and effects of the ideology of intensive mothering, influenced by particular cultural traditions. Some of the most influential traditions are those concerning the position of women in society.

In Japan, unlike the United States, the ideology of intensive mothering has not yet been modified on a large scale by popular demands for alternative lifestyles and the economic emancipation of women. Intensive mothering therefore continues to exert a profound influence over the domestic lives of many Japanese women, especially between the ages of 25 and 35. Expounded by child experts, and imposed by custom and social pressure, Japanese ideology of intensive mothering constrains mothers to devote themselves tirelessly to the well-being of young children from the foetal stage onwards. This ideology has been so successful in shaping expectations of Japanese mothers' behaviour, that it has had the unintended effect of making some young women reluctant to get married and have children (Jolivet, 1997). More Japanese women are delaying marriage in order to enjoy a longer period of personal freedom before accepting the rigours of intensive childcare.

Discussion

Childcare and caregiving are important activities performed by families, not only for family members but also for the larger society. However, their importance is often acknowledged only when it appears that there has been some failure by families to provide appropriate care. In Japan, for instance, concern has been expressed by opinion leaders that rejection of intensive mothering by some young women may lead to population decline and cultural change.

Policymakers everywhere tend to believe that desirable forms of childcare and caregiving can help to prevent social problems. For example, government agencies that are concerned with maintaining public order prefer that children should be brought up as law-abiding citizens. They therefore hope to have parental support in achieving this goal. Other public agencies that are involved in delivering social services and financial benefits to individuals in need also make assumptions about family responsibilities. They expect that families will make only limited demands upon costly government programmes, by looking after their own members with as little public assistance as possible.

In several countries, the combination of a low level of public support for families and rapid family change are creating fears about a *care deficit* (Hochschild, 1998). The demand for care is rising, mainly because people are living longer and there are increasing numbers of elderly people who need long-term care. However, in many cases the supply of public care services is not increasing fast enough to keep up with the demand. This places additional burdens upon family caregivers.

It is possible that the supply of informal care, too, may be shrinking. Divorced and separated fathers are often less involved in childcare than when they were still married and living with their children. As a result, many lone mothers struggle to meet heavy demands of childcare on their own. That burden can make it more difficult for them to participate in activities outside the home, including helping others. At the same time, increased employment of wives, especially in full-time employment, means that care deficits have also developed in some two-parent families. It is true that in some families husbands have substantially increased the time that they spend on caring for children, as well as doing more housework, in order to facilitate their wives' full-time employment. But there are also families in which husbands' domestic activities have not increased enough to compensate for the lesser amount of time that employed wives have for their 'second shift'.

Arlie Hochschild (1989) reports that many American mothers have cut back on the work they do at home by redefining the needs of the house, the marriage, and sometimes the child. Standards of housework may be lowered, and mothers may claim they are meeting the child's needs by providing 'quality time' rather than being available all of the time. This is a strategy for managing the relationship between demand and supply of care by reducing the 'demand'. It draws our attention to the fact that childcare and caregiving are socially constructed activities in every respect.

In the present chapter we have focused on the ways in which childcare and caregiving are organized activities within families. In the first place, caring is structured by family roles, social identities and self concepts. These structures are negotiated among the family members themselves, and they are therefore often fluid and take on various forms. Nevertheless, family structures through which childcare and caregiving are organized are not random. They are influenced by social ideologies upon which family members draw as they construct their joint lines of action. Also, family structures reflect underlying social divisions of resources, preferences and experiences, especially those of age and gender. Although the organization of childcare and caregiving within families has been altered in response to increased employment of mothers, women continue to be responsible for most childcare and caregiving, other than caregiving between spouses.

Women have long held the primary responsibility for looking after children, but their sense of responsibility may have been less onerous in the past. Present-day mothers, and many fathers, are extremely aware of the importance of early childhood years for a healthy and successful adult life. The parents who are most convinced of this are those who have received some education in the health sciences or the social sciences.

Parents today are encouraged to believe they have a special responsibility to ensure that every child grows up happy, strong, confident, articulate, literate and skilled in every possible respect. However, there is a potential problem here for contemporary families. It is a problem that produces internal conflicts over the allocation of time, and external conflicts with employers over inflexible work schedules.

Intensive parenting requires a lot of time from at least one parent. It also takes a lot of other resources, such as books, musical instruments, computers, private lessons, and eventually college or university courses. All of these things must be paid for by someone, often a family member. The immediate consequence of this for any modern family committed to the ideology of intensive parenting is that a family needs a lot of money at its disposal. That means the parents must work a lot of hours in paid employment. In the next chapter we will look at these economic issues of money and work in relation to family life.

7

Money and the Family Economy

Money is involved, directly or indirectly, in most of the things that families do. Making money (for example, employment), the circulation of money (for example, social exchange), and the uses of money (for example, money management) are therefore significant interests for many people. Chapter 7 takes a broad look at these issues and the diverse strategies that are adopted by different groups in different places. Social inequalities are identified, including those between women and men and between people in different types of families, such as lone mothers compared with dual-career couples, and some implications are discussed.

CONCEPTS

family economy   self-provisioning   pooling
money management   financial control   housekeeping
allowance   whole wage system   breadwinner
independent management   rational choice theory   co-
provider   service sector   moral identity   gendered
moral rationalities   strategy   homeworking
family-friendly policies   reciprocity   social exchange

Family life is sometimes idealized as consisting only of intimate personal relations and patterns of care that were described in the last two chapters. But all of these activities are underpinned by economic exchanges. A basic condition of existence is that family members must acquire material resources that are used for familial purposes. For example, many people consider owning a home to be a desirable basis for family life (Saunders, 1990). The main question for them is: can they afford it?

In this chapter we are going to look at the financial resources families need in order to acquire goods such as houses which must be purchased in a market economy. We will also investigate some of the ways in which family members use their financial resources within family life. The main sociological interest here is the way in which acquiring and using resources is organized by social relationships within a *family economy*.

Earned income is the most important economic resource for families in an urbanized and industrialized society, since most of the things that people need have to be bought. Of course, some people can do certain things for themselves such as maintaining and repairing vehicles or renovating their homes. People who have access to land can grow their own vegetables, and sometimes even build their own houses. In rural areas they may be able to supplement their supply of meat by hunting. In these cases, *self-provisioning* activities can be an important part of the family economy.

Self-provisioning is a valuable supplement to buying goods and services, since it increases the standard of living a family can obtain from the same income. It is therefore somewhat surprising to find that it is not the families with the lowest incomes who provide the most for themselves (Pahl, 1984; Nelson and Smith, 1999). Although the poorest families might seem to benefit the most from access to non-monetary resources, it tends to be the families with at least one worker in a stable and well-paid job who engage in the most self-provisioning. The reason for this is that productive work requires tools and raw materials, and they all cost money. Furthermore, some of the most cost-effective activities, such as home renovations, are really only worth doing by people who own their own homes. Therefore, it tends to be families who have a steady income and who own property who take the most advantage of opportunities for self-provisioning. Lack of money, on the other hand, limits practically everything that family members might want to do.

Financial Practices

Money is such a basic resource in daily living that husbands and wives with earned incomes are expected to support one another financially. The most common way of doing this is by *pooling* their incomes. The majority of couples in the United States expect to pool some or all of their earnings (Blumstein and Schwartz, 1983). In practice there are large differences in the ways in which couples handle their money. A study of financial practices among couples in Canada found a great deal of diversity, and it has also been shown that this diversity has implications for the amount of economic inequality within marriage (Cheal, 1993b; Woolley and Marshall, 1994).

How much of their money couples actually pool is an important question. It is a question that has implications for family interaction, as well as for how much economic and social equality exists between spouses. Feminist sociologists have often questioned the fairness of income sharing and property sharing between spouses. From this perspective, the tendency for many women to depend financially upon men within marriage is seen as the result of an historical structure of gender inequality (Mossman and Maclean, 1997). Husbands and wives often earn different amounts of money, with husbands typically earning more than wives. This imbalance in economic resources has the potential to create an imbalance of power within marriage (Pahl, 1991). The partner who earns the most money may expect to have the most say about how it is spent. When wives and husbands are not financial equals, gender divisions can therefore develop concerning control over money.

In cases of extreme economic inequality within marriage there is a division of labour over money and its different uses. One partner engages in the day-to-day management of money to meet the family's needs by shopping for food and household supplies. The other partner decides how much money is to be allocated for daily necessities, as well as making all the decisions about major purchases. This particular financial relationship shows a sharp division between *money management*, which is usually the wife's responsibility, and *financial control*, which is typically the prerogative of the husband. This economic system was quite common during the middle decades of the past century. Its main feature was a *housekeeping allowance* that a breadwinner husband gave to his wife to meet the daily needs of the household (Zelizer, 1997).

The allowance system is much less prevalent today than it was in the past. That is largely because there are more women now who use their own earnings to meet part or all of the family's needs. Employed wives are generally less dependent upon their husbands for financial support. Furthermore, couples with two reliable incomes tend to find other ways of managing money that make better use of their combined resources. Another cause of change is the cultural ideal of companionate marriage that has grown stronger in the past half century. The ideology of companionate marriage tends to favour egalitarian and democratic relationships between wives and husbands. In Britain today, only one in ten couples continue to practice the allowance system for allocating money in marriage (Laurie and Rose, 1994).

The most common system of allocating money in contemporary marriages is through income pooling, or shared management. This system has grown in popularity in recent decades, despite the tendency of many people to follow the system their parents used when they were growing up (Vogler and Pahl, 1993). Approximately half of British couples, and the majority of Canadian couples, practice this system today. Partners who pool their incomes put all or most of their earnings into a common fund, such as a joint bank account from which either partner may draw. In Winnipeg, Canada, four out of five couples have a joint account at a bank or similar financial institution (Cheal, 1993b).

It is important to note that the widespread preference for shared management of money does not necessarily mean that there is complete equality
between husband and wife (Pahl, 1989). Partners may pool all, or only a
portion, of their earnings. Furthermore, they may agree that one partner in
fact manages most of the money most of the time (Hertz, 1986). She, or he,
may be thought to be the one who has the greatest knowledge and interest in
financial affairs. Or, it could be that the less involved partner does not have
much time to spend on money management activities, due to heavy demands
of employment or housework.

In Britain, money management by wives seems to be more common than
money management by husbands. The *whole wage system* in which a husband
turns over all, or most, of his earnings to his wife seems to be followed by a
little over one third of British couples (Laurie and Rose, 1994). Many couples
see this as a relatively efficient system. Since the wife is responsible for most of
the day-to-day expenditures, she is able to keep track of how much money is
available. At the same time she has a realistic understanding of how much
money can be put aside for paying major bills, or for long-term savings such as
a down-payment toward buying a house. In working-class families, the whole
wage system can be particularly important for economic survival. Working-
class husbands in manual occupations may lack familiarity with record keeping
and be uninterested in dealing with financial institutions. Furthermore, careful
management is required if a modest income is to cover all of the family's needs.
Low family income therefore tends to be associated with female money management (Vogler and Pahl, 1993).

Husbands in middle-class families, who have more education and who are in
white-collar or managerial occupations, are more likely to want to manage a
significant portion of the family income and to control how it is used (Pahl,
1989). That is especially so if they earn considerably more than their wives and
is usually the situation when a wife is non-employed, or employed only part-
time. Here, a discourse of income pooling in the family may obscure the fact
that it is the husband who has the larger influence over how money is used in
the family. That is because he is defined as the family *breadwinner.*

Whether or not most married couples are actually equally involved in money
management and control, many of them want to believe in income pooling as a
feature of their relationship. Pooling a couple's resources is a way of expressing
unity in marriage. It involves deliberately ignoring economic differences which
exist between most wives and husbands (Singh and Lindsay, 1996). Pooling
first became popular around the time that the ideology of the companionship
family emerged. Today, pooling is most prevalent in middle-class families
where the ideology of companionate marriage has had the greatest appeal.
The meaning of pooled money within companionate marriage is that allocation
of money is based on trust, as well as a suppression of any calculation about
who gains the most or who benefits the least. Open recognition of difference
in marriage is generally avoided by companionate couples since it can be

threatening. However, there are some circumstances that make the suppression of separate interests difficult or impossible.

Recognizing different economic interests in marriage tends to occur in couples where both partners have substantial earnings or they possess significant financial assets acquired before marriage, and when they are both highly educated and equally confident of their financial skills (Hertz, 1986). Under these conditions, the need to rely upon someone else financially in order to get things done is not very strong. As a result, partners sometimes keep their earnings entirely separate and manage their financial resources independently. To date, this pattern of *independent management* seems to be rare in most countries. However, it may become more important in the future as women gain more education and earn higher wages. If it is to become more common, its advocates will have to overcome the powerful influence of the ideology of companionate marriage. In Britain today, independent money management is practised by only about two per cent of couples (Laurie and Rose, 1994).

Recognition of separate economic interests is common in couples who are cohabiting, especially if they have only recently begun living together. A study conducted in Melbourne, Australia, concluded that money has a different meaning in cohabiting couples than in legally married couples (Singh and Lindsay, 1996). Money in cohabiting couples is separate and calculable. Each person manages her or his money independently, and each expects to pay a fair share of the bills (ideally 'half and half'). If the relationship lasts, however, the pattern of money management is likely to change in the direction of income pooling. As the couples' commitment becomes deeper and more explicit, financial calculations of their costs and benefits become more vague. Discussions of precise rights and obligations are likely to be blocked by assertions of common interest. Partners' individual incomes are subjectively redefined as part of a 'family income'.

Family Income

A critical factor in most family economies is how many people earn an income from paid employment, and how much money they are able to earn. That is an especially important consideration for families with children, since raising even one child is a costly undertaking today. When children get older, they may be able to earn modest sums of money which help to cover their personal expenses including some food and clothing. Their income can therefore alleviate part of the financial burden on parents. Children's earnings are particularly important in adolescence when their financial demands grow (Aronson et al., 1996). Some older children may also give money to their parents, but they are only a small minority in America today. Very few children contribute to meeting the family's basic shelter costs, especially when they are young.

Among families with children, single-parent families with only one adult worker are at a relative disadvantage in income earning compared with many two-parent families (Cheal, 1996a). Families headed by lone mothers tend to have below average incomes in most countries, although there are a few notable exceptions such as the Netherlands (Whitting, 1992). In countries such as the United States and Canada where public supports for families are generally limited, the incomes of female-headed families tend to be much below average (Sidel, 1996; Hunsley, 1997). Not surprisingly, single-parent families tend to have greater difficulty than other families in making ends meet.

The largest item in most families' budgets is the cost of housing, and this represents a major hurdle for many lone mothers. In the United States, single-parent families are more likely than two-parent families to be living in less desirable forms of housing, such as older housing and in multiple-units and apartments rather than detached houses (Cheal, 1996a). Also, separated and divorced mothers are much less likely than married couples with children to own their own homes. After a relationship breakdown, many separated and divorced women do not have enough income to maintain ownership of their homes, unless mortgage repayments are low or they receive substantial financial support from their ex-husbands (Morris and Winn, 1990). In Britain and the United States, families headed by lone mothers are more likely than other families to rent public housing and to be marginalized at the bottom of the housing market (Crow and Hardey, 1991; Mulroy, 1995).

Dual-career couples are most likely to be found at the upper end of the housing market. Their combined incomes give them with a wide range of choices about how to live and where to raise their children. Indeed, having more money to spend on children is one reason why many couples prefer that both partners should earn an income throughout marriage. In this respect, large financial resources that are necessary for intensive parenting have helped to change the contemporary family economy. Parents who are committed to intensive parenting tend to create work-intensive families in which both parents are employed for many hours.

Mothers and fathers are naturally affected by all the demands upon their time and energy in work-intensive families. However, combining employment and family life has a notably larger impact upon the lives of mothers, as they are usually more involved in intensive childrearing. The combination of intensive parenting and income earning creates a 'double burden' for many mothers today, especially those who are employed full-time.

In the recent past, men tended to be the main family breadwinners. That was partly because they were less involved in meeting the everyday needs of children. Also, it was partly because they had gained more education on average and so could earn higher wages. In most families it was thought to be a rational economic strategy to stress male employment as the way to maximize family income. (See **Box 7.1**). However, in recent decades great changes have occurred in amount of female education and in average wage levels gained by women. Economic calculations about the value of women's work are therefore changing.

Another factor affecting economic calculations in contemporary families is higher rates of marital separation and childbearing outside marriage. Many women are now sole providers for their families. Lone mothers are typically more dependent than married mothers upon public income transfers, such as social security or welfare payments (Dooley, 1993). Nevertheless, employment is an important part of the survival strategies of lone mothers, especially among those who have older children (Hardey and Glover, 1991; Lero and Brockman, 1993).

In contemporary Canada, most women of working age are regular participants in the labour force and full-time employment has become normative for Canadian women. In recent years, the largest increases in employment have been among married women. There has been a very rapid growth in the employment of women with children, and mothers are increasingly likely to be working full-time (Ghalam, 1993; Logan and Belliveau, 1995). With the exception of women with children under six months old, children are no longer the deterrent to female labour force participation that they once were. Detailed research into children's effects on labour-force participation of women at different ages shows that the traditional relationship between childbearing and reduced employment for women has changed dramatically (Townson, 1987). It used to be the case that many women left the labour force when they had their first child, and then returned to paid employment only when their youngest child was old enough to be left at home alone. That pattern is much less common in Canada today. Nevertheless, it remains the case that even now women do not participate in the labour force on exactly the same basis as men.

Among women in the labour force, parenting is associated with interrupted employment spells as well as reduced hours of paid work, and women are more likely to be working part-time than men (Marshall, 1994; Cook and Beaujot, 1996). Women who are living in a family with children are less likely to be working full-time than men who are living in a family with children. Also, the younger the children are the more likely it is that men will be working full-time, and the less likely it is that women will be working full-time (Beaujot, Gee, Rajulton and Ravanera, 1995). Obviously gender continues to be a significant factor in the organization of the family economy. However, its relevance is changing and the boundaries between gender roles are increasingly blurred (Potuchek, 1997).

Employment and Gender

As women's working lives have changed, so too have the lives of men. Men's lives have not changed as dramatically as those of women in the majority of

Box 7.1   Gender and the division of labour: Rational choice?

One of the most influential branches of social theory in recent years has been that of *Rational Choice Theory* (Coleman, 1990). Rational Choice Theory is an interdisciplinary approach which is based on the principles of neo-classical economics. It assumes that almost all human behaviour can be explained as a result of individuals making rational choices as they seek to maximize their benefits and minimize their costs. That line of argument has been extended to the gender division of labour in family life, notably by the American economist Gary Becker (1985; 1991[1981]).

Becker argued that a division of labour will always emerge in families as a result of rational decision-making by family members, whenever there are differences of skill between them in market work versus domestic work. It will be rational for the person with the greater skills in market work to devote more time to it, since that person's wage level will be higher and therefore the income earned for the family will be larger. Husbands who have only limited responsibilities for children can 'invest' their time in acquiring market skills. However, wives usually spend more time on childcare, Becker observes, and therefore they have less time available to develop market skills. It follows that men will specialize more in market work, and women will generally specialize more in domestic work.

Becker's approach to decision-making in families has been widely emulated, and it has also been heavily criticized (Owen, 1987; Menaghan and Parcel, 1990; Cheal, 1991). Some of the critical comments question the concepts of rationality that are employed in studies of this kind, and other comments question how much free choice men and (especially) women actually have in their family lives. As an example of the former, consider the negative impact of divorce upon many wives. Is it really rational for women to specialize in domestic work within marriage, if marriage may end and leave them unqualified to earn a decent income on their own? The second line of critical comment points to the way in which many families create gendered experiences for their members, and thus shape the 'preferences' that men and women develop for different activities.

Finally, economic concepts of rationality assume that the ultimate goal in life is to maximize the quantity of goods and services acquired for the lowest possible cost and effort. But is there also a 'rationality of caring', as Kari Waerness (1984) has suggested?

cases, but change has nonetheless occurred. One reason why we hear little about men and family change is because there is no simple, compelling story to tell about them. It is hard to identify any linear trend that could describe how men as a group have responded to new issues in family and work. Instead, what we find is that men's lives have become more diverse, and different groups of men are moving in different directions. It has therefore become more and more difficult to summarize male behaviour in terms of sociological general-izations about gender and work.

Kathleen Gerson (1997) concluded from her research in the United States that men's connections to work and family have become looser in recent decades. It is hard to predict men's lifestyles on the basis of their gender alone. In practice, Gerson suggests, American men seem to have evolved three different patterns for balancing their involvements in work and family.

Some men continue to follow the pattern of male breadwinning. These men tend to marry women who think that having children is important, and who want to spend a lot of time at home with their children. Whether or not they intended to do so when they got married, many of these couples gravitate toward a gender division of labour when they have their first child, producing a breadwinner/homemaker family.

Male breadwinners think of fatherhood primarily in economic terms. They see their main responsibility as providing an income on which the family can live, and this means they need to earn high wages. In addition, it means they must have secure jobs with stable incomes, which can provide a steady flow of money to meet the constant demands of feeding and clothing an entire family. Male breadwinners therefore tend to be in regular employment, and to be relatively successful economically. Because these economic advantages are both highly correlated with education in today's economy, contemporary breadwin-ners who have homemaker wives also tend to be better educated on average (Cheal, 1996a).

In contrast, other men in North America today have clearly detached them-selves from the role of breadwinner because their main goal is personal and economic independence. In order to keep to a minimum any commitments that might limit their freedom of action, they may prefer to remain unmarried and to have few or no children. If they do get married and have children then they are likely to accept, or to expect, that their wife will be an equal *co-provider* in income earning. They are unlikely to share equally in the domestic tasks of childrearing, however, with the result that their partners have the double burden of childcare and wage earning.

Sharing the financial burden of raising a family relieves these men of what might otherwise be a crushing responsibility (Mandell, 1989). Being a co-provider cushions them against the consequences of taking financial risks, including that of being between jobs. These men have frequent job changes, whether by choice or because they are employed in short-term positions or because they are self-employed. To some extent, the increased prevalence of men who avoid traditional breadwinning is an effect of the economic restruc-turing that occurred in the 1980s and 1990s. Organizational and occupational changes left many young men with diminished job prospects and less income security, especially if they had below average education. As a result, being the sole financial supporter for a family has often seemed to be an unattractive, or simply unavailable, option.

Between the two extremes of family breadwinners and men who seek autonomy from family life lies a group of men whom Gerson refers to as 'involved fathers'. These men are committed to raising their children and they are usually committed to doing so with a partner. Unlike male breadwinners, however, involved fathers do not define their parental role mainly in economic terms. Rather, they see themselves as sharing the overall responsibility for raising a family. Sometimes that responsibility may involve more employment and less childcare, and at other times it may involve more childcare and less employment. Where exactly the balance is struck between employment and childcare by involved fathers depends upon a negotiated agreement between spouses. Negotiation over the division of labour in such families takes into account individual preferences as well as economic opportunities, or lack of opportunities.

Male unemployment is a major factor which has the potential to shift a family's division of labour and allocation of income earning away from male breadwinning. That seems most likely to occur in economically depressed regions, where unemployment spells typically involve being out of work for a long time (Wheelock, 1990). Some men clearly resist changing their role in the family, even under desperate financial circumstances. Other men, however, take on new responsibilities at home so that their wives can take advantage of employment opportunities in the *service sector* of the economy.

A long-term consequence of economic change has been a decline in typically male jobs, such as miner or manual labourer, and an increase in typically female jobs in the service sector. The latter include jobs such as secretary or day-care worker. As industries such as financial services and personal care services have expanded, employment opportunities have improved for many women. In some countries that shift in opportunities is reflected in changing opinions about women and work, especially concerning mothers and work.

In the past, being a good economic provider was not considered to be part of the *moral identity* of a good mother. That is to say, the set of moral rules that defined appropriate behaviour for a 'good mother' did not include having paid employment. Most mothers were thought to be unavailable for employment, due to heavy family responsibilities. That situation still exists in Japan, where mothers are expected to give up their careers for at least five years in order to devote themselves entirely to the care and supervision of a young child (Jolivet, 1997). In most other countries, however, public expectations have shifted considerably as average family size has fallen, and as the economy has changed to make a wider range of jobs available to women.

Raising children is no longer automatically accepted as a reason why a woman should not be employed. On the contrary, the widespread availability of effective contraceptive techniques has led to a hardening of attitudes in some places. It is now thought that fertility is, or should be, a voluntary choice. Since that is the case, it is believed that a socially responsible woman should only have children if she can afford to support them. Public opinion in countries such as Canada has therefore shifted toward expecting mothers to take on greater responsibility for meeting the costs of raising their children.

Margrit Eichler (1997) argues that as gender ideologies and family structures have changed, public policy has changed from a 'patriarchal model' based on assumptions about a male breadwinner to an 'individual responsibility' model. The patriarchal model assumed a two-parent family, in which one parent (the male) earned the family income and the other parent (the female) provided care for her husband and children. In contrast, the recent trend toward an individual responsibility model assumes that both male and female parents have the same responsibilities. Fathers and mothers are considered to be equally responsible for meeting the economic and personal needs of themselves and their children.

In countries such as Canada, which do not have a strong tradition of collective responsibility for children, the result of this shift is an increased burden of individual responsibility. Since both parents are assumed to be capable of fulfilling care and provider functions today, it follows that either parent must be capable of doing both. From this, the conclusion is drawn that one parent should be able to do both. This is not only the dominant way of thinking among public policymakers, but it is also how the majority of mothers think about their own lives today. Many mothers, too, believe that they should make a significant financial contribution to the family economy, now that they have the opportunity to do so. In short, motherhood no longer shields women from public *or* private pressures to find paid employment. One consequence of this is that employable lone mothers who are not in fact employed, but who rely on welfare, are often treated as undeserving of financial support by taxpayers (Lord, 1994; Brodie, 1996; Evans, 1996).

Lone Mothers

Public policies concerning employment and lone motherhood have the potential to generate controversy and conflict, because not all mothers have accepted a sweeping redefinition of their economic role. Some lone mothers continue to define their role mainly as providers of care for children in the home, often with the support of relatives and neighbours. In Britain, Simon Duncan and Rosalind Edwards (1999) concluded from their research that lone mothers think about paid work in terms of a system of moral identities. The authors refer to these moral identities as *gendered moral rationalities*. Duncan and Edwards argue that there are three sets of moral rules which lone mothers use to construct moral identities for themselves. Lone mothers may define themselves primarily in terms of a moral obligation to provide full-time care for their children in the home; or they can define themselves primarily in terms of personal achievements in paid employment that enable them to be self-sufficient. Finally, they may see themselves as fulfilling their responsibilities to their children through a combination of both childcare and income earning.

Duncan and Edwards suggest that whether or not lone mothers seek paid employment is often a moral choice, rather than an economic calculation. The particular choice that lone mothers make is based on reasoned arguments about the relative importance of claims for the cultural value of 'good mothering' compared with the cultural value of individual autonomy. Lone mothers who stress good mothering and who believe that they should care for their children at home are likely to resist taking up paid employment, unless forced to do so by policies that cut their income supports. Those policies were in fact adopted in a number of countries at the end of the twentieth century, as one way of lowering government expenditures. That policy direction has intensified concerns among some social activists about how contemporary mothers balance responsibilities to children with responsibilities to employers.

Balancing Employment and Family Life

Balancing responsibilities to employers and children may be somewhat easier for two parents who live together than it is for a lone parent, but in reality it is a challenge for practically every parent. Everywhere we can see that employed parents struggle to work out solutions to their childcare problems. The primary responsibility for making appropriate childcare arrangements usually falls on mothers (Brannen and Moss, 1987, 1992).

A variety of solutions can be devised to problems of balancing employment and family life. Long-term solutions tend to be worked out in a *strategy* that is adopted by one or more family members. There are six main strategies which parents with children seem to adopt:

1. employment at home;
2. working non-standard hours;
3. altering work practices and conditions of employment;
4. reducing the amount of paid employment;
5. reallocation of labour within the household and between kin; and,
6. use of commercial or state childcare services.

Sometimes people try all six of these approaches. More often than not, they select one or two strategies that are particularly successful in their local communities or that are strongly supported by local customs and institutions. The six types of family/work strategy will be described next, and some suggestions will be made about conditions that favour one over another.

Working at Home

In theory, the simplest choice for parents who need employment would be to find paid work that they can do at home. When the centre of family life is also the primary work site, then work time can be adjusted to take account of children's activities. Also, older children can sometimes be included in work tasks so that they do not feel separated from their parents. Working at home means that employment and family life can be integrated in ways that are otherwise impossible (Beach, 1989). However, *homeworking* is not very common in practice as a way of balancing family responsibilities with earning a wage.

The main reason why homeworking is uncommon in an industrial society is that it is not easy to find suitable, well-paid jobs which can be done within the physical limitations of the home. As a result of industrialization, most work became divided between domestic labour in the home and employment in factories and offices. In factories and offices, large numbers of people can work together in order to gain the benefits of higher productivity. As they do so, they use machinery and quantities of raw materials that require large amounts of space and protected working environments. Homeworking has therefore declined, especially in the early industrial societies of Europe and the United States where industrialization took the classical form of mass production in large factories.

Industrialization has not followed the path of mass production everywhere. This economic variation produces interesting social differences in the world today. Sometimes industrialization is based on small, family-owned factories and workshops, in which family members provide much of the labour. In order to compete with large corporations, these small businesses must find other ways of cutting costs than buying large, expensive machinery. They therefore tend to contract out some of the work to people in neighbouring households who work at home, usually for low wages. Taiwan is one country in which this model of industrialization has been very successful. As a result, large numbers of Taiwanese women have been employed in businesses where living rooms are also factories (Hsiung, 1996).

There is also growing interest in homeworking today in the post-industrial societies of contemporary Western Europe and North America (Phizacklea and Wolkowitz, 1995). Improved telecommunications and computer technologies are making it possible for more people to work at home in occupations such as telemarketing, telephone support services, and data entry. Nevertheless, most homeworkers continue to be employed in traditional low-technology (and low wage) occupations, such as finishing and packing, machine knitting and as providers of in-home daycare. These kinds of jobs do not usually have the fringe benefits associated with standard employment in a factory or office, such as medical benefits or a company pension. They are therefore unattractive to most parents whose educational qualifications give them access to better opportunities outside the home. If such parents want to have an adult present in the home on a full-time basis, they usually look for a more financially rewarding strategy.

Working Non-standard Hours

Two-parent families in which both parents work outside the home can sometimes maintain something close to a full-time adult presence within the home by arranging for one parent to work non-standard hours. While one parent works a standard daytime shift from Monday to Friday, the other parent is employed on a night shift or at the weekends. Alternating their hours of employment in this way means that as one parent is leaving for work, the other parent is returning home in order to be available for the children. In Canada, more than a third of employed parents work non-standard shifts (Lero et al., 1992). Much of this non-standard employment is involuntary, being done in order to meet the demands of employers. However, research in the United States suggests that non-standard shift-work is sometimes chosen deliberately as part of a family strategy. Women who are attracted to the traditional ideal of a stay-at-home mother in a nuclear family, but who need to work outside the home for economic reasons, may adopt this employment strategy as a way of being at home during the day (Garey, 1995). We see here, once again, the importance of the home as a socially constructed basis for family life. Mothers who work night shifts in order to be at home during the day define the home as a safe place for their children. They believe that a child's home should be permanently open and available for the child to turn to, at any time of the day or night, whenever the child becomes sick or has some other emergency.

Permanent availability of at least one adult at home is a demanding requirement in families containing just two adults. When the only way it can be done is by having one parent work non-standard hours, then the almost inevitable result is stress in some other area of family life. Parents who work night shifts in order to spend more time with their children during the day tend to get less sleep than other parents. They also tend to spend less time sleeping with their partners. Clearly, this is not a strategy that every parent will to want to follow.

Altering Work Practices

Two-parent families, in which both parents are employed full-time, grew rapidly in numbers in western societies during the last four decades of the twentieth century. As they did so, the difficulties these families encountered led to growing demands upon employers to alter their work practices. Perennial problems for employees who are also parents include: what to do when children are sick and are sent home from school; who will look after the children when there is a rush job and employees have to work overtime; and, who cares for children in the school holidays, especially when the babysitter or childminder takes a vacation? (VandenHeuvel, 1993).

As a result of these problems, many parents and social policymakers have exerted pressure upon employers to adopt *family-friendly policies* (Raabe, 1996). Family-friendly policies include flexible hours of employment, extended maternity leave or parental leave with a guarantee of re-employment, and discretionary use of 'sick days' that enable parents to attend medical appointments for their children or other family members with frequent health problems. Such policies are very useful. However, they only help parents to cope with short-term difficulties in balancing employment and family responsibilities. In the long term, most employers still expect a substantial work commitment from their employees in return for security of employment. Workers who are unable to make that level of commitment, because of a higher priority that they attach to family needs, are likely to end up taking a slower and less lucrative career path. They will almost certainly have reduced opportunities for promotion. It may also be suggested, or expected, that they should they give up their job and find another job with lower expectations.

Employment Reduction

In the absence of major changes to work practices by employers, the task of assimilating a new child into a family's work system typically falls upon the family itself. This means that employment must either be relinquished or reduced by at least one family member. Alternatively, the family's tasks must be reallocated in order to reduce the time stress experienced by an employed parent. The particular route which is taken will depend, among other things, upon the extent of gender role segregation.

Japan is one society in which the predominant adjustment to demands of family and work continues to be based on the gender segregation of roles. This inevitably leads to lesser employment by married women. Japanese women are expected to relinquish employment when they have children, and many of them in fact give up full-time employment as soon as they get married (Jolivet, 1997). The heavy demands that employers place upon male employees, combined with a strong cultural emphasis upon gender difference, produces a situation in which Japanese wives are mainly engaged in domestic responsibilities. Japanese mothers of young children are less likely to be in paid work than mothers in other industrialized countries. If they are in paid employment, then they are more likely to have doubts about combining it with responsibilities to children and home (Stockman, Bonney and Xuewen, 1995). Those doubts are no doubt partly due to the fact that husbands in Japan are among the least likely to help their wives with childcare and running the home (Tsuya and Bumpass, 1998). Most Japanese wives seem to accept this situation as inevitable, and to accept that their primary role is as mother and housekeeper. However, attitudes are changing to some extent in the younger generation. The fascinating sociological question is, how much longer can Japanese families continue to follow a traditional path which has diverged from that taken in most other countries?

In western societies today, an employment reduction strategy is less likely to involve complete cessation of work by married women. Rather, it takes the principal form of mothers working part-time (Duffy and Pupo, 1992). Part-time employment is especially popular among women with pre-school-age children, and among married women who have a relatively traditional attitude toward the gender division of labour (Tam, 1997). Women with less traditional attitudes tend to prefer a different strategy.

Reallocation of Domestic Labour

In many economically developed countries, a variety of jobs are now open to women. Practically all women, except those with newborn babies, are therefore encouraged to take advantage of employment opportunities. In order for a new mother to return to full-time employment without exhausting herself, part or all of the extra workload created by the child must be shifted away from her and onto someone else (Daune-Richard, 1988). Reallocation of domestic labour within the family can be one way of ensuring that an employed mother's burden of childcare and housework is not overwhelming.

In nuclear families, the possibilities for reallocation of labour are typically rather limited. Career-oriented wives must call upon their husbands to do more housework and to take equal responsibility for raising children. Many husbands have been slow to respond to their wives' demands, partly because they face career pressures of their own. The typical outcome in the United States is a patchwork of compromises between mothers and fathers, which rarely satisfies everyone (Stacey, 1990).

In societies where extended families are more prevalent than they are in the United States or Europe, the options for familial reallocation of labour are correspondingly larger. In urban India, for example, where joint families continue to be enjoyed by large numbers of people in the middle classes, an employed mother may renegotiate the division of labour not only with her husband but also with her mother-in-law (Sekaran, 1992). In practice, the possibility of persuading Indian husbands to do much more domestic labour seems to be rather limited in most cases. Therefore, a mother's mother-in-law, or other female relatives with children, are the ones who are most likely to take on the responsibilities of looking after her children and other domestic tasks while she is at work.

In Singapore, too, most employed mothers rely heavily on their relatives for support (Yuen and Lim, 1992). Here, grandparents play an especially import- ant role. However, other non-employed female relatives who are living nearby may also be called upon for help. The difficult question faced by families in countries like Singapore is, as more women enter the paid labour force there are fewer non-employed relatives who have the time to participate in others' domestic responsibilities.

Paid Childcare Services

Help from relatives is often the preferred means of handling competing demands of domestic labour and wage labour. However, families who are unable to turn to relatives may have to turn to the paid services of childcare providers instead. In Singapore this includes childcare centres and home day- care providers similar to those found in many other countries. In addition, some Singapore families use foster parents who provide day-and-night care outside the home, except on weekends. Or, they may employ domestic ser- vants who provide childcare and other services inside the home (Yuen and Lim, 1992). Nevertheless, social changes are underway in Singapore that are leading to a decline in distinctively Chinese traditions of foster-parenting.

Growing numbers of educated women in Singapore are influenced by national and international ideals of intensive mothering. This includes a strong emphasis upon the importance of family preparation and support for children's education. Mothers are often heavily involved in supervising their children's homework. As a result, middle-class mothers in Singapore are making less use of foster mothers for their children. Furthermore, suitable foster mothers are becoming more difficult to find as more women are now employed outside the home. Domestic servants remain popular among those who can afford to employ them. But here, too, increased job opportunities for women and restrictive immigration policies are exerting increasing pressure upon families to find alternative solutions. Similar, though less intense, pressures exist in urban India where good domestic help is getting harder to find in some places (Sekaran, 1992). One emerging solution may be for employed mothers to use daycare centres to look after their children.

In the Scandinavian countries, publicly organized daycare, provided in centres that are financially supported and managed by government agencies, has emerged as the preferred means of practical support for employed parents (Leira, 1992). In Sweden, for example, the shift toward the collectivization of childcare that occurred from the 1960s onwards was part of a 'new family paradigm' based on gender equality (Sandqvist, 1992). According to this paradigm, income earning is held to be a normal and expected part of mother- hood as well as fatherhood. An important factor here is that the well-being of individuals in their family lives is thought to be a public responsibility as well as a private responsibility. Recognition that families need collective support to carry out their tasks has gone beyond mere rhetoric in the Scandinavian welfare states. It includes large-scale policy interventions and public funding of social programmes. In countries where public financial support is less available, families must look to different sources of support. One important source of support that is found in many places is exchanging goods and services with members of a support network.

Social Exchange

The ability to call upon help from others often depends on whether or not the individual has given help to them on an earlier occasion. People are more willing to help someone if they have received help from that person in the past. In countries where a strong cultural norm of *reciprocity* exists, it is almost always expected that individuals who receive support will make an appropriate return at some point in the future. In the Philippines, for example, a general-ized norm of reciprocity is acknowledged to be very strong. It reinforces the customary expectation that adult children should support elderly parents, because adult children are reminded of how much they owe to their parents for the care they received when they were young (Domingo, 1994). A perva-sive concept in Filipino society is 'utang na loob', or debt of gratitude. Children are said to incur an 'utang na loob' to their parents. This requires them to support their parents in a variety of ways in later life.

Give and take is a fundamental aspect of family life, although the importance of reciprocity is sometimes overlooked in modern societies (Jones, 1992). In order to receive, it is also necessary to give. Membership in social networks too involves obligations to provide suitable returns for favours received. This is especially the case in poor communities, where hardly anyone has surplus resources (Edin and Lein, 1997). In these communities, mothers who need help generally have to provide something in exchange for what they receive. Mothers who are unable to pay back the money they 'borrow' must provide whatever practical assistance they can. For example, a woman who pays her sister's utility bill might expect some free babysitting or house cleaning in exchange for her financial contribution.

Mothers who depend upon relatives and friends for support must also invest their time and energy in other ways, in order to keep supportive relationships going. They must demonstrate the value they attach to these relationships, through symbolic interactions that demonstrate appropriate feelings of grati-tude and appreciation. This may include having to express polite agreement with a donor, despite real differences of opinion, in order to maintain the relationship. The recipients of aid may therefore come to fear that they risk losing their independence. Because of this, an over-reliance on help from one family member can breed resentment. Many low-income mothers therefore try to develop as wide a social network of family and friends as they can, so that they do not become too dependent upon any one person. They are also likely to be cautious about the kinds of aid that they accept.

With the exception of support from older to younger generations, financial support is usually the least common type of support between extended family members or other members of support networks. It is generally preferred that help should take the form of exchanges 'in kind' (that is, exchanges of practical assistance) rather than gifts of money. Even people who need money the most, namely those who have low incomes, will often accept money only as a last resort (Kempson, Bryson and Rowlingson, 1994).

Research conducted in low income, inner-city areas in England found that people's attitudes about giving and receiving form a hierarchy of acceptability (Kempson, Bryson and Rowlingson, 1994). The most acceptable type of help is in-kind assistance, such as help with decorating or passing on an old stove that is no longer needed. Passing on children's clothes when they are outgrown is a particularly common practice. Money is less often asked for, or accepted, especially if the person who is giving the money is much better off. A financial contribution from a rich relation can feel too much like charity for poor people. It tends to be a source of embarrassment, and it can lead to loss of face. As a result, research in Britain has shown that unemployed men are more likely to accept help in-kind from men who are employed than they are to accept financial aid from such a source (Morris, 1995).

Gifts of any sort are not a preferred solution to financial problems, except sometimes between parents and children. Financial support that can never be repaid reveals an inequality between family members that can make the receiver feel inferior (Graham, 1992). The most acceptable transactions, therefore, have the appearance of equality because they involve *social exchange*.

In an exchange relationship people swap things backwards and forwards over long periods of time. Many exchange transactions, such as the provision of food, occur in the context of visiting and other sociable activities. Considerable support can be given in this way. Unequal transactions are seamlessly worked into the everyday fabric of social life, without drawing attention to who has given the most or who has received the most. Nevertheless, everyone is expected to give something in return for what they have received. In an exchange relationship, receiving is not only acceptable but giving is also compulsory. Using a relative to provide childcare, for example, significantly increases the probability of returning other services or giving a gift or loan to relatives (Folk, 1994).

Discussion

In this chapter we have followed a 'transactions approach' to family life. That approach stresses how individuals in families acquire, manage and consume resources by interacting with each other and with various groups in the family's environment (Cheal, 1998). We have seen that a family can be studied as an economic unit which formulates strategies about how to use the opportunities provided by structures in the social environment, such as social networks and business organizations. Internally, a family can be analyzed as a group of individuals who engage in a variety of transactions with one another. Those transactions are often characterized by long-term reciprocity.

Transactions that occur within a family are connected to other transactions that go on at the same time between family members and other groups in the environment. For instance, the redistribution of money between family members by means of income pooling is frequently used to compensate for the effects of unequal incomes earned by different individuals in the labour market.

A familiar example of this occurs when adult children with low incomes depend upon their parents for free, or low-cost, accommodation in the parental home. Housing is an indirect financial benefit that is transferred from parents to children. This type of transaction is in one sense a 'free choice' made by the parents about how to use their money. At another level, the choices made by parents are responses to pressures from the family's environment (Hartley, 1989). Relevant pressures upon parents include: demands of employers for higher educational qualifications, and therefore the necessity for prolonged education of children well into adulthood; employment difficulties for new entrants into the labour market; falling wage levels in recent years for some young workers; and reluctance by some governments to pay social security benefits to young people.

As the above examples illustrate, families can be affected by a variety of groups such as business organizations, schools and government departments. In the next chapter we shall consider some more general questions about how families are connected to the groups around them. An important conclusion to be drawn from the present discussion is that families are often pressed into adapting to the requirements of more powerful institutions. Most business organizations make only relatively minor adjustments to their work practices in order to accommodate working parents. They are afraid that if they were to do more they would incur additional costs, which might make them uncompetitive in a competitive market economy. Families are therefore left to cope on their own, for the most part. Family members have to negotiate between themselves an acceptable balance between family obligations and work commitments that will also satisfy the needs of employers. From time to time the needs of families do find support in civic organizations, such as churches, and in the political processes of democratic welfare states. However, those institutions have their own agendas and they leave their own footprints on family life.

8

Family Environments

The many influences of different social environments upon families have been described throughout this book. Chapter 8 draws explicit attention to this feature of family life by discussing four ways in which families are connected to other social groups. Market economies provide opportunities, but they also produce inequalities that may create social problems. Discourses about social problems may shape public responses to families, and are important in the formation of social policies. Welfare states develop and apply social policies that have multiple effects on families. Finally, social networks can provide people with resources that help their families to cope with the challenges of daily living.

CONCEPTS

market economy   spurious correlation   human capital   commodification   public sphere   the state   discourse   reflexivity   social inclusion   social exclusion   welfare state   liberal welfare state   universal programmes   targeted programmes   means testing   corporatist welfare state   social-democratic welfare state   social network   social capital   remittances   decommodification

In the preceding chapters of this book, we have seen that there are many ways in which families are affected by their social environments. For one, family life is affected by individuals' reactions to new opportunity structures that are created by changes such as urbanization and industrialization. Many of these changes have had the long-term effect of loosening traditional family ties and traditional family obligations. Greater opportunities for a more rewarding existence in a business organization, or in a new relationship, can draw people away from their homes and the people who live there. From time to time, this long-term trend of more choices and looser family ties is punctuated by revitalization movements that re-emphasize family values under changed social conditions. One historically important example of this was the influential movement to re-establish permanent marital ties on the basis of companionship, which reached its peak in certain western societies in the middle of the twentieth century.

Today, the idea that transitions into family roles are based mainly on customary social obligations is being challenged in many places by individual demands for freedom of choice. Those demands are supported by a surging global economy that includes commercialized international adoption of children, and new opportunities to be upwardly mobile through marriage. The latter phenomenon includes 'mail-order brides' from low-income countries in Asia and Eastern Europe. Tensions between personal morality and economic interests are often most visible in places where average incomes are low, and there is rapid social and economic change. But such tensions are not found only in those places. They exist everywhere that we find a modern market economy.

Markets

A *market economy* is a network of interconnected individuals and organizations who buy and sell goods that are referred to as commodities. The principal use of money here is as a medium of buying and selling. Money is mainly a medium of commercial exchange between individuals and between businesses. As such, it is associated with business-like motives, including motives of profit-seeking and rational calculation of how to get the most for one's money. Those motives are very different from the generosity which is expected to exist between close family members (Zelizer, 1997). Giving money as a present is therefore often felt to be an unsatisfactory way of expressing social ties that are based on feelings of sympathy and caring, and which are contrasted with the impersonality of market exchange (Cheal, 1988).

Markets of various kinds are the central institutions in societies based upon private ownership of property, which we refer to as capitalist societies. Critical analysis of capitalism and its implications for political and social relations, such as family relations, is known as political economy. (See **Box 8.1**). Studies in the political economy of capitalism tend to stress the prevalence of inequality and conflict.

The goal of a buyer in a market economy is to purchase goods and services for the lowest possible price. On the other hand the goal of someone who has goods to sell, or who is offering to sell their work for a wage, is to get the highest possible financial return. Clearly, there is an opposition of interest here. The lowest possible price for a buyer must mean that a seller does not get the

Box 8.1 Political economy

Studies in the political economy of family life stress the crucial importance for survival of productive labour, or in other words work (Seccombe, 1974). They therefore examine the various forms of work
performed by family members, whether they are paid or not, and how
much they are paid. This involves understanding how labour markets
work, and the different ways in which different social groups are connected to labour markets (Morris, 1995; Luxton, 1998).

A fundamental feature of modern societies is the division between
paid work that is rewarded in the market economy, and unpaid work
which is performed as a 'labour of love' in the home. This division within
modern societies has different, and unequal, implications for women
and men. Implications of that division for women receive special attention in feminist political economy (Maroney and Luxton, 1987). Insofar as
women on average spend more time on childcare in the home than men,
they do not compete on an equal footing with men in the labour market.
Their financial rewards therefore tend to be lower.

Studies in political economy also examine the impact that changes in
commodity and labour markets have upon changing family relationships. For example, a greater need for labour in the service sectors of
postindustrial societies created an increased demand for female employees. In turn, this resulted in more employed wives and mothers who must
balance responsibilities to both their families and their employers. It may
also be argued from this perspective that increased economic independence of employed wives is a factor that facilitates easier divorce.

Political economy has been criticized for its theoretical assumptions, in
particular for economic determinism. It is believed to neglect the independent influence of ideas and their importance for crosscultural comparisons.

highest possible return. Inevitably, in the competition between buyers and
sellers some people will be winners and other people will be losers.

A very visible effect of a market economy is economic inequality between
winners and losers. Economic inequalities are mainly due to unequal earnings
between people who work for shorter or longer periods, and between people
who receive unequal pay for the work that they do. For example, employment
and earnings of less skilled and less educated workers in the United States fell
during the 1980s and 1990s, by comparison with more skilled and better
educated workers (Bianchi, 1993). This trend created a growing income gap
as more working-class men (young men in particular) were unable to earn
wages sufficient to keep their families above the poverty line.

Income differences receive special attention whenever economic inequalities between adults also affect children. Anxieties about inequalities in market incomes are often focused upon concerns about the quality of life for children in low-income families (Cheal, 1996a; Lichter, 1997). Low family income means that children in some families are disadvantaged consumers in markets such as the housing market (Mulroy, 1995).

Child Poverty

Children who grow up in low-income families do not do as well on average as children who grow up in high-income families (Ross, Scott and Kelly, 1996a; Brooks-Gunn, Duncan and Maritato, 1997). The differences between these children begin early – in the womb, in fact. Amount and kind of nutrition, and prenatal care received by unborn children, vary according to family income. Babies born into poor families have lower birth weights on average than babies born into affluent families. Low birth weight has been shown in numerous studies to be associated with a variety of developmental difficulties, including unexpected death in infancy ('sudden infant death syndrome' – or SID), greater vulnerability to childhood infections (including ear infections), more learning problems in childhood, and lower school performance. Sociologists have been especially interested in the latter two, since they can affect adult social placement such as occupational achievement.

Research into the effects of poverty upon children is complicated by the fact that poor families differ from affluent families on other dimensions besides low income. In particular, lone-parent families are more prevalent than two-parent families among families with low income, whereas two-parent dual-career families are more common among high-income families. It is therefore conceivable that the apparent correlation between child outcomes and family income may really be due to the effects of a 'third variable', namely family composition. Sociologists refer to this type of analytical problem as *spurious correlation*. The only way to resolve that analytical problem is to examine the relationship between two variables of interest (here, family income and child outcomes), while controlling statistically for the suspected 'third variable' (for example, family composition).

Research in the United States shows that there are no easy answers to questions about the causes of child well-being (McLanahan, 1997). In many instances, coming from a single-parent family seems to reduce a child's chances of success, even after low income is taken into account. In other cases, low family income appears to have a stronger negative effect upon children. In general, the strongest independent effect of amount of family income on children's lives has been demonstrated for cognitive and educational performance, rather than emotional or behavioural issues.

The amount of money in the home affects children's cognitive development through the unequal capacity of parents to provide an intellectually stimulating environment for them and to support their emerging interests and skills. Lack of money in the home means such things as having fewer books, a lower probability of access to a home computer, fewer school trips, and less participation in organized sports. That is because poor parents have less money to 'invest' in their children's knowledge and skills than affluent parents. Children from poor families therefore grow up having reduced *human capital* (Watts, 1993). That is to say, their stock of knowledge and set of skills relevant to school performance and adult occupational success tends to be smaller than it is among children from more advantaged family backgrounds. In that sense, economic inequalities between families in one generation can reproduce economic inequalities in succeeding generations.

Economic inequalities in market economies can also affect children in other ways, by affecting the interaction dynamics of family life. This often happens when the family's economic situation is deteriorating and family members are subject to increasing economic pressure.

Economic Stress

An environment of economic decline places families under increasing pressure due to an intensified struggle to make ends meet. Under these conditions, economic survival may depend upon increased cooperation between family members. Unfortunately, emotional consequences of dealing with economic anxieties can make cooperation difficult. Tension, depression and hostility can all spill over into interactions between family members who see each other on a daily basis. Interaction difficulties may include fights over money, especially when one partner uses scarce resources without letting the other partner know.

Economic stress can be found in many situations in a market economy, including on family farms. In the 1980s, American farmers in states such as Iowa were hit hard by falling prices for their crops. As the income to be derived from farming dropped, so the value of farmland also decreased. This made it difficult for farmers to sell up, pay off their debts and move into some other line of work. As a result, some farmers went bankrupt. However, most farm families simply endured the hard times by taking on more debt and making do. The consequences of this situation for Iowa farm families were studied by Rand Conger and Glen Elder and their colleagues in 1989 (Conger and Elder et al., 1994). The researchers found that indicators of economic pressure, such as having unmet needs and the inability to make ends meet, were associated with feelings of depression and hostility. In married couples, these moods were often accompanied by feelings of unhappiness and dissatisfaction with the marriage.

Anomie

Marital relationships are not only affected by hard times and the strains this imposes upon economic cooperation in marriage, but they are also affected by good times and unexpected opportunities which become available to some people but not to others. Emile Durkheim again referred to this kind of situation as anomie. Durkheim claimed that under conditions of rapid social or economic change, traditional norms cease to be seen as relevant, with potentially disturbing consequences for some people.

Contemporary examples of anomie can be seen today in several countries where there was an abrupt shift from a centrally planned socialist economy to an open-market economy at the end of the twentieth century. China is one such country. The new market economy has brought unprecedented prosperity to some parts of China. However, prosperity has not always had favourable effects upon family life. Choices must now be made about many things that previously had to be accepted. Some of the choices that are being made disrupt established relationships, and they are therefore challenging traditional understandings about family loyalties.

In the special economic zone of Shenzhen in China, the sudden emergence of a market economy has changed not only people's economic existence but also their modes of thinking about family and sexual relationships (Weijie, 1995). Middle-aged men from rural, peasant backgrounds who have become economically successful overnight and who have acquired great wealth, now want to enjoy all the pleasures that life has to offer. This includes having sexual relationships with much younger women. The 'third person', as these mistresses and concubines are publicly referred to by local people, is creating a marriage crisis for many middle-aged women in Shenzhen. Most of these women followed a traditional path of hard manual labour at home and on the land, as well as bearing multiple children. This way of life has left them at a disadvantage in competing for their husbands' affections with younger women. The experience of competitive sexual relationships in marriage is quite new for these traditionally oriented middle-aged women. They are confused by it, and do not know how to act under contemporary conditions. Appeals to authority figures to save their marriages, which were often effective in the past, now fall upon deaf ears.

The marriage crisis in Shenzhen has arisen in part because the opportunity to enjoy an affluent lifestyle in a modern consumer society has drawn many young women into the city looking for husbands who will improve their material existence. Zhao Weijie (1995) claims that the visible wealth of Shenzhen compared with isolated rural areas creates a huge temptation for these young women. Furthermore, the market ideology of rational economic exchange of commodities has encouraged the formation of new attitudes. The exchange of youth and beauty for a comfortable lifestyle and modern consumer goods is seen as a fair exchange by some young migrant women and middle-aged men.

Commodification

The relationship between economic exchange and family life is changing in many places, in a variety of ways. For example, new reproduction technologies mean that new choices are available concerning the very traditional business of having children. Traditionally, adoption was the main alternative to conception as the method for adding children to a family, when children were wanted but could not be produced naturally. Today there is another option, namely surrogacy.

Surrogacy is a social relationship in which one woman produces a child, or children, for another woman. Some infertile couples desperately want to have children, and they will do whatever is necessary to achieve that goal. This includes being prepared to spend large sums of money at private reproductive clinics or on hiring the services of a surrogate mother. Sometimes, the way in which money is used to acquire a child through commercial surrogacy may give the appearance of an economic exchange, in which a newborn baby seems to be purchased for money. In that case, the child becomes a commodity which is bought and sold in a specialized 'baby market'. The process by which moral goods such as babies become part of a baby market is referred to as *commodification*.

Commodification of family role entry, by offering a financial incentive to gain a child as if it were just like a commodity, has been widely condemned. However, it is not rejected by everyone. The legal situation surrounding surrogacy is therefore complex. In practice, considerable variation exists between different legal jurisdictions. In the United States, for example, individual states vary significantly in how they handle surrogacy involving a commercial contract in which money is paid to a surrogate (Rosen, 1999). In some other countries, such as Canada, the impact of new reproductive technologies has been slower due to legal barriers and political delays (Canada, Royal Commission on New Reproductive Technologies, 1993a, 1993b). Systemic differences have arisen because there is often a difference of interpretation over role transitions in which money passes from a family that receives a new member to the provider.

Two contrasting systems of meaning can be identified. On the one hand, there is the system of meanings associated with a market economy. The market economy is based on rational calculation about how to make the most money, or how to get the best value for money that is being spent. On the other hand, there are systems of meanings based on moral values and personal feelings that are conventionally assumed to be the basis for family life. From the latter point of view, it is emotion and not economic calculation that is expected to bring people together in the intimate relationships of family life. This point of view clearly became the dominant one in western societies during the past century. It has influenced how many societies have responded to the possibility of commercial surrogacy (Anleu, 1990). In countries like Sweden, that place a strong emphasis upon consensus on important matters, public regulation of family life is often the preferred solution to such moral dilemmas.

Public Discourses

Public regulation of family life is based upon influential systems of ideas, which have often been advanced by modernizing elites. Over the last two centuries many of those influences came to be defined through an expanding and increasingly active *public sphere*. The public sphere of social life involves government, law, education, business, social movements and mass media. Many of these groups have specialized interests in families. For example, the topic of 'intimate violence' within families is the subject of a public discourse among lawmakers and law enforcement agencies. Those particular groups are part of an interlocking system of government known as *the state*.

Groups such as law enforcement agencies, which have the backing of the state, have a great deal of power to affect what goes on within families. Sometimes they exercise that power by direct intervention. More often, it is done by some combination of moral persuasion and practical incentives for compliance with public policy. The 'rewards' of compliance with public policy can include relief from negative sanctions, such as avoiding the stigma of being labelled as a 'bad mother' or a 'deadbeat dad'. Negative labels are sometimes followed by public punishments, such as the removal of children from the home or denial of state benefits. Because these negative labels can have serious consequences they are often resisted by the people who are affected by them. If there are enough people who are affected in this way, and they are fortunate enough to have supporters, they may subsequently appeal to people in power for a change of policy.

Within the public sphere there are extensive networks of people who are interested in issues like family violence, child support or divorce law reform. They attempt to define what the issue is about, and they negotiate over what should be done about it. Groups with different points of view on the issue attempt to influence public opinion by communicating their own point of view in as persuasive a manner as possible. Each group discusses its own perspective on the issue in a particular way, which we refer to as a *discourse*.

Public policies on families are profoundly influenced by the kinds of discourses that are conducted about them (Rodger, 1996). For example, in the 1990s, government policies toward lone mothers shifted in the United States, as well as in Canada and Britain. These families became the objects of new discourses, which portrayed them as potential threats to social order. Financial benefits for single-parent families were reduced, and measures were introduced to encourage more lone mothers to enter the labour market. Lone mothers who were not in the labour force, and who were not looking for work, were pressured to get off welfare benefits and into paid employment as fast as possible.

Duncan and Edwards (1999) describe four discourses about lone mothers that were active in Britain during this period. Those four discourses contributed unequally to the public debates about family and society that ultimately shaped government policy. All four discourses were concerned with the increased prevalence of lone motherhood at the end of the twentieth century, but the nature of their concerns differed.

One discourse looked at lone motherhood as a 'lifestyle change'. This approach located the origins of lone motherhood in the increased freedom of choice that many people claim for themselves today, including decisions about divorce and raising children outside marriage. The second approach was also concerned with the causes of lone motherhood, but in this case mothers were seen as 'escaping from patriarchy'. Inspired by feminism, this approach described the difficulties experienced by many women in marriage. It stressed how separation could be a rational choice for women seeking a better life for themselves and their children. Third, people who saw lone mothers as the victims of circumstances tended to focus on lone motherhood as a 'social problem'. The main concern here was the low income level experienced by many single-parent families, and the need for public income transfers to bring these families up to an acceptable standard of living. Finally, there was the discourse of lone motherhood as a 'social threat'. In Britain, this discourse was linked to the American discourse about an emerging urban underclass containing a disproportionate number of single-parent families. Negative social consequences of this situation were emphasized. Undesirable outcomes were believed to include lack of male authority over children, especially sons; the public costs of supporting a large number of lone mothers; and the potential for welfare dependence to be passed on from one generation to the next in a cycle of disadvantage.

Two points are worth making immediately about discourses on single parenthood. The first point is that social scientists, including sociologists, have been deeply involved in elaborating and communicating all four of the competing discourses described above. In fact, elements of each of these discourses have already been encountered in earlier chapters of the present book. Clearly, sociological analysis and public policy discourse are connected when sociological work becomes a part of public discourse. This example illustrates what is sometimes referred to as the *reflexivity* of modern societies. In modern societies there is a socially organized process of critically examining current conditions in order to decide how they should be changed. Evidence from social research is used to support, or to dispute, various arguments for change that are debated in universities, in the mass media and in democratic political institutions.

The second point to make is that not all discourses are equal. The discourse of lone motherhood as 'social threat' became the dominant one in Britain in the 1990s. It helped to shape the policies not only of the Conservative Government at that time, but also of the subsequent Labour government. In particular, increased costs of supporting lone mothers and their children came to be seen as an unjustifiable burden upon the state (Millar, 1999).

Discourses which focus on perceived consequences of change tend to receive a great deal of public attention if the consequences are described as being very negative. Amid the constant chatter of public discourse, people pay the most attention to those discourses that describe some threat to themselves, or which demand immediate action to solve some problem. Dramatic stories about social crises and the costs of family change are therefore much more likely to attract attention than stories about individual problems. Politicians and policy-makers have to be seen to do something about public crises if they want to be viewed as effective managers of a modern welfare state.

Welfare States

Some modern states, notably in continental Europe and in Scandinavia, have explicit and coherent policies about family life (Haas, 1996). Other states, such as Britain, the United States and Canada either do not have well-developed policies concerning families, or their policies are fragmented and inconsistent (Lewis, 1993; Skrypnek and Fast, 1996). However, governments in the latter countries do make important decisions which affect families.

Decisions about such matters as income taxation and tax credits, and income support payments, are based on judgements concerning the form of family life that policymakers consider to be 'normal' (Eichler, 1997). Inevitably, distinctions are made between those types of family arrangements which are recognized in state policies, and types of family arrangements which are not recognized. Dimensions of *social inclusion* and *social exclusion* are therefore important issues in studies of families and their environments. Are all families equally supported by the state? That is, are they all equally included in government programmes? Or do some kinds of families receive much support, while the needs of other families are largely ignored ?

One interesting example of social exclusion is the treatment of large families which have many children. They tend to receive little attention in public policy in North America today (Cheal, 1996a). Average family size has fallen dramatically over the past half century, and a 'normal' family in many countries now has only one or two children. The fact that there are still some families with many children tends to be overlooked. Public perceptions of children today are based on the assumption that they live in small families in which there is little competition for resources. That assumption can be seriously misleading. Donald Hernandez (1998) has illustrated just how badly perceptions of children's lives can be skewed under current demographic conditions in the United States.

Hernandez points out that it can make a big difference whether families or children are taken as the unit of analysis in social research. (The 'unit of analysis' is a social object about which information is collected, which may be a single person or a social group containing a number of individuals). If 'the family' is chosen as the unit of analysis then we would say that in the United States in 1993, 41 per cent of families with children had only one living child at home. However, if we took the child as the unit of analysis then we would conclude that just 22 per cent of American children in 1993 lived in families where they were the only child. The reason for this apparent discrepancy is that although there are not many large families in America today, those large families which do exist account for a disproportionate number of American children. Thus, in the United States in 1993 only 20 per cent of families with children contained three or more children. But, 37 per cent of all children actually lived in families having at least three children present. An important practical consequence of this methodological point is that official statistics on family income almost always underestimate the number of children who live in poverty. Children in large families are more likely to be poor than children who live in small families. However, it is children in small families who are the most visible in statistics based on the family as the unit of analysis.

Welfare State Regimes

Government income transfer programmes should always be examined to see how they may affect families of different kinds, such as large families compared with small families. They should also be examined to see how they may affect different family members, such as children compared with adults. This aspect of the politics of family life emerged as an important issue in the relationship between families and welfare states in the 1990s.

The term *welfare state* is used to describe a system of government in which the state plays an important role in meeting a variety of needs. Politicians and policymakers are expected to provide public policies which deal with a wide range of social problems. Exactly how wide the range of policies is depends upon the particular image of the welfare state that is favoured by opinion leaders in a given country. Images, or models, of the welfare state can vary considerably from one country to another.

Sociological discussions of public policy environments for families have been greatly stimulated by an analysis of the welfare state presented by a Swedish sociologist, Gøsta Esping-Andersen. He classified the welfare states which emerged in western societies during the twentieth century into three types (Esping-Andersen, 1990, 1992). Countries like the United States, Australia, Britain and Canada are what Esping-Andersen refers to as *liberal welfare states*.

In these countries the state tends to play a minor role in social life, including family life. The state does not aim to intervene in family issues, unless family members are clearly unable to solve their own problems. In that case the issues may be redefined as social problems. Even when the existence of social problems is widely recognized, however, state involvement is likely to be limited if public solutions would require higher levels of taxation.

Liberal welfare states tend to avoid *universal programmes* that provide the same benefits to everyone who is a citizen of the state. Instead, they favour *targeted programmes* which help a limited number of people in greatest need. In order to receive support from a targeted programme it is necessary to demonstrate personal and family need to government officials. For example, the level of a family's financial need may be judged through *means testing*. This requires the applicant to provide detailed information about financial resources as well as personal relationships with people who might be expected to support them financially.

The United States is often considered to be the classic liberal welfare state. Compared with other western countries, families with poor children in the United States are much less likely to receive government support, the average amount of support is much smaller, and it is more likely to flow from means-tested welfare programmes than to come from more broadly based social programmes (Hernandez, 1995).

Liberal welfare states such as the United States and Britain provide limited public support for single-parent families. The social problems discourse in these countries identifies single-parent families as a needy group, but at the same time there is a great deal of concern about the public cost of supporting lone parents (Duncan and Edwards, 1997). Individuals in a liberal welfare state do not expect to pay heavy taxes in order to support other people's families. Needy families that require a lot of support are therefore seen as creating problems for 'normal families' by imposing unacceptable burdens upon them.

The second type of welfare state described by Esping-Andersen is the *corporatist welfare state*. A corporatist welfare state is one in which voluntary organizations, such as churches, non-profit insurance funds or employers' associations, assume a major role in helping people to develop their family life under the guidance of the state. Countries such as Austria, France, Germany and Italy fit this description. However, there are also some important differences between these countries.

In Germany, public support for families has traditionally been provided through employment-related insurance contributions. An insurance-based system assumes a stable family income that is earned by a full-time employed male breadwinner, who then supports a non-employed housewife and their children. This system is changing, as female employment has increased in Germany in recent years. Still, the majority of married German women with children either do not work a full week or they are not employed at all. Lone mothers in Germany, on the other hand, must work longer hours because they do not have a husband's income on which to depend. The dominant discourse about single motherhood in Germany is therefore a sympathetic discourse of social problems. Lone mothers are pitied because they are poor and over-worked (Klett-Davies, 1997).

Finally, the third type of welfare state described by Esping-Andersen is the *social-democratic welfare state*. This type of welfare state is found in the Scandinavian countries, with Norway and Sweden as the clearest examples. Here, the state is actively involved in developing social programmes that are intended to alleviate social inequalities and other social problems. However, the image of the interventionist welfare state in these countries is sometimes exaggerated (Leira, 1994).

A high level of employment by everyone is encouraged in Sweden. The general aim of public policy has therefore been to equalize mothers' employment, regardless of their marital status. For example, the children of lone mothers are given priority access to public childcare, partly in order to give these mothers the opportunity to support their families through full-time employment. The dominant discourse of single motherhood in Sweden is that it is a lifestyle choice that is to be expected of some women under current conditions of social change and individualization (Björnberg, 1997). As such, they are considered to be deserving of public support. However, even in Sweden the dependence of lone parents upon their own unaided earnings or upon state benefits makes them vulnerable to market changes and to cuts in public funding. Difficulties in the Swedish economy in the 1990s, combined with a fiscal crisis in the Swedish welfare state, were followed by financial constraints for some lone mothers.

Ultimately, it is not possible for any state, even a social democratic state, to meet the needs of everyone at the same time or to solve every social problem. Choices must be made about how government resources are to be allocated. The key sociological question is: who benefits the most from the political choices that are made about economic and social policies? And, what consequences do those choices have for family life?

Intergenerational Relations in the Welfare State

Pensions and other income support programmes for the elderly are among the most generous programmes offered by many governments. A major consequence of the welfare state in a number of western countries is therefore that it has changed the relationship between the generations (Cheal, 1996a). The growth of public pensions has reduced the need for private financial support for older people. This has the indirect effect of reducing financial pressures upon adult children with aged parents. To a lesser extent, adult children have also benefited from the expansion of publicly funded services for the elderly, such as home help and home nursing. Public services, like the municipal homemakers in Finland, relieve adult children of some of the caregiving for elderly parents that they might otherwise have to do themselves (Simonen, 1990).

In Finland, public support for the care of elderly people living in their own homes went even further in the 1990s with the introduction of the Informal Carer's Allowance. This allowance is a financial benefit awarded to a caregiver, including pension rights, which is granted on the basis of an elderly person's needs (Jenson and Jacobzone, 2000). Care allowances, and the public provision of domestic services for incapacitated elderly persons, are likely to be of great benefit to daughters and daughters-in-law of elderly people. As significant caregivers for aged parents, they might otherwise have to choose between caregiving and paid employment.

In addition to Finland, Norway is another good example of a country in which the rapid expansion of social services for the elderly has led to changes in family interactions (Daatland, 1990). Older Norwegians are more receptive to public services today than they were thirty or forty years ago. More of them now prefer public help instead of help from family members. It seems that when public services are readily available, older people in Norway are reluctant to make heavy demands upon their children's time, even if the children are living nearby. Interestingly, a distinction has emerged between short-term assistance, which is acceptable from adult children, and long-term care which it is thought that the state should provide.

Long-term care provided by state programmes is expensive, and it is not always available even in affluent countries. In recent years, the main emphasis has tended to be on controlling the costs of such programmes in order to reduce the amount of public debt and lower taxes. In Britain, which has been heavily involved in this trend, the welfare state today is no longer expected to be the major provider of care. Rather, agents of the state such as social workers are involved in organizing 'care packages'. This may include some state services, but the main component is likely to be family care supplemented by the work of volunteers and commercial service providers (Dalley, 1993; Rodger, 1996). The overall effect of this shift has been to re-emphasize 'traditional' obligations of family members as primary caregivers.

The dominant ideologies in Britain today are those of individualism and communitarianism. These ideologies favour individual responsibility and informal social support rather than state provision. Individual free choice within an unfettered market economy is preferred. This means lowering taxes, controlling the costs of public services, and articulating a discourse of community altruism and family obligation. In this respect, Britain today is ideologically more similar to the United States than it is to its geographically closer neighbour Norway.

In the United States it is estimated that four out of five disabled elderly persons live in some kind of non-institutional private setting, usually in their own homes (Coward, Horne and Dwyer, 1992). Family members represent the largest source of support for elderly Americans who need assistance with daily living at home. The primary caregivers for older people who live in their own homes are their spouses, when available. If a spouse is not available, then other close family members usually take on the family's obligation to care, especially female family members.

In most developing countries today, the provision of social services is even further restricted by limited government revenues from taxation, and by the fact that public funds tend to be directed toward projects that foster growth in the market economy. As a result, programmes to assist older people are normally given a low priority by governments in these countries. In the Philippines, for example, the elderly must rely heavily upon their families for support when their productivity declines and their health deteriorates (Domingo, 1994). One vital means of support in many cases is coresidence. Only a small minority of elderly Filipinos live alone, whereas the majority live with at least one of their children.

In the Philippines, sons are assumed to be mainly concerned with making a living and they are therefore expected to help their parents financially. All family members have an obligation to assist a parent who is in poor health, but in practice most of the responsibility for daily caregiving falls upon daughters. Daughters are thought to be more available than sons, as well as being more reliable and more caring. In this example, we see how the weak development of the welfare state in a low income country has different implications for sons and daughters. Similar questions can also be raised about gender relations in more affluent countries.

Gender Relations in the Welfare State

Feminist commentators have raised a number of questions about gender differences in developed welfare states (Leira, 1992; Lewis, 1992; Orloff, 1993; 1996; Sainsbury, 1996; Evans, 1997). Of special interest here is gender analysis of income transfer policies which may have implications for women's financial dependence in marriage. That issue emerges from a considerable critical literature in recent years, on the interconnections between the market economy, family, gender and the state (Cheal, 1997a; Luxton, 1997; Pulkingham and Ternowetsky, 1997).

The conceptual foundations of public income support policies have typically included assumptions about income pooling in families, on the grounds that any money earned by any family member is part of the 'family income'. The precise nature of a 'family income' is typically unstated, but it is generally understood to mean a pool of money which is used to benefit all of the members of the family more or less equally. Thus, it is implicitly assumed for policy purposes that family incomes are used to meet family needs, and that married persons with low individual incomes will be fully supported by their partners. Relationships of economic dependence between spouses are considered to be a normal part of family life, and the social-psychological dimensions of dependence are conventionally deemed to be of little or no relevance. Feminist perspectives have sometimes been at odds with this point of view (Hobson, 1990; Lister, 1990, 1994; Ginn and Arber, 1992; Baxter and Kane, 1995; Vosko, 1995).

Leah Vosko (1995) argues that family income testing in government programmes is highly gendered. Wives are presumed to be formally equal partners in marriage, who are entitled to a substantial portion of the family income. However, Vosko suggests that women do not necessarily have their own financial resources in families with seemingly adequate incomes, due to unequal power over the distribution of money within the family. Therefore, she claims that family income testing produces a state of dependency at home when unemployed female claimants must rely on spousal support. If such support is not forthcoming, then wives may have to turn to other sources of help such as their social networks.

Social Networks

Mothers whose own earnings are not large enough to support their families may receive emotional and material support from members of their *social network*. A network can consist of friends, neighbours, relatives and sometimes boyfriends, as well as their children's fathers and *their* relatives (especially the children's paternal grandmothers). Women's personal networks tend to be focused more on family than are men's networks, and they often contain a greater proportion of kin (Moore, 1990). In many cases a mother's relationship with her own mother is a particularly important source of help, as illustrated in a study of low-income single mothers in four American cities (Edin and Lein, 1997). The majority of these mothers got some financial support from members of their networks that supplemented their low wages or limited welfare payments.

Married women can construct large social networks under favourable conditions of high fertility and stable residence. These networks are composed of their own kin, their husband's kin, their friends, and the friends of both sets of kin. Unlike their married counterparts, lone mothers do not have the resources of a husband's kinship network on which to draw. However, they may sometimes maintain limited relationships with ex-in-laws. More often, lone mothers lack a direct relationship with a mother-in-law, and they also lack indirect ties that could be accessed through a husband's interactions with his kin (Lamphere et al., 1993). To some extent lone mothers can compensate for their lack of indirect ties by strengthening relationships with their sisters, and with their friends. Lone mothers are more involved with non-relatives than are mothers living with a partner (Gunnarsson and Cochran, 1990). However, such a network building strategy is likely to be of limited value in populations where fertility is low. One consequence of a low birth rate, and small family size, is that some women will have no sisters. Research in Sweden and the United States shows that lone mothers have smaller networks than mothers in two-parent families (Gunnarsson and Cochran, 1990). Much of the difference is accounted for by the fact that the networks of lone mothers contain fewer relatives than the networks of married mothers.

Studies in the United States, as well as in Australia, show that homeless families tend to be poor families that lack effective social support networks (Kryder-Coe, Salamon and Molnar, 1991; McCaughey, 1992). Separated and divorced female single-parents are particularly vulnerable to homelessness at the point when a relationship breaks down. At that time they may experience a very sudden decline in income. Lone mothers who lack significant social ties to relatives or friends, including those whose own mothers are dead, may have no one on whom to rely for temporary housing, financial assistance, information about housing and jobs, or low cost childcare.

Childcare provided by relatives is often done for no monetary payment, or it may be done at a cost that is well below the market rate for commercial childcare services (Folk, 1994). This can be a significant element in the survival strategies of low income families. Having access to relatives can be a factor which distinguishes those low income families which do well from those that struggle to get by.

The network of social ties which helps to sustain many mothers and their families is sometimes referred to as part of a woman's *social capital* (Maclean and Eekelaar, 1997; Duncan and Edwards, 1999). A person's social capital is the accumulated set of social supports which she or he uses to gain access to resources that could not be obtained independently. For example, immigrants usually lack information about the labour market in their new country. They are therefore likely to have some initial difficulty in finding employment. Social ties to people who migrated earlier, and who are already established, are often important in helping new migrants to find work and other economic opportunities (Wong and Salaff, 1998).

Social capital is an important factor in the well-being of most families. It is an especially important factor for immigrant families and low income families who have little access to financial capital (Sanders and Nee, 1996). Lower-class mothers who are not employed often need to swap practical assistance and everyday household supplies in order to make ends meet, especially if their husbands are unemployed or earn low wages. Social capital can also be important for middle-class families, notably in countries where many public services are not readily available. In India, for example, employed mothers in all classes tend to rely on members of their social networks to look after their children while they are at work (Sekaran, 1992).

Important class differences exist in the size and nature of social networks, as shown in a number of countries. In the United States, Wales, Sweden and

Germany, mothers from white-collar families all have larger networks than mothers from blue-collar families (Cochran and Gunnarsson, 1990). Perhaps this class difference is a result of differences in resources. Mothers from white-collar families have more resources for meeting and entertaining other people, and they may therefore be less concerned about the possibility for embarrassment in not being able to return the generosity of others. Another important class difference is that social networks of mothers from blue-collar families contain more relatives than non-relatives, whereas the reverse is true for mothers from white-collar families. White-collar families tend to have a wider range of social contacts that extend beyond the family and neighbourhood into the community. This gives them greater advantages in access to new resources, such as information about job opportunities. When children get older, parents' social contacts can help them to find a job and get established in other ways. Assistance in finding first jobs is often vital for young people, since they lack the work experience that is essential for obtaining most kinds of employment.

Parents are not the only people who might want to use their social capital to gain access to resources such as jobs. Men and women in a variety of situations rely on network contacts when they are looking for work. Network ties seem to be particularly important for people with relatively little education, and who live in areas with high unemployment (Allatt and Yeandle, 1992). Many jobs are never advertised by employers, because they are quickly filled by people who are introduced to the employer by someone who is already working in the business. Family members often pass information about new employment opportunities to one another. They may also convince prospective employers about a relative's ability to do a job. In these ways family members are often an important part of a worker's social support network (d'Abbs, 1991).

In some regions of the world, such as the Caribbean, help provided by support networks is not enough for everyone to get a job, because there are simply not enough jobs to go round. When unemployment is very high, some people will therefore emigrate in order to obtain employment outside their country of origin. Occasionally migrants lose contact with their families, but usually they carry their family obligations with them wherever they go. Large numbers of migrants send *remittances* back to the family members they leave behind. These are cash transfers from relatives living abroad, which are often of great value to people in low-income countries like Jamaica and Haiti (Itzigsohn, 1995). Many families depend upon these remittances as a regular part of the family income because local sources of income are often unreliable.

Families with children tend to receive multiple forms of support, including support from relatives living nearby as well as relatives living abroad. In Canada, young couples with children and lone mothers are especially likely to receive financial help from family members. It is noteworthy that they receive material help much more often than do elderly persons (Cheal, 1996a). In earlier times, older people were often in dire financial need and they had to turn to their families in order to survive. Today, most people in high-income countries who retire from the labour force benefit from income supports such as public pensions. Some of them also have other financial assets, such as equity in a home or retirement investments. As a result, some older people give financial help to family members in younger generations even into advanced old age.

Discussion

In the present chapter we have explored four social environments that affect how family members achieve their individual and collective goals. We have seen that markets, public discourses, welfare states, and social networks each have their own distinctive features, but they are also interconnected in a number of ways. Those connections often have important effects upon families.

Welfare states have a large impact upon family life in a number of countries, because policymakers often pay deliberate attention to what is happening in families. Goals such as strengthening family ties, helping families that are overburdened, and correcting problems of family abuse, are all tasks that welfare states have undertaken at different times and in different places. We have seen in this chapter that government services and income support pro- grammes can affect family relationships. They may alter the demands that family members make upon one another, by empowering some family members with resources they would not otherwise have enjoyed. Welfare states can also help to redress historic social inequalities, such as gender inequalities, as the social democratic welfare states of Norway and Sweden have attempted to do. On the other hand, welfare states can also deepen and strengthen existing inequalities through public programmes that are based on assump- tions about a particular type of family as the natural form of 'the family'.

Single-parent families are the ones most affected by the contrasting policies pursued by governments under different kinds of welfare state regimes. As we saw earlier in this chapter, public discourses of social problems and social threats differ between different countries, and they have changed over time. Are lone parents merely the symptoms of a set of social problems created by uncontrolled social change; or are lone parents a threat to social order because of the problems they create? Public debates about that question raise funda- mental issues of family values. They also touch upon other issues that arise from the connections between families, welfare states and markets.

For most families, the most important market is the labour market. Lone mothers have been the subject of so much public concern partly because they often have greater difficulty than mothers in two-parent families over how to balance the competing demands of children and employers. Employment in the paid labour force is clearly a critical issue in a capitalist society. Welfare states may therefore compensate for deficiencies in earned incomes by providing income transfers from public resources.

Some welfare states provide extensive services to families, such as homecare for the elderly. Those services are provided by employees of the state, rather than being provided by family members themselves or being purchased from private service suppliers. The historic takeover in some countries, in which services such as medical care were largely removed from the market and placed under the control of the state, is referred to by Esping-Andersen as a process of *decommodification*. More recently, governments in many countries, including Sweden, have either cut back on government programmes or they have re-privatized certain government services (Acker, 1994). This shift might be referred to as one of 'recommodification'. A distinctive characteristic of this process is that it has been accompanied by a renewed emphasis upon family responsibilities (Oppenheim and Lister, 1996). Faced with greater need to provide care for their members, many families have responded by drawing upon their inner resources as well as the external resources of social networks.

In contemporary welfare states, caseworkers recognize that they have to develop partnerships with social support networks in order to provide an adequate level of care, especially for growing numbers of elderly people with disabilities. In some cases, public social services are stretched so thin that caseworkers no longer attempt to provide any direct care. Rather, they merely act as the catalysts and coordinators of pre-existing social networks. Families which have always relied upon assistance from social networks composed of friends, neighbours and kin are the least likely to suffer from this development.

Conclusion

The final chapter raises questions about the place of the sociology of family life within the discipline of sociology, especially in relation to ideas about social progress. Images of progress, and therefore expectations of future developments, have often influenced the ways in which sociologists study current social events. Problems with this approach are briefly discussed, notably with respect to modernization theory. It is recommended that sociologists should begin with questions about group life, such as life within family groups. The questions raised in this book were:

■ Who are family members?

■ What do families do?

■ How are families connected to other groups?

CONCEPTS

modernity   postmodernity   high modernity
family life

In this book we have seen that sociologists are engaged in trying to answer three main questions about families. Those questions are: Who are family members? What do families do? And, how are families related to other social groups? There are many different answers that can be given to those questions depending upon the time and place in which families are located, and according to the different interests that motivate sociologists to study family life. In this book we have sampled some of the many answers given by sociologists, with special emphasis on regional variations in sociological studies from a number of different countries. We have also seen that different theoretical approaches influence sociological studies of family life. That is particularly visible at the present time in areas such as divorce and post-divorce relationships, where feminist and non-feminist points of view often raise different concerns (Cheal, 1989, 1991).

Underlying each of the questions asked in this book there is also usually some concern about family change. At the most basic level, people everywhere face the same fundamental choice – between maintaining family life as they know it or reinventing family life along new lines. Sociologists are therefore always very interested in the choices that people make about their family lives when they face new opportunities and new constraints. We also want to know about the ways in which powerful groups, such as governments, respond to change and attempt to shape the choices that people make. Both as sociologists, and as users of sociological research in fields like social policy, we have an urgent need to know more about trends of family change. We need to know the direction in which winds of change are blowing, in order to provide up-to-date advice to governments and social agencies about policy development. That desire to anticipate and control the future by understanding current trends is very important in sociology, including the sociology of family life.

Sociology, Modernity and Family

One way of thinking about sociology and social change, that has been widely discussed in recent years, is to claim that the proper subject matter for sociology is the study of *modernity*. Modernity is a type of culture which favours technological and social changes that are thought to bring about human progress. Those changes include industrialization, urbanization, the growth of market economies and the expanded influence of the state. We have seen evidence of the effects of these influences upon family life in various parts of this book. However, it is necessary to be aware that the sociology of family life cannot be reduced to the study of modernization. Sociological emphases upon modernity (including, perhaps, the concept of modernity itself) place certain restrictions upon the development of the sociology of family life. (See **Box 9.1**). That is the final issue to be taken up in the concluding pages of this book.

Family life is clearly not one of the main sources of modernization. The major institutions of modernization such as science, formal education, markets and welfare states are all relatively recent developments in historical terms, but family life has existed for much longer. Furthermore, modern institutions have developed autonomously within a public sphere that is outside of, and sometimes contradictory to, family life. The immediate consequence of this is that family studies does not occupy a central place within the sociology of modernity. As a result, the sociology of family life tends to have a marginal position within the discipline of sociology as a whole. That is despite the considerable

---

Box 9.1 Modernity or postmodernity?

Concepts of modernity have exerted an increasing influence in social theory, but they have also been subjected to critical examination. Increased diversity in some areas of social life and a sense of directionless change, as well as doubts about progress, encouraged the idea that modernity is being replaced by postmodernity. *Postmodernity* is conceptualized as a type of culture in which an accelerated rate of change produces unpredictable outcomes, and modern social institutions lose much of their capacity to control events. Postmodernity is an incoherent juxtaposition of contrasting images, experiences and ideas (Bauman 1992). Not surprisingly, applications of this approach in family studies have also been diverse and sometimes contradictory. In some versions of this approach, children are seen as being especially vulnerable to the effects of uncontrolled change upon families (Denzin, 1987; Elkind, 1995; Cheal, 1996a). Other concepts of postmodernity have placed more emphasis upon the unexpected opening up of personal choices and opportunities for new forms of pleasure, and the dilemmas that sometimes follow from this (Stacey, 1990, 1991; Cheal, 1993a).

In opposition to concepts of postmodernity, Anthony Giddens has proposed that current social and psychological changes should be seen as consequences of the extension of modernity, or in other words *'high modernity'* (Giddens, 1991). Greatly increased capacities for communication and the use of information (for example information technologies and expert systems), and massive growth in the circulation of goods and people (for example, globalization of trade and international travel), are creating a world in which social organizations – and social relationships – are constantly being created, redesigned, discarded and reconstituted. A critical issue for personal relationships in this context, Giddens believes, is trust (Giddens, 1990).

---

importance of family life for personal happiness and sense of well-being, as well as for a variety of social and economic policies.

The second point to make about the awkward relationship between the sociology of family life and modernity is that family life is often of interest to sociologists mainly in relation to their beliefs about future progress. For example, a variety of hopes have been pinned upon the idea that the welfare state can provide social programmes which will liberate family caregivers from the limitations of a narrow existence within the family. From this point of view, services such as the public provision of subsidized daycare for working mothers are thought to be essential vehicles for social progress. Margrit Eichler (1997) refers to this approach as the 'social responsibility model'. Sweden is often held out to be the lead society in the social responsibility model for family development.

The difficulty posed by this modernist viewpoint is that the sociology of family life is made to depend upon a particular image of the future. That is to say, it tends to be based upon a utopian image in which priorities for family studies are defined by assumptions about a constant expansion of state services. Unfortunately, that expansion appears to have come to an end in most western societies (including Sweden), if not permanently then at least temporarily. Realistically speaking, it is no longer possible to believe that Sweden constitutes the lead society for trends in western family life, let alone families in non-western societies.

It is important to recognize the enormous political and social changes, which occurred at the end of the twentieth century, that raised many new questions about the direction of progress. A notable example concerns the collapse of the German Democratic Republic (East Germany), and its effective take over by the Federal Republic of Germany (the former West Germany). The state socialism of the GDR used to provide a high level of material support and moral encouragement for employment of mothers. GDR state policies constituted one of the most effective demonstrations of the potential advantages for women of Marxist family politics. The disappearance of the GDR, as well as other regimes that were once based upon official Marxism, has created a void in modernist accounts of the future of social policy. There is no longer in existence any convincing demonstration of the total modernization of family life through state policy. That void may be difficult to fill. Successful capitalist nations such as Canada are moving only slowly, if at all, toward large-scale public provision of daycare and other social services for families. It may therefore be necessary for the sociology of family life to anticipate a twenty-first century social world in which progress through the expansion of the welfare state is either minimal or non-existent.

A third troubling consequence arising from the identification of sociology with the study of modernity is that the comparative study of families in different societies is ultimately shaped by some version of modernization theory. According to this approach, different societies and their families are seen as lying at different stages of development along a universal path of modernization. Among other changes, modernization theory would lead us to expect that industrialization and urbanization are consistently followed by the loosening of extended family ties. However, that is not always the case. For example, a study of families in Taipei, Taiwan, has concluded that although feelings of obligation to support distant relatives are indeed getting weaker, actual frequency of interaction with them has in fact increased at important ritual events, such as ancestor worship, the New Year, weddings, birthdays and funerals (Marsh, 1996). Useful as modernization theory may be for certain purposes, it has the serious disadvantage of oversimplifying processes of family change in some non-western societies.

Discussion

The sociology of modernity is an unreliable framework within which to study family issues. It is therefore necessary to approach family studies from a different direction. That is what we have attempted to do in this book, by directing attention to the sociology of *family life*. Instead of looking at families from the perspective of the future of modern societies, we have looked at families from the perspective of the one thing that guarantees a future of any kind, namely life itself.

From the moment we are born we are social beings. Somebody picks us up and holds us, comforts us, cleans us, and feeds us. That 'someone' is almost always a woman. From that moment on we spend most of our lives in social groups of one kind or another. Despite the many changes which we experience in our lives, family groups are often among the most enduring of our social experiences. The particular family group to which we belong may be small, consisting perhaps of only two people such as mother and child. Or, our family group may be very large, providing us with extensive social ties upon which we draw for many social purposes. Either way, there is a common experience of participation in a family group of some kind.

It is for this reason that the present book has taken family groups as basic units of analysis for social enquiry. We have asked, who belongs to family groups and what forms do they take? What do people do in family groups, and what effects does this have upon them? And what are the connections between families and other kinds of social groups, especially those which are the major sources of change in family life today? Those questions will inevitably be answered in different ways, in different countries and in the light of different social goals and different social experiences. But the questions are always worth asking.

Glossary

Abuse: An act is considered to be abusive if it has a high probability of causing long-term harm to the recipient. (*See also* **sexual abuse**).

Anomie: This is a situation in which traditional social norms no longer serve as effective guides to conduct, due to rapid social or economic change.

Anticipatory Socialization: Anticipatory socialization is self-directed learning in which individuals seek out experiences that they think will help them to become the kind of person they expect, or want, to be in the future.

Arranged Marriage: In an arranged marriage the bride and groom do not choose each other as partners, but the decision about who they should marry is made for them. This decision is usually made by the parents, but other kin may also be involved.

Breadwinner: A breadwinner is someone who assumes the responsibility for earning all or most of the family income on a regular basis.

Breadwinner/Homemaker Family: The breadwinner/homemaker family is a type of **nuclear family** based on a sharp **division of labour** between husband and wife. The husband has the sole responsibility for earning the family income, and the wife has the sole responsibility for housework and most of the responsibility for child care.

Bridge Generation: In multigenerational families, a bridge generation is one that links a junior generation (for example, children) with a senior generation (for example, grandparents).

Care Deficit: A care deficit is a lack of care which is due to an imbalance between the demand for care and the supply of care.

Caregiving: This is the term that is used to describe all the activities by which someone helps another person to meet the basic needs of daily living. (*cf.* **caring about**).

Caring About: Caring about someone is a feeling of interest and concern for their well-being that motivates awareness and attention.

Childcare: Childcare is **taking care** of children.

Cohabitation: Cohabitation occurs when two people live together and engage in sexual and economic relationships without being legally married.

Cohort: The term cohort refers to a group of people who were all born in the same period of time.

Commitment: Commitment is a feeling of being obligated to perform certain activities for another person because the individual has accepted and fulfilled similar responsibilities in the past.

Commodification: Commodification is a social process whereby things that were previously excluded from a **market economy** become subject to rational economic exchange mediated by monetary transactions. (*cf.* **decommodification**).

Companionate Marriage: Companionate marriage is based on the cultural ideal that a husband and wife should spend a considerable amount of time in each other's company, and that they should endeavour to meet each other's needs and engage in open communication about all aspects of their lives.

Conjugal Family: A conjugal family is the domestic unit consisting of a couple, with or without children.

Conjugal Relationship: A heterosexual partnership, traditionally confirmed by legal marriage that is the basis for the **conjugal family**, is called a conjugal relationship.

Co-provider: A co-provider is someone who shares the responsibility of earning a joint family income with at least one other family member.

Corporatist Welfare State: A corporatist welfare state is one in which voluntary organizations, such as churches or employers' associations, assume a major role in helping families to develop their **family life** under the guidance of the state.

Cultural Alternative: A cultural alternative is a particular design for living provided by a given culture, which exists alongside other cultural alternatives in a competitive relationship with them.

Cultural Contradiction: A cultural contradiction occurs when two or more values or social norms within a given culture conflict, and neither of them is strong enough to replace the other.

Custodial Parent: The custodial parent is the parent who gains sole legal custody of a child or with whom the child resides after divorce.

Decommodification: Decommodification is a social process whereby things that were previously bought and sold in a **market economy** become subject to state regulation and public provision through government agencies. (*cf.* **commodification**).

Demography: The social scientific study of human population is known as demography. The key factors studied in demography are births and deaths. Since childbirth often occurs in the context of marriage, demographers are also interested in marriage and divorce. Recently, they have also begun studying non-marital cohabitation.

Dependence: A situation in which most of the financial and/or psychological supports for someone are provided by one other person, or by one group of persons, is a situation of dependence upon that person or group.

Discourse: A discourse is a way of talking about a social object, such as lone mothers. It defines what the object is, and it identifies themes in the object that are considered to be important topics for discussion.

Division of Labour: In most social groups, different kinds of work are divided up and allocated to specific persons who specialize in doing a particular set of tasks. This specialization of task performance is known as the division of labour.

Dual-Career Couples: Dual-career couples are two-earner couples in which both partners work full-time.

Economic Determinism: Economic determinism is a method of analysis which stresses how economic processes involving work and money determine what happens within systems of interaction, such as families.

Economy of Pleasure: An economy of pleasure is an exchange of gratifications, including sexual gratifications, that stimulate emotions and heighten each individual's sense of well-being.

Emotion Work: When individuals attempt to manipulate their emotions, by suppressing emotions that are socially undesirable and expressing emotions that are socially preferred, then they are said to engage in emotion work.

Encapsulation: Encapsulation is a social process in which the range of an individual's effective relationships is drastically narrowed, as a result of spending much time with one individual or group to the exclusion of all others.

Endogamy: Endogamy is a social rule, or norm, of preferred marriage between members of the same social group. Norms of endogamy are found most often in religious groups and in ethnic groups.

Ethnomethodology: Ethnomethodology is a sociological approach which is concerned with the techniques, or 'methods', of interaction by which individuals carry out, or 'do', social life.

Extended Family: An extended family is a large family group containing more than one couple, or more than one parent–child dyad, and whose members are linked by a discourse of family ties and by exchanges of practical support. The principal family ties in extended families are descent ties. Extended families are therefore usually inter-generational families, typically involving three generations of family members.

Family: A family is a group consisting of people who have close personal relationships which are believed to endure over time and across generations. Family relationships involve careful social construction of links between persons in the past, the present and the future. Those links frequently include marriage and descent ties, but they may include other ties such as adoption and special ritual relationships.

Family Boundaries: Family boundaries are barriers that separate people who are inside a family from people who are outside the family. Sometimes those barriers are very visible, such as the walls of a dwelling. Other barriers may be less visible, such as interaction processes by which some people are included in family activities while other people are excluded.

Family of Choice: A family of choice is a family structure created by non-heterosexuals who want to emphasize continuity and mutual support in a loving and caring relationship.

Family Composition: Family composition refers to the number and kinds of people who belong to a family.

Family Dynamics: The general term used to refer to all changes that occur within families, either when **family composition** changes or when family members alter their relations with one another, is 'family dynamics'.

Family Economy: A family economy is a system of **transactions** through which family members acquire and use material resources that are needed in **family life**.

Family Formation: The term family formation refers to some **transition** that initiates the creation of a new family. Traditionally, a new family was understood to be created by marriage. Subsequently, other transitions, such as beginning to cohabit, or unattached parenthood, have also been recognized as types of family formation.

Family-Friendly Policies: Family-friendly policies are arrangements made by employers to help their employees cope with tasks of childcare or eldercare.

Family Life: Family life is a way of living in which individuals seek to achieve personal goals they believe are important for their happiness and sense of well-being by actively participating in family relationships.

Family Life Cycle: The family life cycle is a particular sequence of stages in the life course that is believed to be the standard pattern for people living in a given society. In a society where the **nuclear family** is the cultural ideal, the family life cycle includes leaving the **family of origin**, getting married, and having children, in that order.

Family of Orientation: A person's family of orientation is a family to which she or he has chosen to belong, usually through marriage.

Family of Origin: The family of origin is the family into which an individual was born, and in which he or she was raised.

Family of Procreation: The family of procreation is the family in which a person has her or his own children.

Family Strategies: Family strategies are organized attempts by the members of a family to maintain or to improve their collective situation. (*See also* **strategy**).

Fertility: In the study of human population known as **demography**, fertility refers to the number of children a woman has in her lifetime. Average fertility is often expressed as the fertility rate, that is the number of births per thousand women.

Filial Piety: Filial piety is a devout attitude of respect from a child toward a parent, accompanied by a strong sense of the child's duty to follow the wishes of the parent.

Filial Responsibility: Filial responsibility is a sense of personal obligation to assist a parent who needs help.

Financial Control: Financial control means having the largest say over how money is spent. This is done either by managing all of the available money directly, or by supervising how someone else uses it and holding them accountable for what they do.

Function: A function performed by a social unit is the activity it carries out which fulfills some need, either for one or more members or for some larger social unit. The family is sometimes considered to be a basic social unit, which performs essential functions for its members (such as physical care) and for society (such as the reproduction of the next generation of citizens and workers).

Functional Prerequisite: A functional prerequisite is an element of a society that is essential to the maintenance of that society.

Functionalism: Functionalism is a theoretical approach which stresses the positive benefits of families, and which claims that families exist because of the ways in which they meet individual and collective needs.

Gendered Moral Rationalities: A gendered moral rationality is a set of moral rules which is used to construct a **moral identity** that reflects different expectations and situations for women and men.

Heteronormative: This concept refers to the taken-for-granted dominance of social assumptions based upon the typical experiences of heterosexuals.

High Modernity: High modernity is a late era of modernity in which social organizations and social relationships are constantly being created, redesigned, discarded and reconstituted due to increases in communications and growth in the circulation of goods and people. It is characterized by widespread scepticism, and awareness of the risks and dangers as well as benefits of modernization.

Home: A home is a private space in which family members can interact with one another without external interference.

Homeworking: Homeworking is paid employment that is carried out within the home.

Household: A household is a group of people who live together for the purpose of meeting their daily needs, particularly food and shelter. Household members almost always share at least some food, typically by eating meals together.

Housekeeping Allowance: A housekeeping allowance is a fixed sum of money that a **breadwinner** husband gives to his wife to meet the family's daily needs.

Human Capital: An individual's human capital is the stock of knowledge and set of skills that she or he possesses, as a result of the investments that have been made in his or her development, mainly by other people such as parents.

Ideology: An ideology is a shared system of beliefs and values that defines and justifies a particular way of life in opposition to other ways of living. It also identifies an ideal set of goals that people are expected to achieve in their private and public activities, in order to preserve and advance that way of life.

Illusion of Control: Illusions of control are unrealistic judgements about an individual's capacity to influence another person, due to accepting ideological assumptions about a harmony of interests between them.

Independent Management: Independent management of finances within families involves each person having a separate bank account and paying a share of the bills that reflect the individual's own expenses.

Individualization: Individualization is a collective process of change in which large numbers of people reject traditions, as well as religious and political definitions of social obligations, in favour of creating unique patterns of life for themselves by making individual choices about employment and personal relationships.

Industrialization: Industrialization is a process of technological and social change in which new machines are invented that use non-human sources of energy, such as steam power or electricity, to produce large quantities of goods.

Intensive Mothering: Intensive mothering is a self-sacrificing commitment made by a mother to focus most of her time and energy upon managing every aspect of the child's relationship with its environment.

Interhousehold Transactions: These are **transactions** that are carried out between people who live in different households.

Intrahousehold Transactions: These are **transactions** that are carried out between people who live in the same household.

Joint Actions: The term 'joint action' refers to any collective form of action that is a result of the participants fitting together their individual lines of behaviour.

Joint Family: A joint family is a family consisting of parents, their sons and daughters-in-law, and their grandchildren, who all live in one **household**.

Kinship Terminology: People who are related by descent, either directly or indirectly, are identified by kinship terms which classify them according to the kinds of relationships they have.

Legitimation: Legitimation is a social process of justification, whereby individuals seek support for their actions by trying to convince others that what they are doing is reasonable.

Liberal Welfare State: A liberal welfare state is one in which most individuals are expected to look after themselves, with the support of their families, but without a great deal of help from the state.

Life Course: The life course consists of a series of social positions through which an individual moves during the course of her or his life.

Longevity: The term longevity refers to how long someone lives, or in other words the length of a human life span.

Longitudinal Data: Longitudinal studies collect data on the same individuals at several points in time over a number of years. They are used to track the changes in people's lives, and to show the effects of early events on later life.

Marital Status: Marital status refers to an individual's position in a set of social categories defined in relation to marriage. Marital statuses include: single (that is, never married), cohabiting, legally married, separated, divorced and widowed. Today, the marital statuses of 'cohabiting' and 'legally married' are often combined into one category of 'married' persons.

Market Economy: A market economy is a network of interconnected individuals and organizations who buy and sell goods and services that are referred to as commodities. (*See also* **commodification**).

Marriage Work: Marriage work refers to personal reflection and action that is intended to ensure the stability of a marriage, and to produce the impression that it is satisfactory.

Matricentric Family: The matricentric family is a mother-centred type of family, in which the primary tie is between the mother and her children (especially her daughters), and where adult males are occasional visitors or temporary members.

Matrifocal Family: (*See* **matricentric family**).

Means Testing: 'Means testing' is the term used to describe the information that an applicant for welfare, or similar **targeted** income support programme, is required to supply about their financial situation and the extent of their need.

Modernity: Modernity is a type of culture that favours technological and social changes which will bring about human progress, including industrialization, urbanization, the growth of market economies and the expanded influence of the state.

Modernization: Modernization is a continuous process of change in which all social institutions become more specialized in order to become more efficient. This is done because it is believed that, in the long run, modernization guarantees progress in achieving a higher standard of living, a longer average lifespan, greater human health and happiness, and more individual liberty and gender equality.

Money Management: The way in which money is handled in order to meet a family's everyday needs, through shopping, banking, and paying bills, is referred to as money management.

Moral Identity: A moral identity is a social identity which is defined by its relationship to a set of moral rules.

Moral Panic: A moral panic is a sudden and widespread fear that morality has collapsed in certain important segments of society, and that this poses a threat to the social order and to the well-being of vulnerable individuals.

Negotiated Marriage: Negotiated marriage is a modern adaptation of arranged marriage, in which parents take into account the bride and groom's responses to each other in an arranged meeting.

Neolocal Residence: Neolocal residence is a living arrangement in which a newly married couple establishes an independent residence, separate from the **family of origin** of either partner.

Normal Violence: Forms of *violence* that are socially accepted as a normal part of everyday life within a particular culture are referred to as 'normal violence'.

Normative Guidelines: Normative guidelines are social rules about appropriate behaviour, which people are expected to use as guides to decision-making.

Nuclear Family: A nuclear family is a small reproductive group consisting of a wife and husband who live together, as well as the children of the union who live with their parents until they are ready to leave home.

Nurturant Socialization: Nuturant socialization consists of learning the culture of a society through close, caring relationships, such as that between mother and child.

Patriarchy: Patriarchy is the power exercized by older men over women and children. In feminist sociology, the term patriarchy is used specifically to describe persistent gender inequalities created by power differences between women and men.

Polyandry: Polyandry is the marriage of a woman to more than one man.

Polygamy: Polygamy is multiple marriage involving more than two spouses. It takes two main forms: **polygyny** (the most common form) and **polyandry** (found less often).

Polygyny: Polygyny is the marriage of a man to more than one woman.

Pooling: Partners' incomes are pooled when they are combined into a single 'pot' of money from which either partner may draw.

Population Aging: Population aging is a process of demographic change in which future populations will have a higher proportion of the population in older age groups than they do today.

Positivism: Positivism is a system of thought for understanding and improving the world, based on science.

Postmodernity: Postmodernity is a form of social life which comes after modernity. It is the result of a period of intensified change that creates uncertainty, ambiguity, cultural fragmentation and diversity.

Private Sphere: The private sphere is the domain of private life which is centred in the home, and that is physically and socially separated from such public institutions as the state and the market economy.

Pseudomutuality: This is a social situation in which two people who claim to treat each other as equals in fact do not give and receive in equal amounts, and they hide this fact from each other.

Public Sphere: The public sphere is an open field of organized human activity in mass societies. Public discourse takes place within diffuse networks of people who are interested in an issue; public opinion is expressed through collective social and political action; and economic exchange occurs in markets through which buyers and sellers who are otherwise unrelated meet to do business.

Pure Relationship: A pure relationship occurs when people enter into a voluntary personal relationship, and remain in it, because they believe it provides each individual with unique satisfactions.

Rational Choice Theory: Rational Choice Theory is a theoretical approach that studies the cumulative effects of choices made by individuals as they pursue their goals.

Reciprocity: Reciprocity is giving something back in return for something that was received earlier. A 'norm of reciprocity' is a social rule which requires a receiver to make a suitable return, either out of a sense of gratitude or a sense of indebtedness. (*See also* **social exchange**).

Reflexivity: Reflexivity is a socially organized practice of critically examining current conditions in order to determine how they should be changed.

Remittances: Remittances are transfers of money that migrants send to their relatives back home.

Rites of Passage: A rite of passage is a collective ritual that publicly marks an individual's **transition** from one role to another.

Role: A role is a socially defined position, for example the role of 'mother' in a family. It is constructed by family members themselves as they interact with one another, and as they are influenced by legal requirements as well as by community expectations and **ideologies**.

Role Conflict: Role conflict refers to contradictory, or incompatible, expectations that are sometimes applied to a person who occupies more than one role at the same time.

Role Differentiation: This is the process of dividing up rights and responsibilities that were once combined within one role, into two or more specialized sets of rights and responsibilities organized as separate roles.

Role Segregation: Role segregation is a sharp division of tasks between different roles, so that a person in one role does not do any of the tasks that are performed by a person in another role.

Romantic Fusion: Romantic fusion is an emotional state that is based on the belief that all of one's being is tied up in a romantic relationship with a partner. As a result, it is impossible to think of oneself as ever being separate from that person.

Secularization: Secularization is the process by which religious institutions and beliefs have less and less influence on social life over time.

Self Concept: An individual's self concept is the image that the person has of himself or herself, and the positive or negative judgement that the person makes about that image.

Self-provisioning: When families carry out tasks in order to produce goods or services that they would otherwise have to buy, they are said to be self-provisioning.

Service Sector: The service sector of the economy consists of industries that provide services to people rather than making things (known as manufacturing).

Sexual Abuse: The primary meaning of the term sexual abuse refers to inappropriate bodily contact of all kinds, including fondling, genital stimulation, oral and anal intercourse, as well as vaginal intercourse. The meaning of the term is sometimes extended to include inappropriate behaviour of a sexual nature that does not involve physical contact, such as exhibitionism ('flashing') and suggestive gestures or remarks. (*See also* **abuse**).

Social Capital: This concept refers to an individual's stock of social 'assets', such as information gained from other people or social supports, through which a person can gain access to other resources.

Social Democratic Welfare State: A social democratic welfare state is one in which the state assumes a major responsibility to support most social groups, in order to equalize their life chances and life conditions.

Social Distribution of Work: The term 'social distribution of work' refers to the way in which work is distributed unequally between people in different groups, or between people who occupy different roles, or between people who belong to different social categories such as men and women.

Social Exchange: In a relationship of social exchange, people are expected to provide appropriate returns for the things they receive from others. However, a return does not have to be immediate, and its value does not have to correspond exactly with what was received. (*See also* **reciprocity**).

Social Exclusion: Social exclusion is an unintended, or unacknowledged, consequence of a society's economic and political processes. Some groups have lesser opportunities than others to participate in major social institutions, due to lack of resources, or discrimination or neglect, and they are left out of government programmes. (*cf.* **social inclusion**).

Social Identity: A social identity is a set of personal characteristics that are believed to be typical of someone who occupies a particular social role, or who belongs to a particular social category.

Social Inclusion: Social inclusion is a deliberate outcome of public policies that are intended to recognize the diversity of groups which exist in a society. Government income supports and social services are delivered in such a way that every group has the opportunity to participate in major social institutions such as education. (*cf.* **social exclusion**).

Social Network: A person's social network is the set of people to whom they are connected, directly or indirectly, and with whom they engage in **transactions** of various kinds.

Spurious Correlation: A spurious correlation is a statistical relationship between three variables, in which an observed correlation between two of the variables is simply due to the fact that they are both correlated with the third variable.

State: The state is the total system of government in a country. It involves the exercise of power that ultimately rests upon means of compulsion. (*See also* **welfare state**).

Stem Family: A stem family consists of a succession of first-born sons, together with their wives and dependent children, who all live in one **household**.

Stepfamily: A stepfamily consists of a legally married or cohabiting couple living in the same household as one or more stepchildren who are the biological children of one of the adults but not of the other.

Stereotype: A stereotype is a highly simplified and inflexible image of the physical and behavioural characteristics of a category of people.

Strategy: A strategy is a sequence of planned actions whose ultimate goal is the well-being of one or more individuals. (*See also* **family strategies**).

Structural Prerequisite: A structural prerequisite is a particular type of social structure that is the only one that can possibly fulfil a particular function.

Structure: A structure consists of an arrangement of the parts of a system. A family structure is thus an arrangement of elements in a family system, such as the family **roles** of mother, father and child.

Surrogate Mother: A surrogate mother is a woman who acts on behalf of another woman who wishes to become a mother, by bearing a child for her.

Symbolic Interactionism: This is a theoretical approach which is concerned with the ways in which individuals define the meanings of their situations, as well as of themselves, in relation to others with whom they engage in joint actions.

Symmetrical Families: Symmetrical families contain couples in which wife and husband are both employed full time, and they share all the housework and childcare equally.

Taking Care of: Taking care of someone means watching over them and protecting them from harm, and providing the practical **caregiving** that enables them to flourish. (*cf.* **caring about**).

Targeted Programmes: Targeted programmes are government programmes that deliver social services or income benefits to selected groups which are recognized as having greater needs than the rest of the population. (*cf.* **universal programmes**).

Time–Space Distanciation: Time–space distanciation is the separation and reorganization of time and space, so that 'being together here and now' is replaced by multiple possibilities for being apart and being together in the future.

Time Stress: Time stress is the feeling that there is too much work to be done, and too little time in which to do it.

Trajectory: A sequence of **transitions** between different statuses in the **life course** is referred to as a trajectory.

Transactions: Transactions are interactions in which a social object such as money or information is transferred from one person to another, or a service such as preparing food is performed by one person for another person. (*See also* **interhousehold transactions** and **intrahousehold transactions**).

Transition: A transition is a change from one status to another; for instance from being without children to having children, or from being married to being divorced.

Universal Programmes: Universal programmes are government programmes that deliver social services or income benefits to everyone who has a recognized social status (for example, mother, elderly person) as a basic right of citizenship. (*cf.* **targeted programmes**).

Urbanization: This is a process of population change in which a growing proportion of a society's population becomes concentrated in cities. It occurs mainly as a result of population migration from rural to urban areas.

Violence: An act is said to be violent if it is intended to cause pain or physical injury to another person. (*See also* **normal violence**).

Welfare State: A welfare state is a system of government which is based on the principle that governments have an important role to play in meeting a variety of needs of many people, by providing public policies intended to deal with a range of social problems. (*See also* **state**; **liberal welfare state**; **corporatist welfare state**; and **social democratic welfare state**).

Whole Wage System: The whole wage system is a system of money management in which the main income earner in a couple (usually the husband) turns over all or most of his earnings to be managed by the other partner.

References

Abbott, P. and C. Wallace. *Family and the New Right*. London: Pluto Press, 1992.

Abdo-Zubi, N. *Family, Women and Social Change in the Middle East: The Palestinian Case*. Toronto: Canadian Scholars' Press, 1987.

Acker, J. 'Women, Families, and Public Policy in Sweden'. In E. N. Chow and C. W. Berheide (eds), *Women, the Family, and Policy: A Global Perspective*. Albany, NY: State University of New York Press, 1994, 33–50.

Adams, B. N. 'Fifty Years of Family Research', *Journal of Marriage and the Family*, 50, 1988, 5–17.

Ahlburg, D. and C. De Vita. 'New Realities of the American Family', *Population Bulletin*, 47, 1992, 2–43.

Al-Haj, M. 'Kinship and Modernization in Developing Societies: The Emergence of Instrumentalized Kinship', *Journal of Comparative Family Studies*, 26, 1995, 311–28.

Al Khateeb, S. 'Male/Female Relationship in Pre-Oil Saudi Family', *Family Perspective*, 30, 1996, 203–19.

Allan, G. *Kinship and Friendship in Modern Britain*. Oxford: Oxford University Press, 1996.

Allan, G. and G. Crow (eds). *Home and Family*. Basingstoke: Macmillan – now Palgrave, 1989.

Allatt, P. and S. Yeandle. *Youth Unemployment and the Family*. London: Routledge, 1992.

Allen, K. 'Lesbian and Gay Families'. In T. Arendell (ed.), *Contemporary Parenting*. Thousand Oaks, CA: Sage, 1997, 196–218.

Ambert, A.-M. *Ex-Spouses and New Spouses*. Greenwich, CT: JAI Press, 1989.

Anderson, E. 'Sex Codes and Family Life among Poor Inner-City Youths'. In W. J. Wilson (ed.), *The Ghetto Underclass*. Newbury Park, CA: Sage, 1993, 76–95.

Anleu, S. 'Reinforcing Gender Norms: Commercial and Altruistic Surrogacy'. *Acta Sociologica*, 33, 1990, 63–74.

Aponte, R. with B. Beal and M. Jiles. 'Ethnic Variation in the Family: The Elusive Trend toward Convergence'. In M. Sussman, S. Steinmetz and G. Peterson (eds), *Handbook of Marriage and the Family*, 2nd edn. New York: Plenum, 1999, 111–41.

Aquilino, W. 'Family Structure and Home-Leaving'. *Journal of Marriage and the Family*, 53, 1991, 999–1010.

Arber, S. 'Unequal Partners: Inequality in Earnings and Independent Income within Marriage'. In L. McKie, S. Bowlby and S. Gregory (eds), *Gender, Power and the Household*. Basingstoke: Macmillan – now Palgrave, 1999, 175–91.

Arber, S. and J. Ginn. 'Class and Caring: A Forgotten Dimension', *Sociology*, 26, 1992, 619–34.

Arber, S. and J. Ginn. 'Class, Caring and the Life Course'. In S. Arber and M. Evandrou (eds), *Ageing, Independence and the Life Course*. London: Jessica Kingsley, 1993, 149–68.

Arber, S. and J. Ginn. 'Gender Differences in Informal Caring'. In G. Allan (ed.), *The Sociology of the Family: A Reader*. Oxford: Blackwell, 1999, 321–39.

Arnup, K. 'In the Family Way: Lesbian Mothers in Canada'. In M. Luxton (ed.), *Feminism and Families*. Halifax, NS: Fernwood, 1997, 80–97.

Aronson, P., J. Mortimer, C. Zierman and M. Hacker. 'Generational Differences in Early Work Experiences and Evaluations.' In J. Mortimer and M. Finch (eds), *Adolescents, Work, and Family.* Thousand Oaks, CA: Sage, 1996, 25–62.

Atmore, C. 'Towards Rethinking Moral Panic: Child Sexual Abuse Conflicts and Social Constructionist Responses'. In C. Bagley and K. Mallick (eds), *Child Sexual Abuse and Adult Offenders.* Aldershot: Ashgate, 1999, 11–26.

Babcock, G. 'Stigma, Identity Dissonance, and the Nonresidential Mother'. In C. Everett (ed.), *Child Custody: Legal Decisions and Family Outcomes.* New York: Haworth, 1997, 139–56.

Baca Zinn, M. 'Family, Race, and Poverty in the Eighties', *Signs,* 14, 1989, 856–74.

Backett, K. 'The Negotiation of Fatherhood'. In C. Lewis and M. O'Brien (eds), *Reassessing Fatherhood.* London: Sage, 1987, 74–90.

Bala, N. 'The Evolving Canadian Definition of the Family', *International Journal of Law and the Family,* 8, 1994, 293–318.

Barrett, M. *Women's Oppression Today.* London: Verso, 1980.

Barrett, M. and M. McIntosh. *The Anti-social Family,* 2nd edn. London: Verso, 1991.

Bartholet, E. *Family Bonds: Adoption and the Politics of Parenting.* Boston: Houghton Mifflin, 1993.

Bauman, Z. *Intimations of Postmodernity.* London: Routledge, 1992.

Bawin-Legros, B. 'From Marriage to Remarriage: Ruptures and Continuities in Parenting'. In U. Björnberg (ed.), *European Parents in the 1990s.* New Brunswick, NJ: Transaction Publishers, 1992, 229–42.

Baxter, J. and E. Kane. 'Dependence and Independence: A Cross-National Analysis of Gender Inequality and Gender Attitudes', *Gender and Society,* 9, 1995, 193–215.

Beach, B. *Integrating Work and Family Life.* New York: State University of New York Press, 1989.

Beaujot, R. *Earning and Caring in Canadian Families.* Peterborough, ON: Broadview Press, 2000.

Beaujot, R., E. Gee, F. Rajulton and Z. Ravanera. *Family over the Life Course.* Ottawa: Statistics Canada, 1995.

Beck, U. *Risk Society.* London: Sage, 1992.

Beck, U. and E. Beck-Gernsheim. *The Normal Chaos of Love.* Cambridge: Polity Press, 1995.

Beck, U., A. Giddens and S. Lash. *Reflexive Modernization.* Stanford, CA: Stanford University Press, 1994.

Becker, G. 'Human Capital, Effort, and the Sexual Division of Labor', *Journal of Labor Economics,* 3, 1985, S33–S58.

Becker, G. *A Treatise on the Family,* enlarged edn. Cambridge, MA: Harvard University Press, 1991[1981].

Beck-Gernsheim, E. 'On the Way to a Post-Familial Family: From a Community of Need to Elective Affinities'. In M. Featherstone (ed.), *Love and Eroticism.* London: Sage, 1999, 53–70.

Bergen, R. *Wife Rape.* Thousand Oaks, CA: Sage, 1996.

Berger, P. and H. Kellner. 'Marriage and the Construction of Reality', *Diogenes,* 46, 1964, 1–24.

Bernardes, J. 'Do We Really Know What "The Family" Is?' In P. Close and R. Collins (eds), *Family and Economy in Modern Society.* Basingstoke: Macmillan – now Palgrave, 1985, 192–211.

Bernardes, J. 'We Must Not Define "The Family"!', *Marriage and Family Review,* 28, 1999, 21–41.

Berrington, A. and M. Murphy. 'Changes in the Living Arrangements of Young Adults in Britain During the 1980s', *European Sociological Review,* 10, 1994, 235–57.

Bertoia, C. and J. Drakich. 'The Fathers' Rights Movement'. In W. Marsiglio (ed.), *Fatherhood: Contemporary Theory, Research, and Social Policy.* Thousand Oaks, CA: Sage, 1995, 230–54.

Bianchi, S. 'Children of Poverty: Why Are They Poor?' In J. Chafel (ed.), *Child Poverty and Public Policy.* Washington, D.C.: Urban Institute Press, 1993, 91–125.

Bittman, M. and J. Pixley. *The Double Life of the Family.* St. Leonards, NSW: Allen and Unwin, 1997.

Björnberg, U. 'Single Mothers in Sweden'. In S. Duncan and R. Edwards (eds), *Single Mothers in an International Context.* London: UCL Press, 1997, 241–67.

Blaikie, A. 'From "Immorality" to "Underclass": The Current and Historical Context of Illegitimacy'. In J. Weeks and J. Holland (eds), *Sexual Cultures: Communities, Values and Intimacy.* New York: St. Martin's Press, 1996, 115–36.

Blieszner, R. and R. Hamon. 'Filial Responsibility: Attitudes, Motivators, and Behaviors'. In J. Dwyer and R. Coward (eds), *Gender, Families, and Elder Care.* Newbury Park, CA: Sage, 1992, 105–19.

Blumer, H. *Symbolic Interactionism.* Englewood Cliffs, NJ: Prentice-Hall, 1969.

Blumstein, P. and P. Schwartz. *American Couples: Money, Work, Sex.* New York: William Morrow, 1983.

Boss, P. 'Family Stress'. In M. Sussman and S. Steinmetz (eds), *Handbook of Marriage and the Family.* New York: Plenum Press, 1987, 695–723.

Boss, P. *Ambiguous Loss: Learning to Live with Unresolved Grief.* Cambridge, MA: Harvard University Press, 1999.

Boyd, M. and D. Norris. 'Leaving the Nest? The Impact of Family Structure'. *Canadian Social Trends*, 38, 1995, 14–17.

Brannen, J. and P. Moss. 'Dual Earner Households: Women's Financial Contributions After the Birth of the First Child'. In J. Brannen and G. Wilson (eds), *Give and Take in Families.* London: Allen and Unwin, 1987, 75–95.

Brannen, J. and P. Moss. 'British Households after Maternity Leave'. In S. Lewis, D. Izraeli and H. Hootsmans (eds), *Dual-Earner Families: International Perspectives.* London: Sage, 1992, 109–26.

Breines, W. and L. Gordon. ' The New Scholarship on Family Violence,' *Signs*, 8, 1983, 490–531.

Brodie, J. 'Canadian Women, Changing State Forms, and Public Policy'. In J. Brodie (ed.), *Women and Canadian Public Policy.* Toronto: Harcourt Brace, 1996, 1–28.

Brooks-Gunn, J., G. Duncan and N. Maritato. 'Poor Families, Poor Outcomes: The Well-Being of Children and Youth'. In G. Duncan and J. Brooks-Gunn (eds), *Consequences of Growing Up Poor.* New York: Russell Sage Foundation, 1997, 1–17.

Bulcroft, K., L. Smeins and R. Bulcroft. *Romancing the Honeymoon: Consummating Marriage in Modern Society.* Thousand Oaks, CA: Sage, 1999.

Burgess, E. 'The Family as a Unity of Interacting Personalities', *The Family*, 7, 1926, 3–9.

Burgess, E. *On Community, Family, and Delinquency.* Chicago: University of Chicago Press, 1973.

Burgess, E. and L. Cottrell. *Predicting Success or Failure in Marriage.* New York: Prentice-Hall, 1939.

Burgess, E. and H. Locke. *The Family: From Institution to Companionship.* New York: American Book Company, 1945.

Burns, A. and C. Scott. *Mother-Headed Families and Why They Have Increased.* Hillsdale, NJ: Lawrence Erlbaum, 1994.

Buunk, B. 'Marriage and Alternatives in the Netherlands'. In L. Shamgar-Handelman and R. Palomba (eds), *Alternative Patterns of Family Life in Modern Societies.* Rome: Collana Monografie, 1987, 317–29.

Call, K. 'The Implications of Helpfulness for Possible Selves.' In J. Mortimer and M. Finch (eds), *Adolescents, Work, and Family.* Thousand Oaks, CA: Sage, 1996, 63–96.

Canada, Royal Commission on New Reproductive Technologies. *Research Studies of the Royal Commission on New Reproductive Technologies, vol. 3: Overview of Legal Issues in New Reproductive Technologies.* Ottawa: Supply and Services Canada, 1993a.

Canada, Royal Commission on New Reproductive Technologies. *Research Studies of the Royal Commission on New Reproductive Technologies, vol. 4: Legal and Ethical Issues in New Reproductive Technologies: Pregnancy and Parenthood.* Ottawa: Supply and Services Canada, 1993b.

Cantor, C. and P. Slater. 'Marital Breakdown, Parenthood, and Suicide', *Journal of Family Studies*, 1, 1995, 91–102.

Caplow, T. *American Social Trends.* San Diego: Harcourt Brace Jovanovich, 1991.

Caplow, T. and H. Mendras. 'Introduction: Convergence or Divergence?' In S. Langlois with T. Caplow, H. Mendras and W. Glatzer (eds), *Convergence or Divergence?* Montreal and Kingston: McGill-Queen's University Press, 1995, 1–21.

Carmichael, G., A. Webster and P. McDonald. 'Divorce Australian Style: A Demographic Analysis'. In C. Everett (ed.), *Divorce and Remarriage: International Studies.* New York: Haworth, 1997, 3–37.

Central Statistical Office. *Social Trends 25.* London: HMSO, 1995.

Chappell, N. 'Aging and the Family'. In G. N. Ramu (ed.), *Marriage and the Family in Canada Today.* Scarborough, ON: Prentice-Hall, 1989, 185–206.

Chayovan, N. 'Elderly Women in Thailand: Their Role, Status and Family Supports', *Australian Journal on Ageing*, 13, 1994, 182–5.

Cheal, D. 'Intergenerational Family Transfers', *Journal of Marriage and the Family*, 45, 1983, 805–13.

Cheal, D. 'The Social Dimensions of Gift Behaviour', *Journal of Social and Personal Relationships*, 3, 1986, 423–39.

Cheal, D. *The Gift Economy.* London: Routledge, 1988.

Cheal, D. 'Theoretical Frameworks'. In G. N. Ramu (ed.), *Marriage and the Family in Canada Today.* Scarborough, Ont.: Prentice-Hall Canada, 1989, 19–34.

Cheal, D. *Family and The State of Theory.* Hemel Hempstead/Toronto: Harvester Wheatsheaf/University of Toronto Press, 1991.

Cheal, D. 'Unity and Difference in Postmodern Families', *Journal of Family Issues*, 14, 1993a, 5–19.

Cheal, D. 'Changing Household Financial Strategies: Canadian Couples Today', *Human Ecology*, 21, 1993b, 197–213.

Cheal, D. *New Poverty: Families in Postmodern Society.* Westport, CT: Greenwood Press, 1996a.

Cheal, D. 'Stories about Step-families'. In Human Resources Development Canada and Statistics Canada (eds), *Growing Up in Canada: National Longitudinal Survey of Children and Youth.* Ottawa: Statistics Canada, 1996b, 93–101.

Cheal, D. 'Sociology and Social Reform', *Canadian Journal of Sociology*, 22, 1997a, 113–22.

Cheal, D. 'Hidden in the Household: Poverty and Dependence at Different Ages'. Presented to the *Conference on Intergenerational Equity in Canada*, Ottawa, February 20–21, 1997b.

Cheal, D. 'Poverty and Relative Income: Family Transactions and Social Policy'. In D. Cheal, F. Woolley and M. Luxton, *How Families Cope and Why Policymakers Need to Know.* Ottawa: Renouf, 1998, 1–26.

Cheal, D. 'Marriage: Barrier or Blessing? Wives' Employment in Canada'. In S. Lee Browning and R. Miller (eds), *Till Death Do Us Part: A Multicultural Anthology on Marriage.* Stamford, CT: JAI Press, 1999, 163–81.

Che-Alford, J., C. Allan and G. Butlin. *Families in Canada*. Ottawa: Statistics Canada, 1994.

Chia, A. 'Singapore's Economic Internationalization and its Effects on Work and Family', *SOJOURN: Journal of Social Issues in Southeast Asia*, 15, 2000, 123–38.

Christensen, D. H. and K. Rettig. 'The Relationship of Remarriage to Post-Divorce Co-Parenting'. In C. Everett (ed.), *Understanding Stepfamilies: Their Structure and Dynamics*. New York: Haworth, 1995, 73–88.

Cochran, M. and L. Gunnarsson, with S. Gräbe and J. Lewis. 'The Social Networks of Coupled Mothers in Four Cultures'. In M. Cochran, M. Larner, D. Riley, L. Gunnarsson and C. Henderson, *Extending Families: The Social Networks of Parents and Their Children*. Cambridge: Cambridge University Press, 1990, 86–104.

Cohen, S. and M.F. Katzenstein. 'The War over the Family Is Not over the Family'. In S. Dornbusch and M. Strober (eds), *Feminism, Children, and the New Families*. New York: Guilford Press, 1988, 25–46.

Coleman, J. S. *Foundations of Social Theory*. Cambridge, MA: Harvard University Press, 1990.

Coleman, M., L. Ganong and S. Cable. 'Beliefs About Women's Intergenerational Family Obligations to Provide Support Before and After Divorce and Remarriage', *Journal of Marriage and the Family*, 59, 1997, 165–76.

Coleman, M., L. Ganong, T. Killian and A. McDaniel. 'Child Support Obligations', *Journal of Family Issues*, 20, 1999, 46–68.

Collier, J., M. Rosaldo and S. Yanagisako. 'Is There a Family?' In B. Thorne and M. Yalom (eds), *Rethinking the Family*, revised edn. Boston: Northeastern University Press, 1992, 31–48.

Conger, R., G. Elder, F. Lorenz, R. Simons and L. Whitbeck. *Families in Troubled Times*. New York: Aldine de Gruyter, 1994.

Cook, C. and R. Beaujot. 'Labour Force Interruptions: The Influence of Marital Status and Presence of Young Children', *Canadian Journal of Sociology*, 21, 1996, 25–41.

Coontz, S. *The Way We Never Were*. New York: Basic Books, 1992.

Coward, R., C. Horne and J. Dwyer. 'Demographic Perspectives on Gender and Family Caregiving'. In J. Dwyer and R. Coward (eds), *Gender, Families, and Elder Care*. Newbury Park, CA: Sage, 1992, 18–33.

Cranswick, K. 'Canada's Caregivers', *Canadian Social Trends*, 47, 1997, 2–6.

Cretser, G. 'Intermarriage Between "White" Britons and Immigrants from the New Commonwealth and Pakistan', *Journal of Comparative Family Studies*, 21, 1990, 227–38.

Crompton, R. *Women and Work in Modern Britain*. Oxford: Oxford University Press, 1997.

Crow, G. and M. Hardey. 'The Housing Strategies of Lone Parents.' In M. Hardey and G. Crow (eds), *Lone Parenthood*. Toronto: University of Toronto Press, 1991, 47–65.

Cuisenier, J. (ed.) *The Family Life Cycle in European Societies*. The Hague: Mouton, 1977.

Daatland, S. ' "What are Families For?" On Family Solidarity and Preference for Help', *Ageing and Society*, 10, 1990, 1–15.

d'Abbs, P. *Who Helps? Support Networks and Social Policy in Australia*. Melbourne: Australian Institute of Family Studies, 1991.

Dalley, G. 'Caring: A Legitimate Interest of Older Women'. In M. Bernard and K. Meade (eds), *Women Come of Age: Perspectives on the Lives of Older Women*. London: Edward Arnold, 1993, 106–25.

Dallos, R. and R. Sapsford. 'Patterns of Diversity and Lived Realities'. In J. Muncie, M. Wetherell, M. Langan, R. Dallos and A. Cochrane (eds), *Understanding the Family*, 2nd edn. London: Sage, 1997, 125–70.

Dalton, S. and D. Bielby. ' "That's Our Kind of Constellation" Lesbian Mothers Negotiate Institutionalized Understandings of Gender within the Family', *Gender and Society*, 14, 2000, 36–61.

Daune-Richard, A.-M. 'Gender Relations and Female Labor'. In J. Jenson, E. Hagen and C. Reddy (eds), *Feminization of the Labor Force*. New York: Oxford University Press, 1988, 260–75.

Dennis, N. and G. Erdos. *Families Without Fatherhood*. London: IEA Health and Welfare Unit, 1992.

Denzin, N. K. 'Postmodern Children', *Society*, 24, 1987, 32–5.

Derné, S. *Culture in Action*. Albany, NY: State University of New York Press, 1995.

Devereaux, M. 'Time Use of Canadians in 1992', *Social Trends*, 30, 1993, 13–16.

Dhruvarajan, V. *Hindu Women and the Power of Ideology*. Granby, MA: Bergin and Garvey, 1989.

Diamond, I. and S. Clarke. 'Demographic Patterns among Britain's Ethnic Groups'. In H. Joshi (ed.), *The Changing Population of Britain*. Oxford: Blackwell, 1989, 177–98.

Dobash, R. P., R. E. Dobash , K. Cavanagh and R. Lewis. 'Separate and Intersecting Realities: A Comparison of Men's and Women's Accounts of Violence Against Women,' *Violence Against Women*, 4, 1998, 382–414.

Domingo, L. 'The Family and Women in an Ageing Society: The Philippine Situation', *Australian Journal on Ageing*, 13, 1994, 178–81.

Donovan, C. 'Who Needs a Father? Negotiating Biological Fatherhood in British Lesbian Families Using Self-Insemination', *Sexualities*, 3, 2000, 149–64.

Dooley, M. 'Recent Changes in the Economic Welfare of Lone Mother Families in Canada: The Roles of Market Work, Earnings and Transfers.' In J. Hudson and B. Galaway (eds), *Single Parent Families*. Toronto: Thompson Educational Publishing, 1993, 115–31.

Duffy, A. and J. Momirov. *Family Violence: A Canadian Introduction*. Toronto: James Lorimer, 1997.

Duffy, A. and N. Pupo. *The Part-Time Paradox: Connecting Gender, Work and Family*. Toronto: McClelland and Stewart, 1992.

Duncan, S. and R. Edwards. 'Single Mothers in Britain'. In S. Duncan and R. Edwards (eds), *Single Mothers in an International Context*. London: UCL Press, 1997, 45–79.

Duncan, S. and R. Edwards. *Lone Mothers, Paid Work and Gendered Moral Rationalities*. Basingstoke: Macmillan – now Palgrave, 1999.

Duncombe, J. and D. Marsden. ' "Workaholics" and "Whingeing Women": Theorising Intimacy and Emotion Work – The Last Frontier of Gender Inequality?', *Sociological Review*, 43, 1995, 150–69.

Duncombe, J. and D. Marsden. 'Whose Orgasm is this Anyway? "Sex Work" in Long-term Heterosexual Relationships'. In J. Weeks and J. Holland (eds), *Sexual Cultures: Communities, Values and Intimacy*. New York: St. Martin's Press, 1996, 220–38.

Durkheim, E. *Suicide*. Glencoe, IL: Free Press, 1951[1897].

Dykstra, P. and C. Knipscheer. 'The Availability and Intergenerational Structure of Family Relationships'. In C. Knipscheer, J. de Jong Gierveld, T. van Tilburg and P. Dykstra (eds), *Living Arrangements and Social Networks of Older Adults*. Amsterdam: VU University Press, 1995, 37–58.

Edin, K. and L. Lein. *Making Ends Meet: How Single Mothers Survive Welfare and Low-Wage Work*. New York: Russell Sage, 1997.

Edwards, S. 'Policing "Domestic Violence". In P. Abbott and C. Wallace (eds), *Gender, Power and Sexuality*. Basingstoke: Macmillan – now Palgrave, 1991, 133–56.

Eichler, M. 'The Inadequacy of the Monolithic Model of the Family', *Canadian Journal of Sociology*, 6, 1981, 367–88.

Eichler, M. *Family Shifts*. Toronto: Oxford University Press, 1997.

Elder, G. *Children of the Great Depression*. Chicago: University of Chicago Press, 1974.

Elder, G. 'Perspectives on the Life Course'. In G. Elder (ed.), *Life Course Dynamics*. Ithaca, NY: Cornell University Press, 1985, 23–49.

Elkind, D. 'The Family in the Postmodern World', *National Forum*, 75, 1995, 24–8.

Esping-Andersen, Gøsta. *The Three Worlds of Welfare Capitalism*. Princeton, NJ: Princeton University Press, 1990.

Esping-Andersen, Gøsta. 'The Three Political Economies of the Welfare State'. In J. Kolberg (ed.), *The Study of Welfare State Regimes*. Armonk, NY: M. E. Sharpe, 1992, 92–123.

Evans, P. 'Single Mothers and Ontario's Welfare Policy'. In J. Brodie (ed.), *Women and Canadian Public Policy*. Toronto: Harcourt Brace, 1996, 151–71.

Evans, P. 'Divided Citizenship? Gender, Income Security, and the Welfare State'. In P. Evans and G. Wekerle (eds), *Women and the Canadian Welfare State*. Toronto: University of Toronto Press, 1997, 91–116.

Ewing, C. *Fatal Families: The Dynamics of Intrafamilial Homicide*. Thousand Oaks, CA: Sage, 1997.

Falicov, C. (ed.) *Family Transitions: Continuity and Change over the Life Cycle*. New York: Guilford Press, 1988.

Farley, R. *State of the Union: America in the 1990s, vol. 1: Economic Trends*. New York: Russell Sage Foundation, 1995.

Faust, K. and J. McKibben. 'Marital Dissolution: Divorce, Separation, Annulment, and Widowhood'. In M. Sussman, S. Steinmetz and G. Peterson (eds), *Handbook of Marriage and the Family*, 2nd edn. New York: Plenum, 1999, 475–99.

Finch, J. 'Family Obligations and the Life Course'. In A. Bryman, B. Bytheway, P. Allatt and T. Keil (eds), *Rethinking the Life Cycle*. Basingstoke: Macmillan – now Palgrave, 1987, 155–69.

Finch, J. *Family Obligations and Social Change*. Cambridge: Polity Press, 1989.

Finch, J. and J. Mason. 'Filial Obligations and Kin Support for Elderly People', *Ageing and Society*, 10, 1990a, 151–75.

Finch, J. and J. Mason. 'Divorce, Remarriage and Family Obligations', *Sociological Review*, 38, 1990b, 219–46.

Finch, J. and J. Mason. *Negotiating Family Responsibilities*. London: Routledge, 1993.

Finch, J. and P. Summerfield. 'Social Reconstruction and the Emergence of Companionate Marriage, 1945–59'. In D. Clark (ed.), *Marriage, Domestic Life and Social Change*. London: Routledge, 1991, 7–32.

Fine, B. *Women's Employment and the Capitalist Family*. London: Routledge, 1992.

Fisher, B. and J. Tronto. 'Toward a Feminist Theory of Caring'. In E. Abel and M. Nelson (eds), *Circles of Care*. Albany, NY: State University of New York, 1990, 35–62.

Flandrin, J.-L. *Families in Former Times*. Cambridge: Cambridge University Press, 1979.

Folk, K. 'For Love or Money: Costs of Child Care by Relatives', *Journal of Family and Economic Issues*, 15, 1994, 243–60.

Foucault, M. *The History of Sexuality, vol. 1*. New York: Pantheon, 1978.

Fox, B. 'Reproducing Difference: Changes in the Lives of Partners Becoming Parents'. In M. Luxton (ed.), *Feminism and Families*. Halifax, NS: Fernwood, 1997, 142–61.

Frederick, J. '*Tempus Fugit*: Are You Time Crunched?', *Canadian Social Trends*, 31, 1993, 6–9.

Frederick, J. *As Time Goes By: Time Use of Canadians*. Ottawa: Statistics Canada, 1995.

Galarneau, D. and J. Sturrock. 'Family Income After Separation', *Perspectives on Labour and Income*, 9 (2), 1997, 18–28.

Garey, A. 'Constructing Motherhood on the Night Shift: "Working Mothers" as "Stay-at-Home Moms" ', *Qualitative Sociology*, 18, 1995, 415–37.

Gelles, R. J. 'Family Reunification/Family Preservation: Are Children Really Being Protected?', *Journal of Interpersonal Violence*, 8, 1993, 557–62.

Gelles, R. J. *Intimate Violence in Families*, 3rd edn. Thousand Oaks, CA: Sage, 1997.

Gelles, R. J. and J. R. Conte. 'Domestic Violence and Sexual Abuse of Children: A Review of Research in the Eighties', *Journal of Marriage and the Family*, 52, 1990, 1045–58.

George, L. 'Sociological Perspectives on Life Transitions'. In J. Blake and J. Hagen (eds), *Annual Review of Sociology, vol. 19*. Palo Alto, CA: Annual Reviews Inc., 1993, 353–73.

Gerson, K. *No Man's Land*. New York: Basic, 1993.

Gerson, K. 'The Social Construction of Fatherhood'. In T. Arendell (ed.), *Contemporary Parenting*. Thousand Oaks, CA: Sage, 1997, 119–53.

Gerstel, N. and H. Gross. *Commuter Marriage*. New York: Guilford Press, 1984.

Ghalam, N. Z. *Women in the Workplace*, 2nd edn. Ottawa: Statistics Canada, 1993.

Giddens, A. *The Consequences of Modernity*. Stanford, CA: Stanford University Press, 1990.

Giddens, A. *Modernity and Self-Identity*. Stanford, CA: Stanford University Press, 1991.

Giddens, A. *The Transformation of Intimacy*. Stanford, CA: Stanford University Press, 1992.

Ginn, J. and S. Arber. 'Towards Women's Independence: Pension Systems in Three Contrasting European Welfare States', *Journal of European Social Policy*, 2, 1992, 255–77.

Glenn, E. N. 'Social Constructions of Mothering: A Thematic Overview'. In E. N. Glenn, G. Chang and L. R. Forcey (eds), *Mothering: Ideology, Experience, and Agency*. New York: Routledge, 1994, 1–29.

Goldscheider, F. and C. Goldscheider. *The Changing Transition to Adulthood: Leaving and Returning Home*. Thousand Oaks, CA: Sage, 1999.

Goode, E. and N. Ben-Yehuda. 'Moral Panics'. In J. Hagan and K. Cook (eds), *Annual Review of Sociology, vol. 20*. Palo Alto, CA: Annual Reviews Inc., 1994, 149–71.

Graham, H. 'Budgeting for Health: Mothers in Low-income Households'. In C. Glendinning and J. Millar (eds), *Women and Poverty in Britain, the 1990s*. Hemel Hempstead: Harvester Wheatsheaf, 1992, 209–24.

Greif, G. and M. Pabst. *Mothers Without Custody*. Lexington, MA: D. C. Heath, 1988.

Grinwald, S. and T. Shabat. 'The "Invisible" Figure of the Deceased Spouse in a Remarriage'. In C. Everett (ed.), *Divorce and Remarriage: International Studies*. New York: Haworth, 1997, 105–13.

Gross, H. E. 'Couples Who Live Apart: Time/Place Disjunctions and Their Consequences', *Symbolic Interaction*, 3, 1980, 69–82.

Gubrium, J. 'Organizational Embeddedness and Family Life'. In T. Brubaker (ed.), *Aging, Health, and Family*. Newbury Park, CA: Sage, 1987, 23–41.

Gubrium, J. and J. Holstein. *What is Family?* Mountain View, CA: Mayfield, 1990.

Gullestad, M. 'Home Decoration as Popular Culture: Constructing Homes, Genders and Classes in Norway'. In S. Jackson and S. Moores (eds), *The Politics of Domestic Consumption*. New York/Hemel Hempstead: Prentice Hall/Harvester Wheatsheaf, 1995, 321–35.

Gunnarsson, L. and M. Cochran. 'The Social Networks of Single Parents: Sweden and the United States'. In M. Cochran, M. Larner, D. Riley, L. Gunnarsson and C. Henderson, *Extending Families: The Social Networks of Parents and Their Children*. Cambridge: Cambridge University Press, 1990, 105–16.

Haas, L. 'Family Policy in Sweden', *Journal of Family and Economic Issues*, 17, 1996, 47–92.

Haas, L. 'Families and Work'. In M. Sussman, S. Steinmetz and G. Peterson (eds), *Handbook of Marriage and the Family*, 2nd edn. New York: Plenum, 1999, 571–612.

Hackstaff, K. *Marriage in a Culture of Divorce*. Philadelphia: Temple University Press, 1999.

Haj-Yahia, M. 'A Patriarchal Perspective of Beliefs About Wife Beating Among Palestinian Men From the West Bank and the Gaza Strip', *Journal of Family Issues*, 19, 1998, 595–621.

Hardey, M. and J. Glover. 'Income, Employment, Daycare and Lone Parenthood'. In M. Hardey and G. Crow (eds), *Lone Parenthood*. Toronto: University of Toronto Press, 1991, 88–109.

Harrison, D. and L. Laliberté. *No Life Like It: Military Wives in Canada*. Toronto: James Lorimer and Co., 1994.

Hartley, R. *What Price Independence? Report of a Study on Young People's Incomes and Living Costs*. Melbourne: Youth Affairs Council of Victoria, 1989.

Hartley, R. (ed.) *Families and Cultural Diversity in Australia*. St. Leonards, NSW: Allen and Unwin, 1995.

Hashimoto, A. *The Gift of Generations*. Cambridge: Cambridge University Press, 1996.

Haskey, J. 'Families and Households of the Ethnic Minority and White Populations of Great Britain', *Population Trends*, 57, 1989, 8–19.

Hays, S. *The Cultural Contradictions of Motherhood*. New Haven: Yale University Press, 1996.

Heaphy, B., C. Donovan and J. Weeks. 'Sex, Money and the Kitchen Sink: Power in Same-Sex Couple Relationships'. In J. Seymour and P. Bagguley (eds), *Relating Intimacies: Power and Resistance*. Basingstoke: Macmillan – now Palgrave, 1999, 222–45.

Heaton, T. 'Socioeconomic and Familial Status of Women Associated with Age at First Marriage in Three Islamic Societies', *Journal of Comparative Family Studies*, 27, 1996, 41–58.

Hendry, J. *Marriage in Changing Japan*. London: Croom Helm, 1981.

Hernandez, D. *America's Children*. New York: Russell Sage Foundation, 1995.

Hernandez, D. 'Children's Changing Access to Resources'. In K. Hansen and A. Garey (eds), *Families in the U.S.* Philadelphia, PA: Temple University Press, 1998, 201–15.

Hertz, R. *More Equal Than Others: Women and Men in Dual-Career Marriages*. Berkeley: University of California Press, 1986.

Hester, M., L. Kelly and J. Radford (eds). *Women, Violence and Male Power*. Buckingham: Open University Press, 1996.

Hester, M. and L. Radford. 'Contradictions and Compromises: The Impact of the Children Act on Women and Children's Safety'. In M. Hester, L. Kelly and J. Radford (eds), *Women, Violence, and Male Power*. Buckingham: Open University Press, 1996, 81–98.

Hill, R. 'Modern Systems Theory and the Family', *Social Science Information*, 10, 1971, 7–26.

Hobson, B. 'No Exit, No Voice: Women's Economic Dependency and the Welfare State', *Acta Sociologica*, 33, 1990, 235–50.

Hochschild, A. *The Second Shift*. New York: Viking Penguin, 1989.

Hochschild, A. 'Ideals of Care: Traditional, Postmodern, Cold-Modern and Warm-Modern'. In K. Hansen and A. Garey (eds), *Families in the U.S.* Philadelphia, PA: Temple University Press, 1998, 527–38.

Hodgson, L. G. 'Adult Grandchildren and Their Grandparents'. In J. Hendricks (ed.), *The Ties of Later Life*. Amityville, NY: Baywood, 1995, 155–70.

Hoem, B. and J. Hoem. 'The Swedish Family', *Journal of Family Issues*, 9, 1988, 397–424.

Hoffmann-Riem, C. *The Adopted Child: Family Life with Double Parenthood*. New Brunswick, NJ: Transaction Publishers, 1990.

Holden, K. and P. Smock. 'The Economic Costs of Marital Dissolution'. In W. R. Scott and J. Blake (eds), *Annual Review of Sociology, vol. 17*. Palo Alto, CA: Annual Reviews Inc., 1991, 51–78.

Holstein, J. and J. Gubrium. 'What Is Family? Further Thoughts on a Social Constructionist Approach', *Marriage and Family Review*, 28, 1999, 3–20.

Hoodfar, H. 'The Impact of Male Migration on Domestic Budgeting: Egyptian Women Striving for an Islamic Budgeting Pattern', *Journal of Comparative Family Studies*, 28, 1997, 73–98.

Horrell, S. 'Household Time Allocation and Women's Labour Force Participation'. In M. Anderson, F. Bechhofer and J. Gershuny (eds), *The Social and Political Economy of the Household*. Oxford: Oxford University Press, 1994, 198–224.

Hsiung, P. *Living Rooms as Factories*. Philadelphia, PA: Temple University Press, 1996.

Hunsley, T. *Lone Parent Incomes and Social Policy Outcomes*. Kingston, ON: School of Policy Studies, Queen's University, 1997.

Hurtado, A. 'Variations, Combinations, and Evolutions: Latino Families in the United States'. In R. Zambrana (ed.), *Understanding Latino Families*. Thousand Oaks, CA: Sage, 1995, 40–61.

Ihinger-Tallman, M. and K. Pasley. 'Stepfamilies in 1984 and Today – A Scholarly Perspective'. In I. Levin and M. Sussman (eds), *Stepfamilies: History, Research, and Policy*. New York: Haworth, 1997, 19–40.

Itzigsohn, J. 'Migrant Remittances, Labor Markets, and Household Strategies', *Social Forces*, 74, 1995, 633–55.

Jagger, G. and C. Wright (eds). *Changing Family Values*. London: Routledge, 1999.

Jamieson, L. 'Intimacy Transformed? A Critical Look at the Pure Relationship', *Sociology*, 33, 1999, 477–94.

Jenson, J. and S. Jacobzone. *Care Allowances for the Frail Elderly and Their Impact on Women Care-Givers*. Paris: Organisation for Economic Co-operation and Development, 2000.

Johnson, H. 'Seriousness, Type and Frequency of Violence Against Wives'. In M. Valverde, L. MacLeod and K. Johnson (eds), *Wife Assault and the Canadian Criminal Justice System*. Toronto: Centre of Criminology, University of Toronto, 1995, 125–47.

Jolivet, M. *Japan: The Childless Society?* London: Routledge, 1997.

Jones, C., L. Marsden and L. Tepperman. *Lives of Their Own: The Individualization of Women's Lives*. Toronto: Oxford University Press, 1990.

Jones, G. 'Short-term Reciprocity in Parent-Child Economic Exchanges'. In C. Marsh and S. Arber (eds), *Families and Households*. New York: St. Martin's Press, 1992, 26–44.

Jones, G. *Leaving Home*. Buckingham: Open University Press, 1995.

Jones, G. W. *Marriage and Divorce in Islamic South-East Asia*. Oxford: Oxford University Press, 1994.

Jordan, B., M. Redley and S. James. *Putting the Family First*. London: UCL Press, 1994.

Júlíusdóttir, S. 'An Icelandic Study of Five Parental Life Styles: Conditions of Fathers Without Custody and Mothers With Custody'. In C. Everett (ed.), *Divorce and Remarriage: International Studies*. New York: Haworth, 1997, 87–103.

Kanjanapan, W. 'The Asian-American Traditional Household'. In F. Goldscheider and C. Goldscheider (eds), *Ethnicity and the New Family Economy*. Boulder, CO: Westview Press, 1989, 39–55.

Karanja, W. 'The Phenomenon of "Outside Wives": Some Reflections on its Possible Influence on Fertility'. In C. Bledsoe, and G. Pison (eds), *Nuptiality in Sub-Saharan Africa*. Oxford: Clarendon Press, 1994, 194–214.

Keating, N., J. Fast, J. Frederick, K. Cranswick and C. Perrier. *Eldercare in Canada*. Ottawa: Statistics Canada, 1999.

Kelly, L. *Surviving Sexual Violence*. Minneapolis: University of Minnesota Press, 1988.

Kelly, L. and J. Radford. ' "Nothing Really Happened": The Invalidation of Women's Experiences of Sexual Violence'. In M. Hester, L. Kelly and J. Radford (eds), *Women, Violence and Male Power*. Buckingham: Open University Press, 1996, 19–33.

Kempson, E., A. Bryson and K. Rowlingson. *Hard Times? How Poor Families Make Ends Meet*. London: Policy Studies Institute, 1994.

Kendall, L. *Getting Married in Korea*. Berkeley: University of California Press, 1996.

Kendig, H. 'Housing Careers, Life Cycle and Residential Mobility', *Urban Studies*, 21, 1984, 271–83.

Kiernan, K. and V. Estaugh. *Cohabitation: Extra-marital Childbearing and Social Policy*. London: Family Policy Studies Centre, 1993.

Kissman, K. 'Noncustodial Fatherhood: Research Trends and Issues'. In C. Everett (ed.), *Child Custody: Legal Decisions and Family Outcomes*. New York: Haworth, 1997, 77–88.

Klett-Davies, M. 'Single Mothers in Germany'. In S. Duncan and R. Edwards (eds), *Single Mothers in an International Context*. London: UCL Press, 1997, 179–215.

Kojima, H. 'Intergenerational Household Extension in Japan'. In F. Goldscheider and C. Goldscheider (eds), *Ethnicity and the New Family Economy*. Boulder, CO: Westview Press, 1989, 163–84.

Kontula, O. and E. Haavio-Mannila. *Sexual Pleasures: Enhancement of Sex Life in Finland, 1971–1992*. Aldershot: Dartmouth, 1995.

Kruk, E. *Divorce and Disengagement: Patterns of Fatherhood Within and Beyond Marriage*. Halifax, NS: Fernwood, 1993.

Kryder-Coe, J., L. Salamon and J. Molnar. *Homeless Children and Youth*. New Brunswick, NJ: Transaction Publishers, 1991.

Kumagai, F. 'Modernization and the Family in Japan', *Journal of Family History*, 11, 1986, 371–82.

Kumagai, F. 'Families in Japan', *Journal of Comparative Family Studies*, 26, 1995, 135–63.

Kurz, D. *For Richer, For Poorer: Mothers Confront Divorce*. New York: Routledge, 1995.

La Fontaine, J. *Child Sexual Abuse*. Cambridge: Polity Press, 1990.

Lamphere, L., P. Zavella, and F. Gonzales with P. Evans. *Sunbelt Working Mothers*. Ithaca, NY: Cornell University Press, 1993.

Langford, W. *Revolutions of the Heart: Gender, Power and the Delusions of Love*. London: Routledge, 1999.

Laurie, H. and D. Rose. 'Divisions and Allocations Within Households'. In N. Buck, J. Gershuny, D. Rose and J. Scott (eds), *Changing Households*. Colchester: ESRC Research Centre on Micro-social Change, 1994, 220–42.

Lawson, A. *Adultery: An Analysis of Love and Betrayal*. New York: Basic Books, 1988.

Lehmann, J. 'Durkheim's Response to Feminism', *Sociological Theory*, 8, 1990, 163–87.

Lehmann, J. 'Durkheim's Women: His Theory of the Structures and Functions of Sexuality'. In B. Agger (ed.), *Current Perspectives in Social Theory, vol. 11*. Greenwich, CT: JAI Press, 1991, 141–67.

Leira, A. *Welfare States and Working Mothers*. Cambridge: Cambridge University Press, 1992.

Leira, A. 'Combining Work and Family: Working Mothers in Scandinavia and the European Community'. In P. Brown and R. Crompton (eds), *Economic Restructuring and Social Exclusion*. London: UCL Press, 1994, 86–107.

Lero, D. and L. Brockman. 'Single Parent Families in Canada: A Closer Look'. In J. Hudson and B. Galaway (eds), *Single Parent Families*. Toronto: Thompson Educational Publishing, 1993, 91–114.

Lero, D., H. Goelman, A. Pence, L. Brockman and S. Nuttall. *Canadian National Child Care Study: Parental Work Patterns and Child Care Needs*. Ottawa: Statistics Canada, 1992.

Levin, I. 'Stepfamily as Project'. In I. Levin and M. Sussman (eds), *Stepfamilies: History, Research, and Policy*. New York: Haworth, 1997, 123–33.

Levin, I. and J. Trost. 'Living Apart Together', *Community, Work and Family*, 2, 1999, 279–94.

Lewis, J. 'Gender and the Development of Welfare Regimes', *Journal of European Social Policy*, 2, 1992, 159–73.

Lewis, J. 'Introduction: Women, Work, Family and Social Policies in Europe'. In J. Lewis (ed.), *Women and Social Policies in Europe*. Aldershot: Edward Elgar, 1993, 1–24.

Lichter, D. 'Poverty and Inequality Among Children'. In J. Hagan and K. Cook (eds), *Annual Review of Sociology, vol. 23*. Palo Alto, CA: Annual Reviews Inc., 1997, 121–45.

Lindsay, C. *Lone-Parent Families in Canada*. Ottawa: Statistics Canada, 1992.

Lister, R. 'Women, Economic Dependency and Citizenship', *Journal of Social Policy*, 19, 1990, 445–67.

Lister, R. ' "She has other duties" – Women, Citizenship and Social Security'. In S. Baldwin and J. Falkingham (eds), *Social Security and Social Change*. London: Harvester Wheatsheaf, 1994, 31–44.

Logan, R. and J. Belliveau. 'Working Mothers', *Canadian Social Trends*, 36, 1995, 24–8.

Lord, S. 'Social Assistance and "Employability" for Single Mothers in Nova Scotia'. In A. Johnson, S. McBride and P. Smith (eds), *Continuities and Discontinuities: The Political Economy of Social Welfare and Labour Market Policy in Canada*. Toronto: University of Toronto Press, 1994, 191–206.

Luker, K. *Abortion and the Politics of Motherhood*. Berkeley: University of California Press, 1984.

Lund, M. 'The Non-custodial Father: Common Challenges in Parenting After Divorce'. In C. Lewis and M. O'Brien (eds), *Reassessing Fatherhood*. London: Sage, 1987, 212–24.

Luxton, M. 'Feminism and Families: The Challenge of Neo-Conservatism'. In M. Luxton (ed.), *Feminism and Families*. Halifax, NS: Fernwood, 1997, 10–26.

Luxton, M. 'Families and the Labour Market'. In D. Cheal, F. Woolley and M. Luxton, *How Families Cope and Why Policymakers Need to Know*. Ottawa: Renouf, 1998, 57–73.

Maccoby, E. and R. Mnookin. *Dividing the Child*. Cambridge, MA: Harvard University Press, 1992.

Maclean, M. and J. Eekelaar. *The Parental Obligation: A Study of Parenthood Across Households*. Oxford: Hart Publishing, 1997.

Maeda, D. and Y. Nakatani. 'Family Care of the Elderly in Japan'. In J. Kosberg (ed.), *Family Care of the Elderly*. Newbury Park, CA: Sage, 1992, 196–209.

Maeda, D. and Y. Shimizu. 'Family Support for Elderly People in Japan'. In H. Kendig, A. Hashimoto and L. Coppard (eds), *Family Support for the Elderly*. Oxford: Oxford University Press, 1992, 235–49.

Mandell, N. 'Juggling the Load: Mothers who Work Full-Time for Pay'. In A. Duffy, N. Mandell and N. Pupo (eds), *Few Choices: Women, Work and Family*. Toronto: Garamond, 1989, 17–43.

Mann, K. 'The Historical Roots and Cultural Logic of Outside Marriage in Colonial Lagos'. In C. Bledsoe, and G. Pison (eds), *Nuptiality in Sub-Saharan Africa*. Oxford: Clarendon Press, 1994, 167–93.

Manting, D. *Dynamics in Marriage and Cohabitation*. Amsterdam: Thesis Publishers, 1994.

March, K. *The Stranger Who Bore Me: Adoptee-Birth Mother Relationships*. Toronto: University of Toronto Press, 1995.

Maroney, H. and M. Luxton (eds). *Feminism and Political Economy*. Toronto: Methuen, 1987.

Marsh, C. and S. Arber. 'Research on Families and Households in Modern Britain'. In C. Marsh and S. Arber (eds), *Families and Households*. New York: St. Martin's Press, 1992, 1–25.

Marsh, R. *The Great Transformation: Social Change in Taipei, Taiwan Since the 1960s*. Armonk, NY: M. E. Sharpe, 1996.

Marshall, K. 'Dual Earners: Who's Responsible for Housework?', *Canadian Social Trends*, 31, 1993, 11–14.

Marshall, K. 'Balancing Work and Family Responsibilities', *Perspectives on Labour and Income*, 6, 1994, 26–30.

Mason, K., N. Tsuya and M. Choe. 'Introduction'. In K. Mason, N. Tsuya and M. Choe (eds), *The Changing Family in Comparative Perspective: Asia and the United States*. Honolulu: East-West Center, 1998, 1–16.

Mason, M., A. Skolnick and S. Sugarman (eds). *All Our Families*. New York: Oxford University Press, 1998.

McCaughey, J. *Where Now? Homeless Families in the 1990s*. Melbourne: Australian Institute of Family Studies, 1992.

McDonald, P. 'Australian Families: Values and Behaviour'. In R. Hartley (ed.), *Families and Cultural Diversity in Australia*. St. Leonards, NSW: Allen and Unwin, 1995, 25–47.

McGlone, F., A. Park and C. Roberts. 'Relative Values: Kinship and Friendship'. In R. Jowell, J. Curtice, A. Park, L. Brook and K. Thomson, *British Social Attitudes: The 13th report*. Aldershot: Dartmouth, 1996, 53–72.

McLanahan, S. 'Parent Absence or Poverty: Which Matters More?' In G. Duncan and J. Brooks-Gunn (eds), *Consequences of Growing Up Poor*. New York: Russell Sage Foundation, 1997, 35–48.

McRae, S. *Cohabiting Mothers*. London: Policy Studies Institute, 1993.

Menaghan, E. and T. Parcel. 'Parental Employment and Family Life', *Journal of Marriage and the Family*, 52, 1990, 1079–98.

Millar, J. 'State, Family and Personal Responsibility: The Changing Balance for Lone Mothers in the United Kingdom'. In G. Allan (ed.), *The Sociology of the Family*. Oxford: Blackwell, 1999, 247–61.

Miller, J. L. and D. Knudsen. 'Family Abuse and Violence'. In M. Sussman, S. Steinmetz and G. Peterson (eds), *Handbook of Marriage and the Family*, 2nd edn. New York: Plenum, 1999, 705–41.

Minow, M. 'Redefining Families: Who's In and Who's Out?'. In K. Hansen and A. Garey (eds), *Families in the U.S.* Philadelphia, PA: Temple University Press, 1998, 7–19.

Mitchell, B. 'Family Structure and Leaving the Nest', *Sociological Perspectives*, 37, 1994, 651–71.

Mitchell, B., A. Wister and T. Burch. 'The Family Environment and Leaving the Parental Home', *Journal of Marriage and the Family*, 51, 1989, 605–13.

Modell, J. *Kinship with Strangers: Adoption and Interpretations of Kinship in American Culture.* Berkeley: University of California Press, 1994.

Modell, J. ' "Where Do We Go Next?" Long-Term Reunion Relationships Between Adoptees and Birth Parents', *Marriage and Family Review*, 25, 1997, 43–66.

Montgomery, R. 'Gender Differences in Patterns of Child-Parent Caregiving Relationships'. In J. Dwyer and R. Coward (eds), *Gender, Families, and Elder Care.* Newbury Park, CA: Sage, 1992, 65–83.

Moore, G. 'Structural Determinants of Men's and Women's Personal Networks', *American Sociological Review*, 55, 1990, 726–35.

Morgan, D. 'Ideologies of Marriage and Family Life'. In D. Clark (ed.), *Marriage, Domestic Life and Social Change.* London: Routledge, 1991, 114–38.

Morgan, D. *Family Connections.* Cambridge: Polity Press, 1996.

Morgan, L. *After Marriage Ends: Economic Consequences for Midlife Women.* Newbury Park, CA: Sage, 1991.

Morley, P. *The Mountain is Moving: Japanese Women's Lives.* Vancouver: UBC Press, 1999.

Morris, J. and M. Winn. *Housing and Social Inequality.* London: Hilary Shipman, 1990.

Morris, L. *Social Divisions.* London: UCL Press, 1995.

Mossman, M. and M. Maclean. 'Family Law and Social Assistance Programs: Rethinking Equality'. In P. Evans and G. Wekerle (eds), *Women and the Canadian Welfare State.* Toronto: University of Toronto Press, 1997, 117–41.

Moynihan, D. *The Negro Family.* Washington, D.C.: United States Department of Labor, 1965.

Mulroy, E. *The New Uprooted: Single Mothers in Urban Life.* Westport, CT: Auburn House, 1995.

Murphy, M. 'Measuring the Family Life Cycle'. In A. Bryman, B. Bytheway, P. Allatt and T. Keil (eds), *Rethinking the Life Cycle.* Basingstoke: Macmillan – now Palgrave, 1987, 30–50.

Murray, C. *Losing Ground: American Social Policy, 1950–1980.* New York: Basic, 1984.

Nazroo, J. 'Uncovering Gender Differences in the Use of Marital Violence: The Effect of Methodology'. In G. Allan (ed.), *The Sociology of the Family: A Reader.* Oxford: Blackwell, 1999, 149–67.

Neale, B. and C. Smart. 'Experiments with Parenthood?', *Sociology*, 31, 1997, 201–19.

Nelson, M. 'Family Day Care Providers: Dilemmas of Daily Practice'. In E. N. Glenn, G. Chang and L. R. Forcey (eds), *Mothering: Ideology, Experience, and Agency.* New York: Routledge, 1994, 181–209.

Nelson, M. and J. Smith. *Working Hard and Making Do.* Berkeley: University of California Press, 1999.

Nicholson, A. 'Husbands, Wives and Partners'. In K. Altergott (ed.), *One World, Many Families.* Minneapolis, MN: National Council on Family Relations, 1993, 43–6.

Ogawa, N. and R. Retherford. 'Shifting Costs of Caring for the Elderly Back to Families in Japan: Will It Work?', *Population and Development Review*, 23, 1997, 59–94.

Oliker, S. *Best Friends and Marriage.* Berkeley: University of California Press, 1989.

Oppenheim, C. and R. Lister. 'The Politics of Child Poverty 1979–1995'. In J. Pilcher and S. Wagg (eds), *Thatcher's Children? Politics, Childhood and Society in the 1980s and 1990s*. London: Falmer Press, 1996, 114–33.

Organisation for Economic Cooperation and Development. *Ageing Populations*. Paris: Organisation for Economic Cooperation and Development, 1988.

Orloff, A. 'Gender and the Social Rights of Citizenship: The Comparative Analysis of Gender Relations and Welfare States', *American Sociological Review*, 58, 1993, 303–28.

Orloff, A. 'Gender in the Welfare State'. In J. Hagan and K. Cook (eds), *Annual Review of Sociology, vol. 22*. Palo Alto, CA: Annual Reviews Inc., 1996, 51–78.

Ouattara, M., P. Sen and M. Thomson. 'Forced Marriage, Forced Sex: The Perils of Childhood for Girls', *Gender and Development*, 6, 1998, 27–33.

Owen, S. 'Household Production and Economic Efficiency: Arguments For and Against Domestic Specialization', *Work, Employment and Society*, 1, 1987, 157–78.

Pahl, J. *Money and Marriage*. New York: St. Martin's Press, 1989.

Pahl, J. 'Money and Power in Marriage'. In P. Abbott and C. Wallace (eds), *Gender, Power and Sexuality*. Basingstoke: Macmillan – now Palgrave, 1991, 41–57.

Pahl, R. *Divisions of Labour*. Oxford: Blackwell, 1984.

Palomba, R. and H. Moors. 'Attitudes towards Marriage, Children, and Population Policies in Europe'. In H. Moors and R. Palomba (eds), *Population, Family, and Welfare*. Oxford: Clarendon Press, 1995, 245–62.

Parsons, T. 'The Kinship System of the Contemporary United States', *American Anthropologist*, 45, 1943, 22–38.

Parsons, T. 'The Normal American Family'. In B. Adams and T. Weirath (eds), *Readings on the Sociology of the Family*. Chicago: Markham, 1971, 53–66.

Peacock, P. 'Marital Rape'. In R. K. Bergen (ed.), *Issues in Intimate Violence*. Thousand Oaks, CA: Sage, 1998, 225–35.

Peters, E. 'The Modernization of the Youth Phase. Educational, Professional and Family Careers of Dutch Youth in the Nineties'. In M. du Bois-Reymond, R. Diekstra, K. Hurrelman and E. Peters (eds), *Childhood and Youth in Germany and the Netherlands*. New York: Walter de Gruyter, 1995, 3–39.

Peterson, P. 'The Urban Underclass and the Poverty Paradox'. In C. Jencks and P. Peterson (eds), *The Urban Underclass*. Washington, D.C.: Brookings Institution, 1991, 3–27.

Phizacklea, A. and C. Wolkowitz. *Homeworking Women*. London: Sage, 1995.

Picot, G., M. Zyblock and W. Pyper. *Why Do Children Move Into and Out of Low Income: Changing Labour Market Conditions or Marriage and Divorce?* Ottawa: Statistics Canada, 1999.

Pilcher, J. *Women in Contemporary Britain*. London: Routledge, 1999.

Pimentel, E. 'Just How Do I Love Thee?: Marital Relations in Urban China', *Journal of Marriage and the Family*, 62, 2000, 32–47.

Pitshandenge, I. 'Marriage Law in Sub-Saharan Africa'. In C. Bledsoe, and G. Pison (eds), *Nuptiality in Sub-Saharan Africa*. Oxford: Clarendon Press, 1994, 117–29.

Potuchek, J. 'Employed Wives' Orientations to Breadwinning: A Gender Theory Analysis', *Journal of Marriage and the Family*, 54, 1992, 548–58.

Potuchek, J. *Who Supports the Family? Gender and Breadwinning in Dual-Earner Marriages*. Stanford, CA: Stanford University Press, 1997.

Pulkingham, J. and G. Ternowetsky. 'The Changing Context of Child and Family Policies'. In J. Pulkingham and G. Ternowetsky (eds), *Child and Family Policies*. Halifax, NS: Fernwood, 1997, 14–38.

Pullinger, J. and C. Summerfield (eds). *Social Focus on Families*. London: The Stationery Office, 1997.

Quddus, A. H. G. 'The Adjustment of Couples Who Live Apart: The Case of Bangladesh', *Journal of Comparative Family Studies*, 23, 1992, 285–94.

Qureshi, H. and K. Simons. 'Resources Within Families: Caring for Elderly People'. In J. Brannen and G. Wilson (eds), *Give and Take in Families*. London: Allen and Unwin, 1987, 117–35.

Qureshi, H. and A. Walker. *The Caring Relationship*. Philadelphia: Temple University Press, 1989.

Raabe, P. 'Constructing Pluralistic Work and Career Arrangements'. In S. Lewis and J. Lewis (eds), *The Work-Family Challenge*. London: Sage, 1996, 128–41.

Ragoné, H. *Surrogate Motherhood*. Boulder, CO: Westview Press, 1994.

Ravanera, Z., F. Rajulton and T. Burch. 'Tracing the Life Courses of Canadians', *Canadian Studies in Population*, 21, 1994, 21–34.

Ravanera, Z., F. Rajulton and T. Burch. 'A Cohort Analysis of Home-Leaving in Canada, 1910–1975', *Journal of Comparative Family Studies*, 26, 1995, 179–93.

Reher, D. *Perspectives on the Family in Spain, Past and Present*. Oxford: Clarendon Press, 1997.

Reiss, Ira. 'The Universality of the Family: A Conceptual Analysis', *Journal of Marriage and the Family*, 27, 1965, 443–53.

Renzetti, C. *Violent Betrayal: Partner Abuse in Lesbian Relationships*. Newbury Park, CA: Sage, 1992.

Robinson, J. and G. Godbey. *Time for Life: The Surprising Ways Americans Use Their Time*. University Park, PA: Pennsylvania State University Press, 1997.

Rodger, J. *Family Life and Social Control*. Basingstoke: Macmillan – now Palgrave, 1996.

Rosen, D. 'American Families and American Law'. In M. Sussman, S. Steinmetz and G. Peterson (eds), *Handbook of Marriage and the Family*, 2nd edn. New York: Plenum, 1999, 553–70.

Rosen, K. 'The Ties That Bind Women to Violent Premarital Relationships'. In D. Cahn and S. Lloyd (eds), *Family Violence From a Communication Perspective*. Thousand Oaks, CA: Sage, 1996, 151–76.

Ross, D., K. Scott and M. Kelly. *Child Poverty: What Are the Consequences?* Ottawa: Canadian Council on Social Development, 1996a.

Ross, D., K. Scott and M. Kelly. 'Overview: Children in Canada in the 1990s'. In Human Resources Development Canada and Statistics Canada (eds), *Growing Up in Canada*. Ottawa: Statistics Canada, 1996b, 15–45.

Rowland, D. 'Family Diversity and the Life Cycle', *Journal of Comparative Family Studies*, 22, 1991, 1–14.

Sadler, A. *Family Violence: Current Controversies*. San Diego, CA: Greenhaven, 1996.

Sainsbury, D. *Gender, Equality, and Welfare States*. Cambridge: Cambridge University Press, 1996.

Salaff, J. *Working Daughters of Hong Kong*. New York: Columbia University Press, 1995.

Sanders, J. and V. Nee. 'Immigrant Self-Employment: The Family as Social Capital and the Value of Human Capital', *American Sociological Review*, 61, 1996, 231–49.

Sandqvist, K. 'Sweden's Sex-Role Scheme and Commitment to Gender Equality'. In S. Lewis, D. Izraeli and H. Hootsmans (eds), *Dual-Earner Families: International Perspectives*. London: Sage, 1992, 80–98.

Saunders, P. *A Nation of Home Owners*. London: Unwin Hyman, 1990.

Scott, J. 'Changing Households in Britain: Do Families Still Matter?' *Sociological Review*, 45, 1997, 591–620.

Scott, J. and A. Black. 'Deep Structures of African American Family Life: Female and Male Kin Networks'. In R. Staples (ed.), *The Black Family*. Belmont, CA: Wadsworth, 1994, 204–13.

Scott, J. and K. Perren. 'The Family Album: Reflections on Personal and Family Life'. In N. Buck, J. Gershuny, D. Rose and J. Scott (eds), *Changing Households*. Colchester: ESRC Research Centre on Micro-social Change, 1994, 263–90.

Seccombe, W. 'The Housewife and Her Labour Under Capitalism', *New Left Review*, 83, 1974, 3–24.

Seccombe, W. *A Millenium of Family Change*. London: Verso, 1992.

Seccombe, W. *Weathering the Storm*. London: Verso, 1993.

Seeley, J., R. A. Sim and E. Loosley. *Crestwood Heights*. Toronto: University of Toronto Press, 1956.

Sekaran, U. 'Middle-Class Dual-Earner Families and their Support Systems in Urban India'. In S. Lewis, D. Izraeli and H. Hootsmans (eds), *Dual-Earner Families: International Perspectives*. London: Sage, 1992, 46–61.

Seltzer, J. 'Consequences of Marital Dissolution for Children'. In J. Hagan and K. Cook (eds), *Annual Review of Sociology, vol. 20*. Palo Alto, CA: Annual Reviews Inc., 1994, 235–66.

Sgritta, G. 'Towards a New Paradigm: Family in the Welfare State Crisis'. In K. Boh, M. Bak, C. Clason, M. Pankratova, J. Qvortrup, G. Sgritta and K. Waerness (eds), *Changing Patterns of European Family Life*. London: Routledge, 1989, 71–92.

Shah, A. *The Family in India*. New Delhi: Orient Longman, 1998.

Shalhoub-Kevorkian, N. 'The Politics of Disclosing Female Sexual Abuse: A Case Study of Palestinian Society,' *Child Abuse and Neglect*, 23, 1999, 1275–93.

Shelton, B. and D. John. 'The Division of Household Labor'. In J. Hagan and K. Cook (eds), *Annual Review of Sociology, vol. 22*. Palo Alto, CA: Annual Reviews Inc., 1996, 299–322.

Sidel, R. *Keeping Women and Children Last*. New York: Penguin, 1996.

Silva, E. and C. Smart. 'The "New" Practices and Politics of Family Life'. In E. Silva and C. Smart (eds), *The New Family?* London: Sage, 1999, 1–12.

Simonen, L. 'The Politics of Caring: The Case of Municipal Homemaking in Finland'. In L. Jamieson and H. Corr (eds), *State, Private Life and Political Change*. New York: St. Martin's Press, 1990, 119–33.

Singh, S. and J. Lindsay. 'Money in Heterosexual Relationships', *Australian and New Zealand Journal of Sociology*, 32, 1996, 57–69.

Skrypnek, B. and J. Fast. 'Work and Family Policy in Canada', *Journal of Family Issues*, 17, 1996, 793–812.

Smart, C. 'Power and the Politics of Child Custody'. In C. Smart and S. Sevenhuijsen (eds), *Child Custody and the Politics of Gender*. London: Routledge, 1989, 1–26.

Smart, C. 'The "New" Parenthood: Fathers and Mothers after Divorce'. In E. Silva and C. Smart (eds), *The New Family?* London: Sage, 1999, 100–114.

Smart, C. and B. Neale. *Family Fragments?* Cambridge: Polity Press, 1999.

Smith, D. 'The Standard North American Family: SNAF as an Ideological Code', *Journal of Family Issues*, 14, 1993, 50–65.

Solomon, C. R. 'The Importance of Mother–Child Relations in Studying Stepfamilies'. In C. Everett (ed.), *Understanding Stepfamilies: Their Structure and Dynamics*. New York: Haworth, 1995, 89–98.

South, S. and G. Spitze. 'Housework in Marital and Nonmarital Households', *American Sociological Review*, 59, 1994, 327–47.

Spruijt, A. 'Adolescents from Stepfamilies, Single-Parent Families and (In)Stable Intact Families in the Netherlands'. In C. Everett (ed.), *Understanding Stepfamilies: Their Structure and Dynamics*. New York: Haworth, 1995, 115–32.

Stacey, J. *Brave New Families: Stories of Domestic Upheaval in Late Twentieth Century America*. New York: Basic, 1990.

Stacey, J. 'Backward toward the Postmodern Family'. In A. Wolfe (ed.), *America at Century's End*. Berkeley: University of California Press, 1991, 17–34.

Stamps, L., S. Kunen and A. Rock-Faucheux. 'Judges' Beliefs Dealing with Child Custody Decisions'. In C. Everett (ed.), *Child Custody: Legal Decisions and Family Outcomes*. New York: Haworth, 1997, 3–16.

Stepick, A. *Pride Against Prejudice: Haitians in the United States*. Boston: Allyn and Bacon, 1998.

Stivens, M. 'Modernizing the Malay Mother'. In K. Ram and M. Jolly (eds), *Maternities and Modernities*. Cambridge: Cambridge University Press, 1998, 50–80.

Stockman, N., N. Bonney and S. Xuewen. *Women's Work in East and West*. London: UCL Press, 1995.

Straus, M. 'Ten Myths That Perpetuate Corporal Punishment'. In K. Hansen and A. Garey (eds), *Families in the U.S.* Philadelphia: Temple University Press, 1998, 641–50.

Sydie, R. A. *Natural Women, Cultured Men: A Feminist Perspective on Sociological Theory*. New York: New York University Press, 1987.

Tam, M. *Part-Time Employment*. Aldershot: Avebury, 1997.

Teachman, J., K. Polonko and J. Scanzoni. 'Demography and Families'. In M. Sussman, S. Steinmetz and G. Peterson (eds), *Handbook of Marriage and the Family*, 2nd edn. New York: Plenum, 1999, 39–76.

Thèry, I. ' "The Interest of the Child" and the Regulation of the Post-Divorce Family'. In C. Smart and S. Sevenhuijsen (eds), *Child Custody and the Politics of Gender*. London: Routledge, 1989, 78–99.

Thompson, R. and P. Amato. 'The Postdivorce Family: An Introduction to the Issues'. In R. Thompson and P. Amato (eds), *The Postdivorce Family*. Thousand Oaks, CA: Sage, 1999, xi–xxiii.

Thorne, B. 'Feminist Rethinking of the Family: An Overview'. In B. Thorne and M. Yalom (eds), *Rethinking the Family*. New York: Longman, 1982, 1–24.

Townson, M. *Women's Labour Force Participation, Fertility Rates, and the Implications for Economic Development and Government Policy*. Ottawa: Institute for Research on Public Policy, 1987.

Trost, J. 'Do We Mean the Same by the Concept of Family?', *Communication Research*, 17, 1990, 431–43.

Trovato, F. 'Sex, Marital Status, and Suicide in Canada: 1951–1981', *Sociological Perspectives*, 34, 1991, 427–45.

Tsuya, N. and L. Bumpass. 'Time Allocation Between Employment and Housework in Japan, South Korea, and the United States'. In K. Oppenheim Mason, N. Tsuya and M. Kim Choe (eds), *The Changing Family in Comparative Perspective*. Honolulu: East-West Center, 1998, 83–104.

Turner, J. 'Saskatchewan Responds to Family Violence: The Victims of Domestic Violence Act, 1995'. In M. Valverde, L. MacLeod and K. Johnson (eds), *Wife Assault and the Canadian Criminal Justice System*. Toronto: Centre of Criminology, University of Toronto, 1995, 183–97.

Ursel, E. J. 'The Winnipeg Family Violence Court'. In M. Valverde, L. MacLeod and K. Johnson (eds), *Wife Assault and the Canadian Criminal Justice System*. Toronto: Centre of Criminology, University of Toronto, 1995, 169–82.

VandenHeuvel, A. *When Roles Overlap*. Melbourne: Australian Institute of Family Studies, 1993.

van Dongen, M. 'Men's Aspirations Concerning Child Care'. In M. van Dongen, G. Frinking and M. Jacobs (eds), *Changing Fatherhood: A Multidisciplinary Perspective*. Amsterdam: Thesis Publishers, 1995, 91–105.

Vanier Institute of the Family. *Profiling Canada's Families*. Ottawa: Vanier Institute of the Family, 1994.

Vannoy-Hiller, D. and W. Philliber. *Equal Partners*. Newbury Park, CA: Sage, 1989.

Velleman, R., A. Copello and J. Maslin. *Living With Drink: Women Who Live With Problem Drinkers*. London: Longman, 1998.

Voegeli, W. and B. Willenbacher. 'Property Division and Pension-Splitting in the FRG'. In L. Weitzman and M. Maclean (eds), *Economic Consequences of Divorce*. Oxford: Clarendon Press, 1992, 163–83.

Vogler, C. and J. Pahl. 'Social and Economic Change and the Organisation of Money Within Marriage'. *Work, Employment and Society*, 7, 1993, 71–95.

Vosko, L. 'Recreating Dependency: Women, Unemployment and Federal Proposals for UI Reform'. In D. Drache and A. Ranachan (eds), *Warm Heart, Cold Country: Fiscal and Social Policy Reform in Canada*. Ottawa: Caledon Institute of Social Policy, 1995, 213–31.

Waerness, K. 'The Rationality of Caring', *Economic and Industrial Democracy*, 5, 1984, 185–211.

Waerness, K. 'Caring'. In K. Boh, M. Bak, C. Clason, M. Pankratova, J. Qvortrup, G. Sgritta and K. Waerness (eds), *Changing Patterns of European Family Life*. London: Routledge, 1989, 217–47.

Walker, A. 'Gender and Family Relationships'. In M. Sussman, S. Steinmetz and G. Peterson (eds), *Handbook of Marriage and the Family*, 2nd edn. New York: Plenum, 1999, 439–74.

Wallace, C. *For Richer, For Poorer: Growing Up In and Out of Work*. London: Tavistock, 1987.

Walzer, S. *Thinking about the Baby: Gender and Transitions into Parenthood*. Philadelphia: Temple University Press, 1998.

Ward, C., A. Dale and H. Joshi. 'Income Dependency within Couples'. In L. Morris and E. S. Lyon (eds), *Gender Relations in Public and Private*. Basingstoke: Macmillan – now Palgrave, 1996, 95–120.

Watts, H. 'Human Capital: The Biggest Deficit'. In J. Chafel (ed.), *Child Poverty and Public Policy*. Washington, D.C.: Urban Institute Press, 1993, 245–71.

Weeks, J. 'Pretended Family Relationships'. In D. Clark (ed.), *Marriage, Domestic Life and Social Change*. London: Routledge, 1991, 214–34.

Weeks, J., C. Donovan and B. Heaphy. 'Everyday Experiments: Narratives of Non-Heterosexual Relationships'. In E. Silva and C. Smart (eds), *The New Family?* London: Sage, 1999, 83–99.

Weeks, J., B. Heaphy and C. Donovan. 'Partners by Choice: Equality, Power and Commitment in Non-heterosexual Relationships'. In G. Allan (ed.), *The Sociology of the Family*. Oxford: Blackwell, 1999, 111–28.

Weijie, Z. 'Economic Development and the Marriage Crisis in the Special Economic Zones of China'. In B. Einhorn and E. Yeo (eds), *Women and Market Societies*. Aldershot: Edward Elgar, 1995, 205–16.

Weitzman, L. 'Marital Property: Its Transformation and Division in the United States'. In L. Weitzman and M. Maclean (eds), *Economic Consequences of Divorce*. Oxford: Clarendon Press, 1992, 85–142.

Weston, K. *Families We Choose: Lesbians, Gays, Kinship*. New York: Columbia University Press, 1991.

Wheelock, J. *Husbands at Home*. London: Routledge, 1990.

White, L. 'Coresidence and Leaving Home: Young Adults and Their Parents'. In J. Hagan and K. Cook (eds), *Annual Review of Sociology, vol. 20*. Palo Alto, CA: Annual Reviews Inc., 1994, 81–102.

Whitting, G. 'Women and Poverty: The European Context'. In C. Glendinning and J. Millar (eds), *Women and Poverty in Britain, the 1990s*. Hemel Hempstead: Harvester Wheatsheaf, 1992, 62–76.

Whyte, M. K. *Dating, Mating, and Marriage*. New York: Aldine de Gruyter, 1990.

Wilson, P. and R. Pahl. 'The Changing Sociological Construct of the Family', *Sociological Review*, 36, 1988, 233–66.

Wilson, W. J. *The Truly Disadvantaged*. Chicago: University of Chicago Press, 1987.

Wilson, W. J. 'The Underclass: Issues, Perspectives, and Public Policy'. In W. J. Wilson (ed.), *The Ghetto Underclass*. Newbury Park, CA: Sage, 1993, 1–24.

Wilson, W. J. *When Work Disappears*. New York: Knopf, 1996.

Wong, S. and J. Salaff. 'Network Capital: Emigration from Hong Kong', *British Journal of Sociology*, 49, 1998, 358–74.

Wood, K. and R. Jewkes. 'Violence, Rape, and Sexual Coercion: Everyday Love in a South African Township', *Gender and Development*, 5, 1997, 41–6.

Woolley, F. and J. Marshall. 'Measuring Inequality Within the Household', *Review of Income and Wealth*, 40, 1994, 415–30.

Wu, Z. *Cohabitation: An Alternative Form of Family Living*. Don Mills, ON: Oxford University Press, 2000.

Wu, Z. and T. R. Balakrishnan, 'Attitudes towards Cohabitation and Marriage in Canada', *Journal of Comparative Family Studies*, 23, 1992, 1–12.

Yip, A. 'Gay Male Christian Couples and Sexual Exclusivity', *Sociology*, 31, 1997, 289–306.

Young, C. *Young People Leaving Home in Australia*. Melbourne: Australian Institute of Family Studies, 1987.

Young, M. and P. Willmott. *The Symmetrical Family*. London: Routledge, 1973.

Yuen, E. and V. Lim. 'Dual-Earner Families in Singapore'. In S. Lewis, D. Izraeli and H. Hootsmans (eds), *Dual-Earner Families: International Perspectives*. London: Sage, 1992, 62–79.

Zelizer, V. *The Social Meaning of Money*. Princeton, NJ: Princeton University Press, 1997.

Zhao, J., F. Rajulton and Z. Ravanera. 'Leaving Parental Homes in Canada: Effects of Family Structure, Gender, and Culture', *Canadian Journal of Sociology*, 20, 1995, 31–50.

Zimmerman, S. *Understanding Family Policy*. Newbury Park: Sage, 1988.

Index